ACCOMMODATION MANAGEMENT
a systems approach

Christine Jones
Val Paul

Batsford Academic and Educational
London

©Christine Jones and Val Paul 1985
First published 1985
Reprinted 1990, 1992

Typeset by Progress Typesetting London
and printed in Great Britain by
Billings
Worcester
for the publishers
Batsford Academic and Educational
an imprint of B T Batsford Ltd
4 Fitzhardinge Street
London W1H 0AH

British Library Cataloguing in Publication Data
Jones, Christine and Paul, Val
    Accommodation management: a systems approach.
    —— (Catering)
    1. Building management   2. Buildings——Great Britain
    I. Title   II. Paul, Val   III. Series
    647.94′068   TX955

ISBN 0 7134 4807 5

Contents

Acknowledgement

Our appreciation and gratitude is expressed to our families, colleagues and friends for their help, understanding and kindness in compiling this book.

CJ and VP 1985

Introduction

This book has been written to develop concepts of Accommodation Management and to consider them in the context of the real world. As any practising manager knows, basic facts can rarely be taken straight from a text book and applied to the working situation. Management requires that many pieces of information be fitted together, theories adapted and prejudices softened, before clear objectives can be set by the manager, and his other functions accomplished. Accommodation Management is no exception to this and our aim is to consider the systems of Accommodation Management in a practical way.

Management is a complex activity and for this reason it was decided to consider the field of Accommodation Management by applying a *systems approach*. No operation within the sphere of control of a manager can be considered in isolation. Any operation will affect something else, and, itself, be open to influence. Suction cleaning a floor surface will, at the very least, affect in some way the operative and the floor surface. This is unlikely to be the end of the story, however. It will probably affect many more people by creating a cleaner environment, generating noise, and bearing maintenance, safety, financial and organisational implications. All these influences may, in turn, imply training needs; equipment, surface and staff selection procedures; supervision; work scheduling and many other consequences with which the manager has to deal.

We set out, then, to consider the functions of Accommodation Management in a way which is intended to develop the student's understanding of the real job and how decisions are reached. At the same time managers may well find the approach valuable and the book useful; particularly in the management of change.

Accommodation

The term *accommodation*, for the purpose of this book, has been taken in a wide context to include any premises, other than a domestic dwelling, where shelter and facilities are provided for use by people. In this wide context, one basic service is a requirement of all users, and this is *housekeeping*; to provide hygienic, comfortable, safe and aesthetically acceptable services and conditions. With respect to the premises itself, provision must be made to ensure its integrity, and the basic service required here is *maintenance*. In addition to housekeeping and maintenance, a third basic service is normally required, particularly when users enter the premise for the first time. This is, at its simplest, some form of *reception* (even if this is only graphical information). Where members of the public frequent the premises, a much more elaborate Front Office facility is required.

Premises provide shelter and facilities for an infinite number of users, and those premises intended for use by some people for more than a few minutes, will often provide some sort of catering service; those intended for use overnight provide sleeping accommodation. As the use of premises vary, so too will the emphasis placed on the services so far mentioned. Although in the real world, jobs do exist for managers who will be responsible for all the basic services of housekeeping, maintenance and reception, examples are taken from specialist establishments to emphasise the value and change of priorities of services to meet the needs of the building's users.

The Accommodation Industry can be categorised into various sectors and, to emphasise the diversity of functions, an analysis of sections is shown below:

Commercial eg
Offices
Retail establishments
Showrooms
Exhibition Halls
Clubs
Garages
Laundries
Markets

Industrial eg
Factories
Warehouses
Hotels/motels
Holiday camps
Restaurants
Bars/pubs
Oil rigs
Laboratories

Transport eg
Air
Bus
Train
Ship/ferry

Governmental eg
Universities
Hospitals and health centres
Armed Services bases
Research centres
Prisons

Local authority eg
Schools
Colleges
Conference centres
Welfare institutions
Public buildings – city halls
            – libraries
            – museums
            – art galleries
Leisure centres.

Another means of classifying accommodation may be by dividing it into profit-making and non profit-making establishments. It can be argued, however, that this bears little relevance to the fields of housekeeping and maintenance. Departmental managers, in any industry, are expected to work within their allocated budget to the greatest effect. In the field of Front Office, however, there will be a significant difference between a department which is endeavouring to increase business, and one which is only trying to cope most efficiently with current input.

Accommodation Management

Accommodation Management, like any other sort of management, involves controlling other people to attain some objectives. Initially it involves the setting out of these objectives, followed by a planning process of how these objectives are to be reached. Management involves identifying and controlling all resources, and controlling people, materials, equipment, time and money. This is achieved through organisation, co-ordination and communication. The resources available to the Accommodation Manager are: personnel; equipment; materials; the building; energy; and his own experience. Each of these must be appreciated and utilised to its maximum effect.

In the field of Accommodation Management then, prime objectives, in the case of the domestic services manager in the Health Service, might be 'provision of a clinically clean environment'. The executive housekeeper in an hotel may set 'provision of an aesthetically pleasing

Figure 1 *Responsibilities of the Accommodation Manager*

Assessing manpower levels
Recruitment and selection of staff
Induction and training of staff
Deployment and scheduling of staff
Supervision
Total quality management
Inspection of premises
Methods of performing tasks
Productivity
Staff welfare
Hygiene control
Pest control
Waste disposal
Selection and purchasing of supplies
Selection and purchasing of soft furnishings
Selection and purchasing of internal surfaces
Stores control
Linen control and laundering
Cleaning and maintenance
Redecoration and upgrading
Capital building projects
Interior design
Health, safety, fire and security
Welfare of the building users
Conferences
Front office operations

environment' as a prime objective.

These objectives may be achieved through planning of manpower requirements and scheduling of staff; selecting suitable equipment and materials; and endeavouring to make the best use of the other resources, including the building itself. In more specific terms, the responsibilities of the Accommodation Manager may include some or all of the items shown in figure 1.

These aspects form the substance of the following chapters, and it will be seen that Accommodation Management requires a considerable degree of specialist knowledge. Management of the accommodation, however, is not always the prime concern of an establishment as it is in the hotel industry. Hotels exist to provide accommodation, and their major source of revenue is from the sale of this product. In other establishments, whilst the *raison-d'être* may be to care for the sick, sell cars, or provide education, accommodation services are a basic necessity.

In the following chapters, consideration is given to the roles of planning and selection, housekeeping and maintenance throughout the life of a building. Terotechnological considerations have been borne in mind. *Terotechnology* being defined by LEE[1] as 'a combination of management, financial, engineering and other practices applied to physical assets in the pursuit of economic life cycle costs'. It requires that all departments within an organisation cooperate to ensure that the physical assets are planned, provided, maintained, operated and disposed of, at the lowest total cost to the organisation.

The Systems Approach

Accommodation Management is a complicated social system and, in common with most, if not all, social systems, many phenomena associated with it cannot be explained in terms of a simple cause and effect relationship. Components associated with Accommodation Management, the type of building; the manpower; the organisational structure; the customer; the local environment, all influence and are influenced by one another. Many elements or situations acting together may cause any of a number of effects. Thus, the method of study applied to Accommodation Management, in the ensuing chapters, is described following a *systems approach*, or an *holistic approach* (looking at all causes and effects).

As defined by BILL MAYON-WHITE and DICK MORRIS[2] a *system* is:

1 . . . an assembly of components connected in an organised way.
2 The components are affected by being in the system and the behaviour of the system is changed if they leave it.
3 The organised assembly of components does something.
4 The assembly has been identified by someone as being of particular interest.

In this case 'the system' is the System of Accommodation Management (see figure 2) and the components are the five sub-systems

Figure 2 *The system of Accommodation Management*

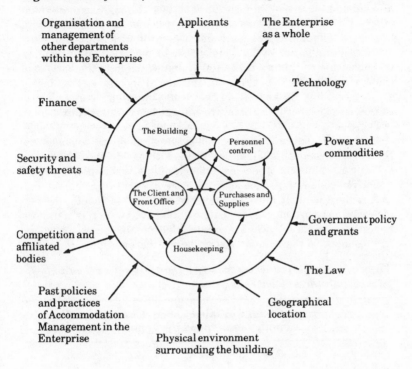

Organisation and management of other departments within the Enterprise

Applicants

The Enterprise as a whole

Technology

Finance

The Building

Personnel control

Power and commodities

Security and safety threats

The Client and Front Office

Purchases and Supplies

Government policy and grants

Competition and affiliated bodies

Housekeeping

The Law

Past policies and practices of Accommodation Management in the Enterprise

Geographical location

Physical environment surrounding the building

⟶ Shows main flow of influence

identified, namely: the Building; Housekeeping Services; Personnel Control; Purchases and Supplies; and the Client and the Front Office.

Existing texts, relevant to the work of the Accommodation Manager, tend to be somewhat specialist in approach, eg involved primarily with cleaning and maintenance or sales of accommodation. It is therefore considered appropriate to look at the full scope of responsibilities of the Accommodation Manager (see figure 1) and consider how work is generally organised. The five main sub-systems have been identified, but the major relevance of the systems approach is the desire to emphasise the point that they cannot be considered in their pure form, isolated from their application. When considered in the field of Accommodation Management they must be applied. The basic practices and procedures of these will be broadly similar to their applications to other fields, but, within Accommodation Management, emphasis will be placed in different areas, and certain techniques utilised in preference to others.

Building design, construction, operation and maintenance is a very involved process concerning many areas and specialisms and, as a specialist in his own right, the Accommodation Manager will be affected and concerned with certain aspects of the building more than others. The five sub-systems can be seen to have separate identities, but only to a limited degree. Each sub-system interacts with the others and, because it is part of the system of Accommodation Management, it evolves in a certain way. The sub-systems each form the basis of a chapter in this book, but are not considered in any way as being self-determining. By identifying their components, a clearer picture can be developed of influences which must be controlled in the real world situation.

As shown in figure 2, the five sub-systems compound to make the System of Accommodation Management. A change in one sub-system will cause a change in others. An example of this, is shown in figure 3.

One component in particular of the system, warrants comment and that is the Client. It must be remembered that the client, whether identified as a customer, guest, patient, student or visitor, is of utmost importance, as the services are provided for him. In operations where management of the accommodation is not the main purpose of the

Figure 3 *Possible influences causing a change in sales policy and possible influences of that change*

	Change in sales policy influenced by:	Change in sales policy influences:
Building	Rooms left unused	Bed configuration
Personnel control	Bad salesmanship of Front Office staff	Staff training Hours of work Manpower requirements
Purchasing and supplies	Excess stocks of consumables demands high turnover of custom to avoid wastage	Increase in stock turnover needed due to higher sales
	Increased speed of room service might enable more frequent lettings	Higher turnover necessitates quicker service
Housekeeping	Inability to achieve desired speed of room servicing	Speed of servicing required and numbers and types of rooms to be serviced
	Non-availability of certain areas undergoing maintenance	May necessitate changes to planned preventative maintenance routine
	Housekeeping services available would meet needs of a more select clientelle	Higher levels of service may be required

operation and does not justify its own existence, accommodation staff may not come in direct contact with other users, eg in a factory, it is easy to lose sight of the fact that the accommodation services are there for the benefit of the user.

Outside the system of Accommodation Management are many more components which will also influence the system and some of these components will, in their turn, be influenced by the system of Accommodation Management. These environmental aspects, shown in figure 2, are now considered.

1 The *enterprise* as a whole, its purpose, aims, policies and its management will inevitably bear considerable influence on the Accommodation Management system and similarly, the Accommodation Management system will influence the enterprise. An outline of these influences is shown in figure 4.

2 The next environmental component is *technology*. As technological advances are made, so the system of Accommodation Management responds. In some cases major developments can be achieved rapidly through application of new, fast-moving technology, eg the application of computers. Other technological changes occur more slowly, or at any rate will take much longer to have an impact on the system, eg development of new building materials.

3 *Consumables* of the system cover all supplies and provisions, including fuel and energy, water and telecommunications. Working to its best efficiency, the system will utilise these available resources to their greatest effect to achieve its overall aims. For best efficiency, the system needs to identify its own specific requirements with respect to consumables and choose from the options available the product most suited to its needs. Working most effectively the system should be influencing suppliers as to the characteristics of products produced and sold rather than finding a use for a product well marketed.

4 Different governments impose different *policies*, sometimes with the assistance of grants, and are another environmental influence which will affect the system. In recent years, policies of privatisation, encouragement of small businesses, development of tourism, implementation of Youth Training Schemes, and reduced government control of wages, are just a few of the policies directly affecting Accommodation Management systems.

5 *Legal implications* of the various aspects of Accommodation Management will generally be mentioned at the appropriate stages in the ensuing chapters and a list of the most relevant laws is included in Appendix 1. Two laws, which have imposed considerable constraints on the system of Accommodation Management, are the Fire Precautions Act 1971 and the Health and Safety at Work Act 1974. The system's response to these constraints is discussed later.

6 Cultural values and patterns associated with the *geographical location* of the accommodation will influence all the sub-systems of

Figure 4 *Influences imposed by the enterprise*

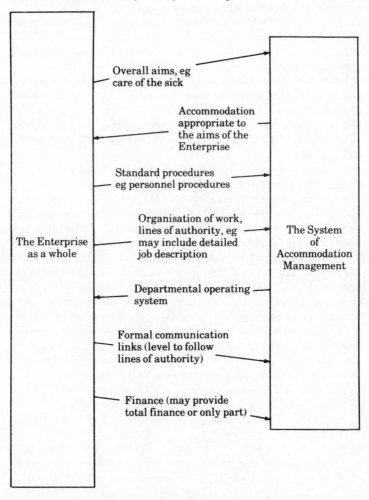

the system of Accommodation Management. The standard of living within the environs of the accommodation will also have its implication. Building styles, materials, furniture, fittings and furnishings, as well as staffing, structures and operating systems will be constrained by such elements as religion, customs and traditions. Similarly the system will affect the environment by creating employment, possibly wealth and other facilities, eg health care, leisure opportunities, depending on the purpose of the enterprise as a whole.

7 Characteristics of the *physical environment* surrounding the building influencing the system, together with possible impacts, are shown in figure 5.

8 *Past policies* of Accommodation Management will have considerable influence on the current methods. Even when some policies are rescinded, considerable time may need to elapse before effects cease to be seen, eg employment of a particular calibre of staff. Results of other policies may outlast the life of the building, eg selection of certain building materials. Past practices will also affect the current system, and again, some practices are more difficult to end than others, eg working hours of staff in some cases may only be changed when a vacancy occurs. Other past practices may automatically dictate current practice, eg the past use of a certain floor seal may eliminate other possible floor maintainance techniques.

9 In profit orientated systems, the role played by *competitors* may be considerable. They may dictate prices charged, facilities offered, images marketed and indeed many practices of the system. Conversely, bodies affiliated to the enterprise, of which the system of Accommodation Management is part, will also create constraints. Operations in other hotels within a group or other hospitals within a Health Authority may determine methods and

Figure 5 *Characteristics of the physical environment and influences on the system*

Characteristic of physical environment	Influence on the system
Climate	Building design Psychological and physical effect on users Heating and ventilation systems Energy useage Selection and care of surfaces
Atmosphere	Polluted atmosphere may affect selection, maintenance and durability of materials May make demands on ventilation system Particularly clean atmosphere will physically and psychologically affect all users and possibly volume of trade
Use of adjoining land	May generate noise or air pollution May create business or competition May improve or detract from visual qualities May affect prestige May affect daylight standards
Access routes	Proximity to main roads or transport terminals may add to or detract from business or affect amenities
Geographical characteristics	Will constrain building structure May affect amentities available

processes adopted. Economic advantages of standardisation can frequently be achieved.

10 *Security and safety threats* imposed on the system must be identified and appropriate action taken. Threats of terrorist attack, fire damage, petty theft or infection risks are a few of the possibilities which need to be identified and action taken as appropriate. Security, Health and Safety and Fire Policies, showing possible responses of the system in this area, are considered in chapter 6.

11 The availability of *finance* is another environmental influence which needs consideration. The system of Accommodation Management both uses money and creates it – by the sale of its facilities. In profit-making enterprises, the profit margin on accommodation sales may be considerable and yet incoming finance may be greatly limited. To make the best use of all monies made available, the system must operate a departmental budget and this is also considered in chapter 6.

12 The system of Accommodation Management in various enterprises will be influenced by different operating departments. In the Health Service, for instance, the Nursing, Medical, Paramedical and Catering systems will impose considerable constraints. In a hall of residence, the teaching system may be the one having most influence and, in an hotel, the accounts system will have an important bearing. Such constraints need to be considered in the development of the system, but similarly, the outgoing influences imposed by the system of Accommodation Management need to be identified before operating methods can be applied.

It can be seen, therefore, that the system of Accommodation Management is complex, being influenced by many environmental factors and itself causing continual changes and responses in the environment. These environmental elements are the constraining influences on the development of the system, and the Accommodation Manager must appreciate that these influences are never static. In response to this the system of Accommodation Management must itself be 'organic', ie ever changing in response to various stimulii.

References
[1] LEE, R, *Building Maintenance Management*, Crosby, Lockwood and Staples 1976

[2] MAYON-WHITE, B and MORRIS, D, *Systems Behaviour*, Open University Press 1974

The Building

Looking at the accommodation system of a given establishment it could be argued that of all the major sub-systems, the one which might exist independently is the building. No matter how admirably it has been designed and built, it could not function as an hotel, a hospital, or a sports complex without the other sub-systems. The building is the slowest system to change and is the least dynamic of all the systems. It is relatively stable (though alterations can be made) and is therefore an appropriate place to start an investigation into an accommodation system.

1.1 ELEMENTS OF A BUILDING

It is useful, first, to determine of what the building is composed. What are the elements of a building? What effect do these elements have on the total system? The elements can be identified as:
   (i) The site;
  (ii) The structure;
 (iii) The fittings.

(i) **The site** The site might be the precise size of the building structure itself or it might comprise acres of land. The site has both physical and environmental characteristics which will influence the structure and the operating of the establishment (see figure 1.1).

(ii) **The structure** The structure consists of:
(a) Foundations, eg footings, pile (the type being dependant on geophysical aspects and building shape)
(b) Walls, either framed (eg timber, steel, concrete with infill panels of glass reinforced concrete, glass reinforced plastic, brick, etc, and an external cladding of brickwork, ceramic, cement rendering, etc) or load bearing (eg concrete, masonry)
(c) Roof, either flat or ridged.

The structure imparts various physical and psychological qualities on the building. Physically, the structure must be firm to resist forces of compression and tension on the building, eg gravity, water, wind and loads. Physical qualities will be achieved by a combination of the characteristics of the materials used and the configuration of these materials, ie the design and shape of the building. The loads on the building may be 'live', eg furniture, water pressure, snow loading,

Figure 1.1 *Site characteristics and their influences on the establishment*

Site characteristics	Influences on the hotel
Geographical location	Proximity to consumers Access Climate Availability of labour and supplies Local planning regulations
Aspect (and other structures in the vicinity)	Amount of sun, shade, wind
Geophysical	Bearing capacity of land Suitability for building Type of structure and foundation Drainage Access
Dimensions	Shape and size of building
Pollutants, eg noise, vibration, carbon, sulphur	Aesthetic desirability of site Building foundations, structure and materials
Other structures	Aesthetic qualities Business

people, or 'dead', eg gravity and the weight of the building. Most elements of the building are designed to transfer these loads through the walls to the ground (hence the importance of the site and the bearing pressure of the sub-soil).

Psychological qualities of the building will be achieved by a combination of design and shape and of the materials used. Frequently buildings are designed to be a symbolic shape, ie designed to meet peoples' (users' and observers') expectations of what a hospital, a restaurant, or a church, looks like. In addition to these, the client (that is, in this case, the person or enterprise who requires a building to be constructed) and designer will usually desire to achieve further qualities, eg an impression of luxury for a top grade hotel or an impression of relaxation for a leisure centre.

A constraining influence on the client and designer will inevitably be finance. The functional characteristics have priority; the building must 'work'. It must also be remembered that clients' priorities vary. One client's first priority might not, in fact, be 'functionability'. He or she may be building for investment.

(iii) The fittings The fittings of a building include:

Partitions	Sanitary fitting
Window frames	Heating and electrical items
Doors	Finishing items, eg architraves,
Gutters	skirtings, etc.

They represent the more flexible items of the building and they may be removed without affecting the integrity of the building itself. Nevertheless, they are vital to the function of the building as an accommodation system. As with the structure, fittings impart physical and psychological characteristics.

1.2 PLANNING AND CONSTRUCTION

Now that an analysis has been made of what the building comprises (both physically and psychologically), it will be valuable to consider how a building comes into existence and how it fits into the accommodation system.

Design systems In the planning and constructing of large public buildings, it is common, if not inevitable, that designs are somewhat stereotyped. These buildings are designed for a wide market and they must satisfy many diverse groups now, and in years to come, when expectations and requirements may have changed. Building designs unlike cars, furniture or clothes, may need to be archetypal, ie stand the test of time, be as useable and satisfactory in 60 years time as they are today.

There are various design systems which can be identified, whether it is a teaspoon which is being developed or a multi-storey office block. The first is the *Vernacular Design*. This is where an individual identifies a need, designs a solution, constructs and then uses it. As the plans and designs are developed, further possible uses are identified and amendments to the original needs are made as the solution is built. Further amendments to the plans or designs may be made in the light of practicalities emerging. The finished product, depending on the individual's abilities, can be exactly what is wanted, and meet requirements precisely. It may be of no use at all to anyone else; the idea may, alternatively, be used by someone else and probably modified and developed.

The next design system is the *Empirical Exchange*. The client analyses his or her own needs, and commissions another to design and construct a solution. There can be a high degree of individual interpretation on the part of the designer/builder. Designs can be amended during construction. Also, communications between the client and the designer/builder can be informal. Again custom-built items can be constructed to meet the needs of an individual.

Another design system is *Direct Patronage*, where the client is also going to be the user of an object. Again an individual custom-built design is required, but in this case, the designer passes the plans to another for construction. As the network becomes more complex, original requirements and requests become more difficult to modify, as the communication process becomes more sophisticated and formal (see figure 1.2).

The final design system is the *Rational Network* (see figure 1.3). The user may not even exist when the product is first considered. The client and the designer must endeavour to predict the user requirements. They must try to satisfy the needs of the maximum number of future users and inevitably individualities must frequently be sacrificed and compromises made. It is, *this* design process which is the norm, when considering large public buildings. The client might be a health authority; the designer is an architect and his team; the constructor usually consists of an enormous number of firms and tradesmen. Inevitably, by the time a building is constructed, the users are rarely all satisfied with the overall design and construction of the building but the building is stereotyped and aims to satisfy most people most of the time.

Design and construction of a building emerge in three separate phases. These are:

1 The problem identification and briefing phase
2 The design phase
3 The construction phase.

1.2.1 Problem identification and briefing

Building design and briefing of a designer must be initiated in some way. The conception of a building first emerges when a problem is identified. Planning predictions in a health authority might foresee too many patients for existing resources; business opportunities for a new hotel are identified; capital is held which a client wishes to invest in a building. In one way or another the client comes to a decision that he or she wishes to build. This problem realisation stage leads the client to consult an architect and explain his or her plans for the future. Such a consultation would constitute the commencement of briefing

Figure 1.2 *Direct Patronage Design Network*

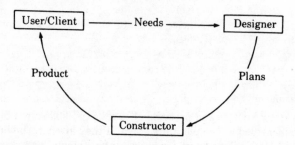

Figure 1.3 *Rational Design Network*

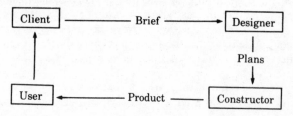

the architect. At the first consultation, the architect would not wish the client to outline any definite plans, rather, briefing on 'the problem' and discussion of the client's general idea is required. A site may or may not have been found at this phase, but detailed planning cannot occur until this element has been acquired.

As has been shown in the Rational Design Network (figure 1.3), the user is not able to represent him or herself, nor to brief the architect. In order to foresee accurately future users' needs the client will usually organise a planning team. This team will comprise representatives of different disciplines of future users. Frequently these representatives are practising specialists. In a very large concern with different users having separate requirements, some members would be co-opted onto the team as and when required. In the planning of an hotel, a food and beverage manager would be invited to join the team when catering departments were to be discussed. An executive housekeeper might be enlisted to give information regarding requirements of a housekeeping department.

It is worth noting that such practising specialists are not always invited onto planning teams. Accommodation Managers in some situations may indeed have to fight for this right. This being so, when given the opportunity, the Accommodation Manager must capitalise on the situation. The accommodation department within the new building can benefit in many ways if a specialist of that discipline has been involved in the planning process. Some information that a housekeeping representative in an hotel or a domestic services manager in a hospital might contribute includes:

(a) Specific requirements of that department; store rooms, linen rooms, laundry, service rooms, periphery stores, changing facilities, rest rooms. Specifications should include dimensions, services, fittings and surfaces required.

(b) Aspects on design which simplify and assist maintenance, servicing and overall standards achieved; siting of power sockets, suitable surfaces and their qualities.

(c) Requirements such as access to upper storeys; service lifts, ramps, etc.

All future activities and procedures to take place within a building must be identified at the planning stage. If they are not, the building may well be erected without some seemingly obvious and very basic components. It would not be the first time that an hotel had been constructed without a kitchen, or a hall of residence without a linen room. The needs of different building users must all be considered, including the needs of the disabled as well as those of the able-bodied. A well organised and informed planning team may well not only avoid such omissions, but could also greatly assist in achieving a more satisfied building user. The planning team's objectives, therefore, are to prepare a comprehensive and appropriate brief, and to assist by representing the user in further stages in the development of building plans.

Figure 1.4 *Building Feasibility Study*

1 The consumer identification	eg Area population, current and predicted population trends, tourism, industry, commerce Population type, eg age, health, wealth Accessibility of the site Communication links of the area Position of the site for accessibility Competition
2 Total capital costs	eg The site Design and construction costs Equipment and furnishings Pre-opening costs, eg stock, salaries, promotion Insurance, rates, rent Debtors
3 Predicted return on capital and running costs	Analysis of expenditure Payback periods Replacement cycles Cash flow

When initial briefing has been completed, early in the design process, a feasibility study, evaluating potential market, usage of the building, capital costs, profits (where appropriate) and overall assessment of the proposed investment must be completed. The feasibility study may have been completed by the client, or he may commission the architect to make the study. Some of the aspects to be considered in such a feasibility study are outlined in figure 1.4.

1.2.2 Design phase
The design phase follows problem identification and briefing, though distinction between the two phases is not clear-cut and a large degree of back-tracking or reiteration will occur. The design phase emerges following clarification of the needs and requirements of the client and is often considered as having five basic aspects:
1 The brief finalisation
2 Analysis of requirements
3 Synthesis of plans
4 Implementation of plans
5 Communication.

Since it is the architect who has prime responsibility for this phase it will be valuable to consider the architect's role. An architect must be chosen carefully (though some large organisations employ their own). Commissioning the 'right' architect will inevitably affect the satisfaction of the client, and the Royal Institute of British Architects (RIBA) publishes a valuable leaflet on the commissioning of an architect.

Architect is a legal term and an architect does, therefore, have various legal responsibilities. He or she is the agent responsible for the client's money and is legally responsible for the building. In carrying out the work, he or she must consider the client, the future building user and those involved in construction. The architect is responsible for the site, the structures, the methods of construction and the materials used.

1.2.2.1 Briefing

The architect may be responsible for the completion of the feasibility study; certainly, he or she must not only analyse the requirements identified by the client, but also aim to assess the future needs of building users, when, perhaps, the main function of the building has changed. Such analysis is necessary in order that identified needs and requirements can be interpreted into a successful building. It must be remembered that the life of a building may be considerable, and flexibility of the structure could well be a valuable, if not an essential asset.

1.2.2.2 Analysis

In the planning and construction of large buildings, such as hotels and hospitals, the design network involves the client, the designer, the constructor and the user. Since the users, as individuals, may not yet have been identified, the client and the architect must together, predict the needs and requirements of those users.

In the planning of new public buildings, the Rational Design Network may become further sophisticated. Standard packages have been developed in the interests of speed of production and economy. The Health Services, for example, have developed, over the years, various standard hospital plans, eg Best Buy, Harness and, most recently, the Nucleus Hospital Plan. The Nucleus set of plans is for a small intensive, first phase hospital, which can stand on its own and be capable of expansion, as and when finance and need dictate. The theory is that whether the unit is required in Lands End or John O'Groats the requirements of the users will be the same. From such a standardised process, an enormous amount of time, duplicated effort and money will be saved. Apart from the physical preparation of plans and the laborious task of preparing specifications, the initial work on user requirements is complete.

User requirements   The users of a building are not just the patients in a hospital, the sportsmen in a sports complex or the customers in a restaurant. The building user includes staff, spectators, tradesmen, firemen and contractors; anyone who is going to use the building at a later date.

User requirements can be considered under two headings:

1 *Individual needs*
  Physical needs, eg shelter, heat, light, food, sanitation, sleeping facilities, ventilation and safety.

Functional needs, ie to enable proposed activities to be carried out, eg furniture and equipment.

Psychological needs, eg privacy, security, efficiency, companionship.

2 *Group needs* eg social interaction requirements, space for business transactions, social functions.

In assessing both group and individual needs, changes in fashion and attitudes and the standards of requirements must be considered. All the identified needs must be analysed, and their implication interpreted by the architect in the form of plans and designs for the new building. A need for sleeping accommodation might have the following space implications:

Appropriate space for beds (single, twin, family or dormitory style)
Space for storing day clothes
Space for appropriate sanitary facilities
Space for linen store
Space for changing clothes and dressing.

In developing plans, the architect must aim to allow individual and group activities to be carried out economically, conveniently, efficiently and comfortably. To achieve this, ergonomic theory must be applied (see 1.2.2.3(2)). Among other things, this will tell the architect how much space, for example, is required by one person using a bed, storing day clothes, using sanitary fittings, etc.

Before any plans can be drawn up, much analysis must be undertaken to prepare data and evaluate and co-ordinate ideas. At the analysis stage, the architect must also be considering what specialists may be involved in further development of the building design (for example, advice may be needed as to what type of linen system is proposed).

1.2.2.3 Synthesis

With all the data which the architect has acquired, at the synthesis stage some conclusions must be drawn and plans developed. At this stage, it should be the architect's aim to offer a variety of possibilities to the client. With the development of Computer Aided Design (CAD), the synthesis stage of design, in particular, has become much more dynamic. Implications of various alternatives can be readily identified. Testing, checking and redesigning work will occur as the client and architect meet and discuss the plans. The plans now developed are only at the sketch plan stage, but, by this time, the architect is likely to have involved others. These will include engineers and a quantity surveyor to advise on practicalities and economic matters respectively. Plans proposed must meet legal requirements and provisional planning permission may be applied for.

1.2.2.3(1) Principles of planning and room layout

To recap, the architect now has information with respect to building users and their activities. Within legal, safety and cost constraints, at the synthesis stage, he must aim to develop designs for a building where all the required activities can take place both efficiently and comfortably. To do this, the architect must consider data on:

Numbers of people
Types of individual activity
Types of group activity
Timing and places of activities.

For example, in a student hall of residence, the architect might consider:

Students – arriving and leaving as individuals and sub-groups
  – grouping together to eat
  – separating out to sleep
  – grouping together to watch television
  – sub-groupings for cooking, washing, etc
  – individual needs for personal hygiene
Visitors – arriving and leaving individually
Domestic staff – arriving and leaving individually and in groups
  – grouping together for instruction
  – separating out for work
  – grouping together for eating
  – individual needs for personal hygiene
Maintenance staff – arriving and leaving individually and in groups
  – working individually
  – grouping for eating
  – individual needs for personal hygiene
Catering staff – arriving and leaving individually and in groups
  – grouping for work
  – grouping for eating
  – individual needs for personal hygiene
Residential staff/Burser – arriving and leaving individually
  – individual needs for work
  – grouping for eating
  – individual needs for relaxation, some eating and personal hygiene.

The architect must consider the noise implications of different activities; siting of radiators and other fittings; how activities coincide (which will involve considering the pattern of movements within the building); and what other activities might occur in the future, depending on social and economic trends. Gradually, a configuration of rooms will be developed which meet individual, group and operational needs.

The detailed planning of room layout can now be considered. The usefulness of a room depends on the shape and siting of doors and windows. These factors limit the size and arrangement of furniture and, therefore, the activities which can operate. Space represents money and cannot be wasted, but adequate space must be available to achieve comfort. This again depends on the activities within the room which, in turn, also determine the furniture and equipment needs.

1.2.2.3(2)   Ergonomic aspects

To achieve user comfort within a building ergonomic theory must be applied at the synthesis stage. Ergonomics is defined as, 'the study of the relationship between man and his environment' and with greater elucidation, 'the study of characteristics of people in order to develop equipment and procedures that are properly suited to these characteristics'. Ergonomics starts with an examination of the capabilities and limitations of people, with respect to gathering and processing information and taking action on that information. Ergonomics is interested in how well people see; how much light they need; what colours they discriminate; how much information they can handle at once; how quickly they deal with it; how people take action (how strong they are, how far they can reach); etc. Ergonomics takes the information gathered and uses it to design equipment, space and procedure, matched to the needs of the user.

Broadly, there are four aspects involved in ergonomics, which are: anthropometrics; kinetics; applied physiology; and applied psychology.

These cover body dimensions, muscle movement, man's physical metabolism, abilities and requirements and man's varying mental states and requirements.

Anthropometrics   Anthropometrics involves measurement of average human dimensions for certain groups, eg soldiers, children 3–5 years old, car drivers, hospital domestic staff, and average dimensions of the adult population as a whole.

Dimensions available are virtually unlimited, eg heights, arm lengths, eye levels, finger lengths. Such information is used by many sectors, eg furniture manufacturers, industrial work place designers and, of course, the architect. It enables the architect to specify dimensions of doors, windows, work surfaces, steps, corridor sizes, room sizes (dependent on usage), and any other building elements to enable that element to be functional, comfortable to use, convenient, efficient and economic.

Kinetics   Kinetics is a study of the muscles of the human body and their use. Architects need to consider how the user's body will be positioned and muscles used when undergoing any activity for which the building is being designed. Dimensions need to be such, that, when a user is, for example, moving a heavy object he or she can (and is, hopefully, encouraged by dimensions) to utilise the larger muscles in the arms and legs, in preference to the smaller back muscles. Consider a domestic assistants' cleaning cupboard. If domestic assistants are going to be expected to pick up heavy buckets, there needs to be, among other things, space in the storeroom for them to bend their knees, enabling the thigh muscles to take the weight.

Applied physiology   Human physiology data also needs to be applied to building design. Here the architect needs to have an understanding of the physical requirements of man, eg fresh air or oxygen requirements; temperature; humidity; lighting requirements; effects of noise; odour; mechanical vibration; visual effects on man (such as changing light intensities, colour, patterns, shapes); needs for sustenance; sanitary requirements; effects of air movement; effects of tactile characteristics. These needs must be analysed and the appropriate responses made in the design work to facilitate them.

Applied psychology Applied psychology is the final aspect of ergonomics and this discipline is concerned with man's mental state and needs, again dependent on the activities carried out, and on the specific user group. Here the architect will need to consider, for example, how much mental stimulation to create in an area, or conversely how to achieve a restful and relaxing environment; how to create an impression of informality, efficiency, opulence, tradition, intimacy, discipline, etc. The mood aimed for may need to be flexible, as indeed, the whole building interior may, but it must be in response to identified needs. Different groups of people have different psychological needs and abilities, and vary in their motivation, concentration, learning patterns, interactive behaviour, etc.

Using a knowledge and understanding of ergonomics, the architect can design practical and economic environments in which the user will feel comfortable.

1.2.2.3(3)   Room sizes and shapes

As the synthesis stage progresses, and the architect develops room plans and layouts, a recommended schedule of furniture may be prepared. This will be needed to achieve a valid assessment of the plans by the client. In the Health Service, where standardisation for economy is a major objective, a standard *Activity Data Base* has been developed, ie given the type of activity within a room, a standard recommended schedule of furniture has been developed. Further than this, given the activity and component (eg activity: emptying or filling a damp mopping bucket; component: a slop sink), *Component Data Base* information provides standard specifications for components.

Actual room sizes and shapes will not only be dependent on the fittings, their dimensions and layout, but also on the shape and site of the building and environment (eg sea view), on the activities of that room, and on the ergonomic needs which have been identified. In the interests of economy, the architect will consider very carefully the use of space. Due to the multiplying effects of costs, even slight increases in room sizes are expensive. There is a definite trend for rooms in newer buildings to be smaller than previously. By careful planning, it may be possible to reduce room sizes, but not reduce space availability. Two single rooms may take up 50% more space than one twin room, yet the useable space may only be in the region of 20% greater in the single room.

Space allocations must reflect market demand. Generally, the higher star rated hotels have, overall, more space allocated to each customer than the lower grade hotels. Within an hotel the ratio of single, double, twin or studio rooms must be based on data collected in the feasibility study (see also chapter 5). The architect will also need to consider standardisation of room sizes within an hotel group. Just as the Health Service aims for economy through standardisation, so hotel groups may stipulate room sizes to enable economies through bulk purchasing, pre-fabrication and the like.

Finally, the architect will be constrained in the design of the building by legal aspects, local bye-laws, and fire regulations. These aspects obviously need to be applied throughout the design phase, but crucially at this synthesis stage, to avoid abortive work. As options are eliminated, a general agreement is made as to the route to follow, and the architect's brief should not alter after this.

1.2.2.4 Implementation

The presentation by the architect of final designs and plans to the client can be considered as the implementation stage (in some cases, alternative proposals may be submitted). Data has been interpreted in plans, and a definite proposal has been developed. If the client chooses now to change the brief, much work will be wasted and ultimately the client will bear the cost. Working drawings will have been developed, so that following acceptance of the plans, tenders can be invited, contracts made and building can commence.

In evaluating plans submitted to him or her by the architect, the client must be satisfied with respect to the following:

(a) Overall shape and appearance of the building

(b) Convenience of entering and leaving (various different entrances may be needed, eg for customers, tradesmen, staff, deliveries)

(c) External facilities for visitors and building users

(d) Relation to the external environment

(e) Efficiency of circulation system

(f) Convenience of activity areas in relation to one another

(g) Privacy, quiet and other psychological needs

(h) Detailed provision of heating, lighting and ventilation

(i) Facilities for changing demands, eg weekends/weekdays, summer/winter.

1.2.2.5 Communication

Throughout the design process, communication is vital. It has been shown that in the Rational Design Network the future user can rarely speak for himself. His needs and requirements must be foreseen. The preparation of the architect's brief is vitally important, but up to the implementation stage, the client should feel free to modify that brief. Even after this stage, as implications become clearer, mistakes and omissions realised, it is preferable for corrections to be made, even at a cost, than, for known faults to be ignored.

Communication between the architect and client must be free-flowing. Communication between the architect and constructor will become more formalised. The client's requirements having been assessed, there is less leeway for negotiations between designer and builder.

A summary of the design phase is given in figure 1.5.

Figure 1.5 *Summary of design phase*

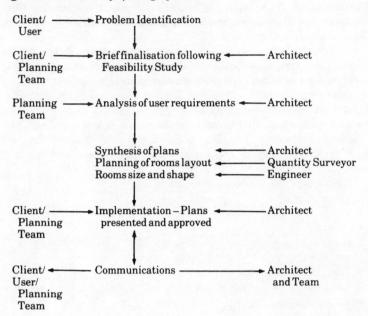

1.2.3 Construction phase

By the completion of the design phase, detailed design of every part and component of the building has been presented to and passed by the client. Complete cost checkings of all designs will have been carried out and approved, and the architect's team will now comprise quantity surveyors and engineers. Planning permission will have been applied for. Approval of the building plans from a practical point of view, as well as a legal necessity, must not only be granted by the local authority (under the Town and Country Planning Act 1954), but also by the:

Police
Fire Authority
British Telecom (or other telephone company)
Health and Safety Executive
Gas Board
Electricity Board
Other specialised authorities, eg Education Authority, Health Authority as appropriate.

The quantity surveyor must now prepare, for the architect, the Bill of Quantities (a complete list of all requirements and their specifications), which will provide basic information needed in the tender documents. Firms can then be invited to tender. Tendering might be 'selective' or 'open' and contractors will fill in their labour costs on the Bill of Quantities. When the contractor has been appointed, various degrees of sub-contracting are likely before site operations commence. The architect will also appoint the clerk of works, a resident building specialist who is responsible for inspecting and controlling work on site.

The construction process will broadly follow the schedule outlined below, depending specifically on the type of construction, but also dependent on availability of labour, materials and equipment.

1.2.3.1 Construction process

1 The building is set out, that is the shape is measured out and defined (the building line, ie nearness to the road, is set by the local authority). Hoardings are erected and site access and services established
2 Excavation and services connections
3 Foundations
4 Erection of walls to the damp proof course. Provision of the dpc or membrane
5 Hard core and return fill (ie excavated material returned to trenches to provide the sub-base for concrete floors)
6 Floor level, eg timber, concrete
7 Basic shell (wood window frames inserted now, steel ones left until later)
8 Timber joists
9 Complete walls to roof
10 Roof carcass
11 Topping out (ie finishing the wall to the roof)
12 Plumbing, eg rainwater guttering and other plumbing to roof
13 Roof covering (approximate half way stage)
14 'First fix' of furnishings and surfaces
eg glazing; plumbing; joining; electric; gas
(the fixing of these is incomplete, as yet, to enable trades to work around one another)
15 Plasterboard, ceilings
16 Partition walls (ie non-load-bearing)
17 Plastering of ceilings and walls
18 Second fix (as first fix)
19 Sanitary appliances, wall fittings and other fittings
20 Painting
21 Floor finishes, eg vinyl tiles
22 Site works, eg drains layed and connected to main services
23 Clearing of site, laying of paths, erecting fences, landscaping.

Such a process, of course, will not always follow an exact pattern. Since there is not one central firm responsible for construction, each must be managed separately. However, these stages of construction can be grouped into three clear areas of work, as follows:

1–13 inclusive comprise the primary units, ie walls, floors, roof
14–17 inclusive comprise the secondary units, eg windows, stairs
18–22 inclusive comprise the tertiary units, ie finishes.

The clerk of works aims to ensure that the work is completed in a logical order, eg walls plastered before floor coverings are layed, to prevent waste, reduce time and to promote co-operation and job satisfaction of different trades.

When tenders are invited, specifications (from the Bill of Quantities) are given to contractors detailing the workmanship which must take place, and where appropriate, detailed sectional drawings are given to show components (eg guttering). Assembly drawings are also prepared to show how components fit together (eg wall joints and ceilings). Specification must be tight to ensure that standards are reached, eg the paintwork specification might detail not just British Standards, colour code, and paint type, but the number of undercoats and topcoats to be applied.

1.2.3.2 Performance specification

To prepare valid specifications, performance details or performance specifications must first be prepared. These give details of the required characteristics of an item. For example, with respect to a floor surface the performance specification might detail the following:

1 Surface suitable for the students' utility room in a hall of residence
2 Resistance to greasy and wet soilage
3 Slip resistance, even when wet
4 Resistance to heat, eg boiling water or fat
5 Noise absorbency with respect to impact sound
6 Good heat insulation properties
7 Comfort to stand on but non-resilient
8 Resistance to cutting and indentation by falling objects
9 Washable surface
10 Attractive appearance, colour variety, etc.

With these criteria in mind, the architect may specify:
1 A particular grade, quality and colour of flooring which he considers most nearly meets all the needs, eg sheet vinyl
2 Adhesive quality, eg waterproof
3 Installation details, eg hermetically sealed joints
4 Finishing details, eg two coats of waterproof seal

1.2.3.3. Quality assurance

To ensure that standards are being achieved, the specification is vitally important. In addition, the clerk of works will regularly be checking work. He will look at materials used, methods used and workmanship, constantly referring to the Bill of Quantities, to ensure that specifications are being met. It is estimated that about 25% of the architect's fees are apportioned to plan supervision, an important quality control system. The architect may also visit the site to check on quality.

1.2.3.4 Completion

When a building is said to be 'practically complete', this is a legal term meaning that it is fit for its intended purpose. The last responsibility of the building contractors is frequently the 'builder's clean'. Once in use, a period of defects liability will operate (eg 6 months for any defect, 12 months for engineering defects). During this period a portion of the funds is retained and the architect is responsible for checking the building for any defects and seeing that such work is made good before 'final completion' of the building.

1.2.4 Commissioning of the building

Once the brief has been finalised and plans accepted at the implementation phase, the client's responsibility with respect to the building design and construction is largely complete. The client may accompany the architect on site visits, but mostly his or her involvement with the building itself now awaits the completion stage and the 'handover'. The building is not the property of the client until this time.

During the construction of the building, the client must plan the functioning of the building and, as building completion nears, he will then be in a position to place orders for inventory, and carry out recruitment, selection and preparatory training of staff. At the date of the handover, insurance liability for the building passes from the architect to the client. Following the handover of the building, as has been stated, there is a period of defects liability, and should the user or the client have cause for complaint, the client must inform the architect who should ensure that defects resulting from a deviation from the specification are made good. (At this stage the housekeeping department frequently becomes involved in identifying defects.)

Frequently, in large buildings, commissioning teams are set up; these usually comprise future users, (often departmental heads). Their responsibilities can be divided into four areas:
1 Checking acceptability of building structure
2 Identifying equipment needs and ordering appropriately
3 Preparing schedules for staffing needs and dealing with selection, recruitment and training
4 Preparing schedules of organisation and operational procedures.

Most of the main work of the commissioning team will occur prior to handover, and it is probable that they will liaise with the clerk of works with respect to building structure matters.

Such is the process of design and construction of the building envelope. In an attempt to ensure that building users (whatever their function) are satisfied with the building, their requirements must be accurately predicted, specifications prepared to meet these requirements, and quality controls applied. The process of preparing specifications is complex, and yet vital if users are going to be satisfied in the future. In chapter 4 the preparation of specifications is considered further, with respect to supplies.

1.3 THE FITTINGS

As has been shown in the pattern of building construction, there are many components within the building. Some of these may be expected to have short lives, relative to the life of the building, eg wall coverings, others will normally be expected to last, and remain throughout the building's existence, eg water and drainage systems. It is the purpose of this next section to consider in more detail those elements of the building with which the users will interface most directly; those items in fact, which the Accommodation Manager will be most likely to be spending much of his or her time on, with respect to maintenance, modification or replacement. In each case possible performance attributes will be considered, specific types identified, the different characteristics analysed, and selection criteria suggested. The fittings have been divided into three areas:

1 Environmental services, ie heating, lighting, ventilation
2 Surface fittings, ie wall, floor and ceiling coverings, windows, sanitary fittings, furniture and furnishings
3 Interior design.

1.3.1 Environmental services
The categories of fittings might also be divided into:
1 Essential features
2 Features which are desirable though not essential.

The environmental services are essential (though not in any specific style) to provide water, oxygen and carbon dioxide exchanges, variable lighting and variable heating. Another essential item to man is food. Provision of food is beyond the scope of this book, except to say that the building will need to provide adequate space and facilities for food storage, preparation, service and eating. The other essential environmental services will be considered under the headings of: Water; Heating; Ventilation; Lighting.

1.3.1.1 Water
Water may be required for any of a number of uses within an establishment eg:
Personal hygiene and sanitation
Culinary uses
Cleaning processes – laundry, environmental cleaning
Manufacturing processes
Heating systems
Fire fighting
Leisure and health pursuits

For each of these uses, the performance specification might vary, eg depending on the degree of hygiene required. Generally, regardless of the use, the source is the same, namely the water mains which enter the building below ground at a depth adequate to give protection from most frosts, and under sufficient pressure to meet fire fighting requirements (though this pressure may be supplemented by a pump in high-rise buildings). Much of British water is classed as hard. Depending on the degree of hardness and subsequent uses from leaving the mains, the water may pass through a softening plant. Softening plants are costly to install but may be necessary where very large quantities of water are used (as in laundries), or where a build up of calcium and magnesium deposits in pipework would occur relatively quickly, so reducing efficiencies.

It is probable that some water will feed a storage tank, eg for hot water installations but water supplying taps for drinking or cooking purposes comes from a direct supply.

1.3.1.2 Hot water supply

Ample hot water is not just a convenience in buildings, but also, under the Offices, Shops and Railway Premises Act (1963), it became a requirement. The temperature of the water needs to be such that it is safe to use, economic to produce and maintain, and sufficiently hot to be effective in use. It is estimated that the hot water requirements are:

Hotels – approximately 115–135 litres/person/day

Hospitals – approximately 130–225 litres/person/day.

An average temperature for hot water is 55°C.

There are four main methods of producing hot water:

1 Central storage plant and distributive pipework, servicing the whole building
2 Remote storage plant, heated from a common heat source, with zone distribution pipework (pipework feeding separate zones of the building)
3 Local storage vessels, heated by independent sources
4 Local instantaneous water heaters.

Due to the quantities used and the peak demands, adequate storage is essential for the first three of these.

Factors to consider when selecting a hot water system are:

1 Economy with respect to
  (a) fuel, fuel storage, heating apparatus installation
  (b) distributive system, minimum 'deadlegs', installation costs
  (c) maintenance costs
  (d) storage of hot water
2 Capacity, ie amount of hot water which can be produced
3 Temperature requirements
4 Aesthetics of visible elements and 'acoustics'
5 Cleanliness and maintenance of storage tanks to control the risk of infections such as Legionnaires Disease.

1.3.1.3 Heating

Heat within a building is derived from:

  (a) The building occupants (the amount depends on their number, age, sex, activity, period of occupation, etc)

(b) Solar gain (here the amount depends on orientation, shape and construction, time of day or year, site of building)

(c) Lighting (dependent on wattage and use)

(d) Electrical and mechanical apparatus (depending on wattage and use)

(e) The heating system.

Conversely heat losses are through:

(a) Building materials and contents (depending on conductivity)

(b) Ventilation (depending on rate of air change, outside and inside temperatures)

(c) Building construction (depending on external radiant temperature and air temperature, wind, moisture in construction)

(d) Refrigeration plant.

Requirements of heating systems vary. Recommendations are made for temperatures within different room types, given a relative humidity of 30–60%; the temperatures are not indisputably suitable in all circumstances, and, in any case, to achieve such average temperatures, heating systems must be flexible and adapt to different conditions. In most situations a 'comfort zone' is aimed for, that is a temperature at which 70% of users feel comfortable.

The performance attributes of the heating system, in general terms, will be to provide optimum room temperatures for given activities, economically and efficiently. More detailed performance attributes will vary with the user, the room use and the building type. Patients in hospital wards, recovering from operations, will usually require higher and more constant temperature than guests in an hotel bedroom. Some attributes which will need to be considered when selecting a heating system include:

1 Maximum, minimum and average temperature requirements

2 Temperature variances required, during a day, a week and a year

3 Speed with which temperatures must be reached

4 Aesthetics of heat emitters

5 Control requirements at point of use

6 Safety aspects

7 Security

8 Economy

9 Maintenance

10 Space requirements.

These attributes will need to be considered, in their turn, with respect to the following:

1 The users: their age, activities, sex, temperature to which they are accustomed

2 Humidity levels and ventilation system

3 Hours of use for given activities, days of use (eg exclusive of weekends) and weeks of use (eg seasonal hotels)

4 General decor of an establishment

5 Degree of flexibility desired in order to meet any one individual's requirements

6 Cost constancy and reliability of supply of selected fuel

7 Installation costs

8 Accommodation and opportunity costs (eg space for boiler room)

9 Running costs (eg fuel and its efficiency, maintenance, insurance decorating)

10 Legislation.

Heating systems Heating systems can broadly be categorised into five types:

1 *Warm air* – air is centrally warmed and fed into the room via ducts. It is filtered before discharge, and cooler air is returned by separate ducts. (Warm air curtains may also be a feature of this type)

2 *Under floor* – heating grids are fitted in the floor screed, and are operated using off peak electricity

3 *Ceiling* – low temperature radiant elements are fitted between the ceiling joists and the final finish

4 *Localised heaters* – small moveable or fixed units, eg gas, electric or paraffin heaters

5 *Radiator system* – comprising a central boiler, distributing pipework and emitters.

The last of these, namely the radiator system, is by far the most commonly used in large buildings, for reasons of economy, efficiency and safety, and there are many variations of this sytem. Variables include:

1 The heat transfer medium, eg pressurised water, steam, air

2 Distribution system, eg gravity, pumps, single or two pipe system

3 Boiler fuel, eg gas, oil, various solid fuels

4 Boiler type, eg new high efficiency boilers

5 Heat emitter, eg pipes, radiators, convectors, skirting heaters.

Whichever heating system is used, to be successful it must fulfil various requirements. The first of these is economy. The efficiency conscious manager will be looking for ways to save energy. The heating system is, generally, the largest user of energy in a building, and it is sensible to look for reductions here. Rooms should never be overheated but be kept as cool as is compatible with comfort. Comfort is dependent not just on air temperature, but also on velocity of air movement (ie feeling of a draught), and relative humidity, as this affects heat exchange. Modern developments, eg harnessing of heat pumps, or use of high efficiency boilers, should be utilised where possible, and flexibility of the heating system also considered. Zoned heating, sensitive thermostatic control, recycling of heat are all methods of energy conservation.

1.3.1.4 Ventilation

The purpose of ventilation is to provide a constant oxygen supply and to remove carbon dioxide and exhaled air, smells and gases. The

ventilation system within a building will be deemed to be satisfactory
or not, depending on:

1 The volume of fresh air provided
2 The distribution of air and speed of air movement
3 The air temperature
4 The relative humidity
5 The purity of the 'fresh' air

The volume of air required depends on the number of people in a
given area and their activities, legislation, use of the room, odours and
condensation. Fresh air needs to be evenly diffused and should not
strike directly on occupiers. There needs to be a feeling of air
movement, but not a draught (ie air speed greater than 0.5 m/sec), and
the temperature of fresh air should not vary greatly from that of the
room, or mixing will not occur. In cold weather, fresh air may need
humidification or conversely in warm weather drying of air may be
desirable.

There are three methods of ventilation:

1 Natural, ie windows and doors, etc, allow air movement which is
   induced by temperature effects or wind
2 Mechanical – air movement is controlled by power driven fans
3 Mixed, ie either the incoming or outgoing air is induced by power
   driven fans.

Air cleaning Air within rooms may be cleaned by various apparatus available today. Some clean by filtration, some by ultra-violet
radiation. The principle is that air is sucked into the unit, cleaned and
returned. Such units may be used to deal with nicotine pollution,
odours and other pollution.

Psychrometry This science is involved with the behaviour of air
and water vapour. When the highest amount of water vapour,
appropriate to the temperature is present, the air is said to be
saturated. At lower pressures, this air would be unsaturated, ie could
theoretically hold more water. The ratio of the two pressures is the
relative humidity, and it is, therefore, the relative humidity which
determines the rate of evaporation from, for example, the human skin,
and affects comfort.

To create comfort, therefore, air must not only provide oxygen but
also a regulated humidity which is important.

Humidifiers Like air cleaners, humidifiers are designed to draw in
air from a room, treat it (in this case correct the moisture content) and
return the air to the room.

Ionisers Ioniser units may be fitted in certain areas to control the
positive/negative ion balance of the atmosphere. High concentrations
of negative ions are claimed to affect both mental and physical health.

Air conditioning Air conditioning goes further than ventilation. It
also aims to control the humidity factor as well as the air temperature,
its purity and gas content. Air conditioning, therefore, provides a
system of control for the total atmosphere of a building, ie heating,

oxygen replenishment, carbon dioxide removal, odour removal, cleaning of air, humidity controls. It may also have an ioniser fitted. It is expensive to install, involving plant at considerable capital cost, and distributive apparatus, but it is a system which is becoming more popular in this country, both from a comfort point of view and from an economic stance, since heat production is carefully controlled and re-cycling can occur. To reduce risk of infections such as Legionnaires Disease, air conditioning plants must be regularly cleaned.

1.3.1.5 Lighting

As with heating and ventilation, the lighting system must meet the needs of the user. It must be remembered that the user can vary, eg customer, domestic staff, maintenance staff, and so may the activities of any one of these groups, eg an hotel guest may use a bedroom for sleeping, reading, watching television, dressing. Each activity has different lighting needs. The lighting system must, therefore, aim to meet a variety of needs. Other requirements of the lighting system include economy, visually attractive fittings, safety, intensity control, creating the 'right' atmosphere, maximising use of space, concealing areas.

There are two types of light within a building:

1 Natural light.
2 Artificial light.

In the interests of fuel economy, use needs to be made of available natural light, but, of course, the quantity of this depends on orientation, cloud cover, time of day, etc. Windows, too, affect not only the amount of natural light, but also its quality. Where windows are placed on only one wall, or use is made of ceiling domes, glare and adaptation demands (the effect of changing light intensities on the eye) can cause problems. Other problems associated with the use of daylight are its conflict with energy conservation, heat loss through windows, heating control, excessive solar heat gain in sunny weather, and conflicts with privacy and security.

Even where maximum use is made of daylight, artificial lighting will still be required. For lighting building interiors, there are three main types:

1 *Tungsten* – fittings are cheap but inefficient in energy use and have relatively short life
2 *Fluorescent* – fittings are more expensive, more efficient and last longer
3 *New generation discharge* – more expensive, more efficient and last longer.

Exterior lighting is somewhat special, and the sodium discharge lamp, together with mercury halogen and tungsten halogen, normally take precedence.

The lighting system hardware comprises the light fitting; light shade; wiring; and control switches.

Other elements in the system are the user, his activities, legal requirements, safety, etc.

When planning a lighting installation, the following points must be considered:

1 Uses of area, light intensities and qualities required, period of use
2 Lighting control
3 Safety, eg of wiring, a night circuit, stairs
4 Structure, shape, aspects of windows, view
5 Window furnishings
6 Reflectiveness of interior surfaces
7 Uniformity of lighting (generally variable levels required)
8 Energy conservation
9 Running costs, replacement costs and replacement cycle
10 Heat generation
11 Visual appearance of fittings and effect on light distribution
12 Colour rendering of light source
13 Siting of fittings, eg wall or ceiling mounted, free standing, concealed
14 Siting of controls.

Recommended lighting levels for given activities are available (see bibliography).

1.3.2 Surface fittings

Characteristics and suitability of surface fittings, eg floors and walls are determined by:

1 The characteristics of the materials used
2 The manner in which the materials are fitted together, installed and maintained.

It is useful to look at the characteristics of different materials. With an understanding of the basic properties, this information can be applied to different types of surfaces.

1.3.2.1 *Properties of materials*

There are three basic criteria involved in the selection of materials: aesthetics; prestige; and cost efficiency.

The fundamental properties of materials are related to three areas inherent within their specific structures. These are:

1 Stiffness – that is the opposite of elastic, ie the ability to recover and this depends on stress
2 Strength – the force needed to break it
3 Toughness – the resistance to cracks.

These basic properties vary in any material depending on its condition, eg whether under compression or tension, temperature, eg steel is usually strong, but, at low temperatures, it is brittle, etc. The properties are determined by the:

Macrostructure	Molecular structure
Microstructure	Atomic structure of the material.

The main adjectives used to describe materials are listed below:
1 Acoustic properties
2 Aesthetic value
3 Colour and pattern
4 Corrosion resistance (ie degradation as a result of chemical action)
5 Cost
6 Durability
7 Electrical resistance
8 Elasticity/flexibility
9 Functional (depends on function)
10 Light reflectance/absorption
11 Porosity
12 Prestige value
13 Resilience
14 Slipperiness
15 Strength
16 Temperature resistance
17 Transparency
18 Toughness

1.3.2.2 Floor coverings
About three-quarters of all costs will, during the life of the building, be spent on floor maintenance. If initial selection is successful much time and money can be saved in the future, and, possibly, common accidents, eg slipping, minimised. Statistics show that, out of every 100 workers hurt, 16 are injured by falls on the level. Under the discipline of terotechnology, the architect, when specifying a particular floor covering, would be considering not only initial costs but also ongoing costs which include maintenance.

In preparing a performance specification for a floor covering, some of the criteria to be considered include those shown in figure 1.6. In addition to these, installation, replacement and repair also need consideration, as does the compatibility of the floor surface with the type and condition of the sub-floor.

Flooring types, characteristics and selection
Hard floor coverings have been classified as: porous; non-porous; and semi-porous, depending on their micro- and macro-structure.

Porous floor coverings include wood, cork, concrete; semi-porous includes many of the plastic variety, eg vinyl, vinyl asbestos, PVC, thermoplastic; non-porous includes epoxy resin, quarry tiles, marble. The porosity of the floor will greatly influence its resistance to soilage and, therefore, the required maintenance. Depending on the maintenance programme, inherent characteristics, eg attractive appearance, durability, chemical resistance, water resistance, slip resistance may

Figure 1.6 *Performance specification for floor covering*

Material property	Possible application to floor covering
1 Acoustic properties	May need to be sound reflecting or absorbing
2 Aesthetic value	More important in prestige areas
3 Colour and pattern	Variety may be important, also retention of this and effect on apparent soilage
4 Corrosion resistance	Consider spillages, sunlight degradation
5 Cost	Dependent on replacement cycle
6 Durability	Dependent on user density and activity
7 Electrical resistance	Important, eg in operating theatres where static electricity may develop
8 Elasticity	Consider quality of sub-floor
9 Functional	Consider maintenance
10 Light reflection	Important in relation to maintenance
11 Porosity	Consider spillages and ease of maintenance
12 Prestige	Consider in relation to aesthetics
13 Resilience	Affects comfort of users
14 Slipperiness	Very important, particularly when wet
15 Strength	Consider impacts (compression), underlying sub-floors could necessitate tensile strength
16 Temperature resistance	Consider spillages, cigarette ends, insulation
17 Transparency	Usually opaque required
18 Toughness	Abrasion resistance, resistance to cutting, etc, from falling objects

be enhanced. Other characteristics, eg acoustic properties, insulation properties, degree of resistance will remain unchanged. In selecting floor coverings, therefore, both inherent and applied characteristics must be considered.

1.3.2.3 Wall and ceiling coverings

Wall coverings are much less vulnerable than floor coverings to the effects of abrasion, spillages and impacts. Wall coverings do need to withstand certain elements, however, eg water in the form of steam; they may be selected for their protective abilities, hygiene qualities, or heat or sound insulation characteristics. Appearance characteristics may prevail also amongst the selection criteria. Some of the performance characteristics which might be applied to wall coverings are shown in figure 1.7.

As with floor coverings, terotechnology must be applied. Installation, maintenance, replacement and repair all need consideration. Replacement cycles of wall and ceiling coverings are, generally, more frequent than that of floor coverings (particularly hard floors), but convenience of replacement might be critical, eg speed of redecorating a room in an hotel to minimise the loss of revenue. Coverings must be compatible with the type and condition of the base wall or ceiling, eg vinyl paints should not be applied to new plaster without the appropriate drying out period.

Figure 1.7 *Performance specification for wall/ceiling covering*

Material property	Possible application to wall/ceiling covering
1 Acoustic properties	May need to absorb radiating noise, eg restaurant
2 Aesthetic value	Appearance can dramatically change a room
3 Colour and pattern	Variety may be important, hide imperfections
4 Corrosion resistance	eg grease and condensation in kitchens. Nicotine stains
5 Cost	Dependent on replacement cycle
6 Durability	Consider resistance to rubbing
7 Electrical resistance	Will contribute to overall static levels in room
8 Elasticity	May need to cover cracks and surface defects
9 Functional	Consider usage of area
10 Light reflection	Dependent on colour, texture, degree of gloss
11 Porosity	Acoustic and soilage resistance properties could conflict. Tactile properties could be important
12 Prestige	Consider visual impact, eg in entrance area
13 Resilience	Impacts in busy corridors, eg from trolleys
14 Slipperiness	Less relevence
15 Strength	Consider impacts. Also consider resistance to insects and pests
16 Temperature resistance	Flammability could be crucial
17 Transparency	Usually opaque required
18 Toughness	Consider abrasion resistance

Wall and ceiling coverings; types, characteristics and selection
Paints There are many types; on some occasions they may be applied directly to the plaster or wall itself, on others, primers and sealers are required. Paints are composed of:

(a) Pigment (insoluble particles)
(b) Vehicle (comprising binder for gloss, toughness, etc, and solvent)
(c) Additives, eg to assist drying or application.

Some paints dry by evaporation of the solvent, though most require an additional chemical reaction, either resulting from air contact or within the paint itself. Some of the varying qualities of paints include:

(a) Ease of application
(b) Adhesion
(c) Strength
(d) Degree of gloss
(e) Durability
(f) Odour
(g) Toxicity
(h) Drying speed.

Some of the different types include water paints, emulsions, alkyd resins, cellulose, etc.

Wall and ceiling papers For contract use, wallpapers are subject to British Standards tests for bursting strength, tearing strength, tensile strength and light fastness. Commonly, 'duplex' papers are used, consisting of a base paper and a top paper. 'Simplex' papers are rarely as durable. Some types include embossed, flock, metallic and relief papers.

Plastic wall and ceiling coverings There are two types of plastic, namely, thermosetting and thermoplastic. An example of thermoplastic wall and ceiling coverings is laminated plastics; thermoplastics include PVC, bonded paper, and expanded polystyrene.

Fabric wall coverings These become more diverse and imaginative as time goes on, ranging from hessian types, through wool, and wool strands to silk.

Other wall and ceiling coverings The range is diverse, and includes wood, cork, ceramic tiles, terrazzo, stone, metal, eg copper, brick and glass.

1.3.2.4 Glazing

Under the heading of glazing, external windows, internal windows and partitions, glass coverings and mirrors might be included. As with the other surfaces, the specific use of the surface will determine the criteria for selection. The performance attributes of glass and glazing are given in figure 1.8.

Certain items of glass and glazing, eg external windows, will be installed relatively early on in the construction of a building. Other items, eg mirrors, will be fitted during commissioning. Replacement cycles will be similarly variable. Glass, the traditional material used for windows, mirrors, etc, is, characteristically brittle. Thus, facilities to ease replacement must be considered.

Glass and glazing types, characteristics and selection
Glass There are many types but the basic constituents for the manufacture are silica, soda and lime. The main types are:
(a) Soda lime glass
(b) Lead crystal
(c) Borosilicate.

It is the first, soda lime glass which is the basis of most flat glass used in windows, doors, etc, specialised types include:
(i) Toughened and laminated – for safety and security applications
(ii) Tinted – to provide colour and protection from solar radiation
(iii) Patterned – for privacy and decoration
(iv) Wired – for fire resistance
(v) Organic coated – for safety and security.

Not only the ingredients for manufacture but the manufacturing process itself will determine the quality and characteristics of the finished product.

Figure 1.8 *Performance specification for glass and glazing*

Material property	Possible application to glass and glazing
1 Acoustic properties	May be required to minimise noise transfer
2 Aesthetic value	Mirrors or windows used as decoration
3 Colour and pattern	Stained or textured glass is decorative
	Tinted glass used to minimise solar heat transfer or vision
4 Corrosion resistance	External windows subjected to air pollutants, eg sulphur, carbon
5 Cost	Probably related to aesthetics
6 Durability	Impact resistance, also compression from window frames and tension on table tops
7 Electrical resistance	Consider light fittings
8 Elasticity	Required when used as coating material
9 Functional	Eg allow maximum vision. Sound insulation
10 Light reflection	Windows usually do allow maximum light transfer
11 Porosity	Minimal for glazing
12 Prestige	To be in keeping with general design
13 Resilience	Impact resistance
14 Slipperiness	To aid cleaning and soilage resistance
15 Strength	Security could be an important feature
16 Temperature resistance	To prevent fire spread. Heat insulation
17 Transparency	May need to be transparent, translucent or opaque for privacy
18 Toughness	Shatter-proof materials may be required

Plastics There are several different types of plastics now available which are used in glazing. The most common are:
   (a) Polymethyl-methacrylate (acrylic) which has good impact properties, used for security and for shower and bath enclosures
   (b) Polycarbonate – virtually unbreakable when glazed
   (c) Polyvinylchloride (rigid PVC) – high resistance to breakage, good clarity and chemical resistance.
Generally speaking, comparing glass with plastics for glazing, plastics have higher resistance to impact and are less heavy; glass has better clarity, fire resistance and chemical resistance. Plastics are available in flat sheet, patterned sheet or thermoformed shaped panels in a wide range of thicknesses and sizes, clear or tinted.

Given the variety of glass and plastics used for glazing, to ensure safety and durability, installation is very important, selection of the correct type for a particular application is also vital. Materials and styles of glazing frames will also need consideration.

1.3.2.5 Sanitary fittings

Sanitary fittings can be defined as 'appliances fitted to a drainage system for the collection and discharge of foul or waste matter'. They are classified into two types:

1 Soil appliances, used for the collection and discharge of excretory matter, eg WCs, urinals and slop sinks.
2 Waste appliances for the collection and discharge of water after use, for ablutionary, culinary or other domestic purposes, eg baths, bidets, lavatory basins, sinks and showers.

The relationship between sanitary fittings, the water supply and drainage system has been covered in the *Environmental services* section 1.3.1. Here the types and characteristics of the fittings themselves will be considered (see figure 1.9). Not only the characteristics of the material, but also the shape and design of the sanitary fitting, will affect selection. To maximise hygiene standards and ease maintenance, sanitary fittings need to be streamlined without corners or crevices where soilage can collect. Also, the internal surface needs to be shaped to drain water, (here installation is important also), and the shape of the fitting should be such as to minimise soiling of surrounding surfaces during use.

Figure 1.9 *Performance specification for sanitary fittings*

Material properties	Possible application to sanitary fittings
1 Acoustic properties	Reverberations can be a problem. Electrical apparatus, eg dishwashers, can be noisy
2 Aesthetic value	Appearance may need to be in keeping with décor
3 Colour and pattern	Colour variety may be required. Smooth surfaces required for hygiene
4 Corrosion resistence	Besides water, uric acid, hypochloride and detergents are common contaminants
5 Cost	Dependent on replacement cycle
6 Durability	Resistance to impacts, particularly service sinks
7 Electrical resistance	Rarely a consideration
8 Elasticity	Rigidity usually required
9 Functional	Must hold water and drain
10 Light reflection	Consider in relation to appearance
11 Porosity	Impervious surface required
12 Prestige	Shape and fittings affect overall appearance
13 Resilience	Impact resistance
14 Slipperiness	To aid soilage resistance, but consider safety in baths and showers
15 Strength	To hold volume of water and user
16 Temperature resistance	Boiling water may be in contact
17 Transparency	Opaque usually required
18 Toughness	Chip resistance

Materials used for sanitary fittings; characteristics and selection

Ceramic (a) Fireclay – strong but semi-porous thus glazing is important

(b) Vitreous china – non-porous with fused ceramic glaze.

Cast Iron Mainly used for baths and coated with porcelain enamel.

Vitreous or enamelled steel Steel is very strong but the enamel may chip, these appliances are noisy.

Stainless steel May be mirror or satin finish, the satin having better resistance to scratching; good corrosion resistance.

Plastics Acrylic or glass fibre reinforced acrylic plastic mouldings are very light weight (which assists installation), slip resistant, with good heat insulation properties, but abrasives, flames, eg cigarettes, and some chemicals, eg solvents, may cause damage.

In selecting sanitary appliances, the appropriate auxilliary fittings such as plugs and taps must also be considered:

Taps Types include the conventional pillar type, spray taps, push-down, elbow action, supa taps and electronically operated types. Selection criteria will include:

(a) Requirements of main users of basin or sink, eg nurses, kitchen staff for vegetable preparation

(b) Hygiene standards required

(c) Hot water conservation

(d) Type of drainage outlet and plug

(e) Material required – eg chromed brass, ceramic topped.

Plugs Types include conventional plugs on chains, captive plugs (which may be raised or lowered), standing wastes (hollow pipe waste fittings). Some installations, eg those fitted with spray taps may not be designed to take plugs. (Hand washing under running water is more hygienic than filling a sink for washing.)

Cisterns Types include bell type and plunger type. Materials include thermoplastics and vitreous china. Cisterns may be close coupled low level or high level, and may be fitted with dual flush syphons to reduce water consumption or automatic flushers, eg urinals. Flushing troughs may be used, which service several WCs or urinals.

In selecting suitable sanitary fittings, many criteria need consideration:

1 Material of the fittings and colour

2 Type of fittings

3 Shape and dimensions of fittings

4 Type, style and material of accessories.

With respect to numbers of fittings, there are specified legal requirements, dependent on the use of an establishment and the number of users.

Following selection, careful installation is necessary if sanitary fittings are to work efficiently and have an acceptable lifespan. Degree of slope to allow correct drainage, suitable jointing materials to provide hygienic finishes, careful attachment to plumbing system, and walls and floor anchorages and buffering are all important.

1.3.2.6 *Furniture*

Furniture may be purchased for an establishment for many reasons. A certain item may be acquired as a focal point in a room, other items might be bought in order to develop a theme, others for prestige or investment. The majority of furniture is, however, bought primarily for functional reasons. It is needed to enable an activity to occur, or to occur with greater comfort, eg a desk at which to write, along with a suitable seat and a filing cabinet for storing paperwork.

It is not easy to define functional furniture, but, certainly, there are a few basic criteria without which furniture cannot be said to be functional. The criteria are listed and discussed below:

1 It must meet customer requirements (in this instance the customer is taken to mean the main user of the furniture, eg the patient in a hospital bed, the clerk in an office, etc). These requirements can be identified by first *analysing the activity* or activities for which the user requires the furniture item and then by applying ergonomic theory. For a chair, required by a secretary to sit on while typing. *Anthropometric data*, eg height, width and depth of seat, degree of slope on seat, etc; *kinetics*, eg siting of back rest, knobs for adjusting heights, varying tilt, etc; *applied physiology*, eg absorptive quality of the material, heat transfer and *applied psychology*, eg does it look like a secretary's chair? would all be applied.

   The relationship between one piece of furniture and another is also important, here, eg the secretary's chair and desk must be considered together.

2 It must meet maintenance requirements (the maintainer could be the room attendant, in the case of tables, chairs, etc, or include an electrician in the case of a television). Again, ergonomic theory can be applied, bearing in mind, that, because the activity has changed, eg cleaning a chair rather than sitting in it, so the requirements change.

3 Furniture needs to be strong if it is to be functional in large establishments. Furniture purchased for use in any large establishment should be *contract furniture*. Weak points are joints but, of course, the main frame material also requires strength.

4 Stability is another requirement of contract furniture. It is an ergonomic requirement of the users, but furniture must also be stable when not in use, eg empty wardrobes.

5 A final basic requirement is durability. Whilst desired replacement cycles of different establishments will vary enormously, eg some may wish to change their theme every two years, contract

furniture, even in a short period of time, will inevitably be subject to much use. The ability to make replacements must also be considered.

It can be seen, therefore, that to be 'functional' furniture must meet the various user's requirements and be strong, stable and durable. Other more specific qualities might include:

Stackability for chairs	Modular co-ordination
Adaptability for different uses	Fitted or free standing.
Manoeuverability	

As well as being functional, furniture needs to be aesthetically pleasing and suit the required décor of an area; and selection will, of course, be influenced by price in relation to standard of quality.

Furniture elements   When considering the qualities of any item of furniture, the individual elements of the item must be considered, namely:

(a) The basic structure material/materials, eg wood in many forms and composition, wicker, cane, plastic, metals, etc

(b) The finish/finishes, eg wax, french polish, nitrocellular, polyester, electroplating, lacquers, etc

(c) The upholstery materials – comprising filling or base and finish.

Bases include foam, resilient webbing, tension springs, and *finishes* include vinyl, wool, fabrics and hide.

In developing performance specifications for furniture, it is necessary to consider the requirements for each of the elements listed above as well as the requirements of the item as a whole (see figure 1.10).

When furniture is successfully chosen it will be fit for its intended purpose, and its appearance will be pleasing. In these circumstances, together with consideration for its appropriate layout, users will be comfortable using the item, and are less likely to misuse it, such as swinging on chair legs, sitting on tables. Furniture is, therefore, more likely to be durable and its 'live costs' reduced.

1.3.2.7 *Textiles*

Of the surface fittings so far considered, textiles are likely to have relatively short lives. By implementing a fairly short replacement cycle on furnishing, the décor of the establishment can be kept reasonably up to date without being unduly costly. Textiles include:

(a) Carpets	(d) Pillows	(g) Uniforms
(b) Upholstery	(e) Napiery	(h) Bed linen and bedding
(c) Cushions	(f) Towels	(i) Curtains.

Obviously, with such diverse uses as floor covering to napkins the performance criteria will vary considerably. Nevertheless, it will be useful to consider the basic material characteristics and to identify some applications. It must be remembered that, when dealing with textiles, many components combine to give the overall characteristics

Figure 1.10 *Performance specification for furniture*

Material property	Relevance to structure	Relevance to finish	Relevance to upholstery material
Acoustic property	●	●	● (particularly bases)
Aesthetic value	● (shape)	●(appearance)	●
Colour and pattern	●	●	●
Corrosion resistance		Most relevance here	Relevance to finish
Cost	●	●	●
Durability	● (joints)	● (corrosion and impact)	●
Electrical resistance		●	● (finish)
Elasticity			● (finish)
Functional	●	●	●
Light reflection		●	● (finish)
Porosity		●	●
Prestige	●	●	●
Resilience		●	●
Slippiness		●	● (finish)
Strength	●		
Temperature resistance		●	● (particularly base material fire resistance)
Transparancy		●	
Toughness		●	

Figure 1.11 *Textiles: process and influence chart*

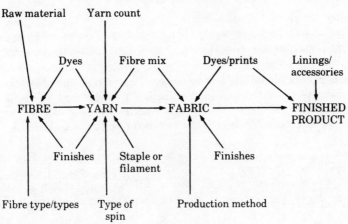

of a finished product, as can be seen in the process and influence chart (figure 1.11).

At each stage in the production ie yarn, fabric, finishing, the product's characteristics are augmented by various other factors.

Fibre Fibres are classified as:
> *natural* eg wool, cotton, silk, flax
> *manmade* – regenerated eg rayon, acetate
> – synthetic eg polyamides, polyesters, acrylics

The fibre type influences the following characteristics of the finished product: micro- and macro-structures, appearance, tensile strength, elongation, elasticity, specific gravity, effect of moisture, thermal properties, effect of sunlight, chemical properties, effect of acid, alkali and organic substance, resistance to insects and micro-organisms and the electrical properties.

Yarn Yarn is conventionally manufactured by the spinning process of drawing and twisting the fibres in a process of wet spinning, dry spinning or melt spinning. The fibres used may be staple (short), mono-filament (one continuous filament), multi-filament (several continuous filaments) or tow (many thousands of continuous filaments). The yarn produced may be simple, ie usually fibres of one kind and colour, although they may be blended; complex, eg slub, knot, loop, flock to give texture, and allow a combination of colours, fibres and thicknesses; textured (where synthetic continuous filament yarns are treated, eg to form crimp, bulk, loops).

Fabric Fabric may be manufactured by weaving, knitting, a weave-knit process, felting or bonding. (A separate section on carpeting types follows.) These processes, too, confer different characteristics on the product such as texture, pattern, longevity, elasticity, tensile strength, specific gravity, thermal properties.

Depending on the particular process applied to the fibre and yarns already, eg dying, bleaching, fire resistance processing, etc, the finished fabric may be treated, eg by dying or printing, and other finishes applied, eg grease resistance, water repellance, etc.

Finished product Other factors affecting quality include, eg quality of braiding round blankets, whether curtaining has bonded lining or requires loose lining, quality of buttons, zips, etc, on uniforms, quality of stitching on hems.

It can be seen, therefore, that when selecting textiles, many factors influence the characteristics of the finished product, and a careful product specification must be proposed. As an example of how the theory works in practice, selection of bed sheets will be considered (see figure 1.12).

Once a choice has been made with respect to fibre and fabric, another factor, influencing comfort, shape retention, cost and appearance is the process of manufacturing and finishing. Depth of hems, whether double hems are used, stitching, application of logos, etc, all

Figure 1.12 *Performance specification for bed sheets*

Possible specification	Relevant fibre/fabric characteristics
1 Comfort	Absorbency, eg cotton, linen, silk
	Smooth soft texture, eg simple yarn, plain yarn or knit
	Low static, eg cotton, linen, silk
	Cool, eg cotton plain weave or warm, eg cotton flannelette
2 Durability	
– resistance to rubbing	eg nylon, silk, eg plain weave or knit
– resistance to snagging	eg simple yarn, plain weave, cotton, linen, silk
3 Withstand high temperatures for laundering	eg cotton, linen
4 Alkali resistance for laundering agents	eg cotton, linen
5 Crease resistance – necessity for ironing	eg Polyester, nylon
6 Suitable for storage – resistant to yeasts, fungi and moths	eg linen (kept dry), polyester
7 Good retention of shape and dimension	Low elastic properties, eg cotton, nylon, linen, terylene, close weaves, bonded fabrics
8 Light weight for ease of bed making	eg silk, polyester, plain knit or weave
9 Low cost	eg rayon, nylon
10 Appearance, eg colour variety	eg polyester, cotton, silk

must be considered before a product is finally selected.

Thus, depending on the specific application, the financial constraints/customer comfort ratio, and the linen system operational, a selection could be made. It must be remembered that this approach is simplistic; there are many different types and grade of cotton for instance; a popular choice is a cotton/polyester mix; processes applied to the fibre will affect its overall attributes, eg Terylene for sheeting may be subjected to singeing, desizeing, scouring and setting before a print, eg transfer print, is applied.

Carpets Much of the above information relating to other textiles is directly relevant to carpeting, eg fibre characteristics and yarn. The carpet manufacturing processes are easily comparable, but, nevertheless, worthy of identification and some comment:

Woven Woven carpets have the pile and backing woven simultaneously and tend to be the most expensive, combining resilience and appearance qualities with durability. There are three main types:

1 *Wilton* Due to the thickness of the backing (produced by carrying yarn under the carpet when it is not required in the pile pattern) and the usual density of the pile, these tend to represent good quality carpeting.

2 *Axminster* Backings are not always as thick as in Wilton carpeting, as colours are inserted only as required in the pattern. Qualities vary enormously depending on fibres, pile tufts per cm and rows per cm. Patterns in Axminsters can incorporate an infinite number of colours, unlike Wilton carpets where the maximum number of colours for practical reasons is five.

3 *Oriental* These are hand woven, if genuine, and are very hard wearing. Their high market values are due, not only to their practical qualities, but also to their aesthetic and ethnic values.

Tufted Tufted carpets are extremely popular, offering the appearance and resilience of a woven carpet at a lower cost. With good pile density and suitable fibre choice, they can compete well with woven types. Their lower cost is a consequence of the cheaper manufacturing process, whereby pile, primary backing and secondary backing/underlay are produced separately, then bonded together. The primary backing is merely a polypropylene or hessian material used, together with latex, to anchor the pile tufts.

Needlepunch These are less resiliant, generally with lower appearance retention, but can represent very hard wearing floor coverings produced comparatively cheaply. A yarn is not required. Staple fibres are bonded together by the needlepunch process, in a comparable manner to the production of felted fabrics.

Adhesively bonded Again, these carpets have relatively low resilience, though in appearance they may resemble a Wilton cord carpet. Spun or unspun fibres (depending on the particular process) are again bonded together, and the result is a low cost carpet, frequently with patterns limited to flecked shades.

Electrostatically bonded These were initially used for car interiors and had rather low durability. Considerable advances have now been made with respect to durability. The carpet is very low pile with low resilience, but one option is for a non-porous floor covering which can withstand high temperatures, frequent cleaning, many chemicals and heavy wear.

Knitted Knitted carpets are not common; drawbacks being, snagging pile and low dimensional stability. Technological development in knitting processes are, however, advancing rapidly, and new techniques may be applied to carpet manufacturing.

A few of the performance criteria to be considered when selecting carpeting have been considered. Figure 1.13 gives a more comprehensive list of these, together with the carpet characteristics most likely to affect them. As can be seen from this chart, the durability of the carpet is not only affected by the characteristics of the carpet itself, but also by the underlay used and the expertise applied to the fixing process. Some carpets need to be adhesively fixed to the floor, others perform better with perimeter fixing. In any case the floor surface to which they are applied needs to be clean, dry and even. The standard of cleaning and maintenance will also have considerable influence on a carpet's life.

1.3.3 Interior design

With respect to the interior of the building, an analysis has now been made of the environmental services and of the surface fittings. It will be useful to consider, briefly, how these two elements, together with the building envelope, and other design elements, may be integrated to produce functional and pleasing surroundings with the right mood, ambience and atmosphere. Comfortable users will be more likely to use the building carefully, and higher standards of cleaning and maintenance will be encouraged. The overall appearance of an establishment is an essential part of merchandising, and of the product image and internal comfort. The appropriateness of the décor and furnishings, and the efficiency of the environmental services are all part of sales promotion and user satisfaction.

The main design elements are shown in figure 1.14. Many of these elements have been discussed earlier, but mainly in a practical vein. It will be useful now to consider psychological aspects as well. Consideration of each element as it integrates with other elements and its effect on the total décor is given below:

Space One objective of interior design will be to maximise the use of space. Space represents capital outlay and other fixed and variable costs. Furniture layout, colour and pattern will encourage the use of space and, as well as being concerned with the efficiency of activities and the practicalities, the apparent shape and the mood or atmosphere can also be affected. Formality or informality within a room can largely be achieved by furniture layout.

Light Once again the practical functions of lighting have already been considered, but this element, too, can go a long way to dictating atmosphere, eg efficiency, intimacy and entertainment. Lighting must be closely integrated with furniture layout and with colour, and it can be used to emphasise features, reveal or conceal, heighten or diminish spaces, create pattern, texture and colour contrast.

Acoustics Practical aspects to consider, with respect to sound, include the reduction of 'noise', ie unwanted sound, and the reflection of other sounds. Machine noises, process noises, traffic noises, etc, need to be minimised (though, in the interests of safety, this is not invariably so – noise can act as a warning). Other sounds, eg a lecturer's voice, musical instruments, television, may need to be reflected within an area but not transmitted outside. Some sounds are more irritating than others; high frequencies cause more annoyance than low frequencies; intermittent noises more than constant. People

Figure 1.13 *Performance criteria of carpets and the carpet's characteristics most likely to affect them*

Performance criteria	Pile fibre	Pile density	Pile height	Loop or cut pile	Colour/pattern	Manu-facturing process	Backing	Underlay	Fixing	Special treatment	Comments
Acoustic properties	●	●	●	●			●	●			Depending on specific qualities required
Appearance retention	●	●	●		●		●	●			
Colour fastness	●				●					●	
Compression and resilience	●	●	●	●		●	●	●	●		May be short or long term loading
Dimensional stability						●	●		●		
Fire resistance	●					●	●	●		●	
Soiling resistance	●				●					●	May be real or apparent soilage
Static properties	●						●	●		●	Associated with low humidity
Thermal insulation	●	●	●	●				●			With underfloor heating low insulation required
Thickness retention	●	●	●	●		●	●	●	●		
Wear	●	●	●	●		●	●	●	●	●	

Figure 1.14 *Integrated design*

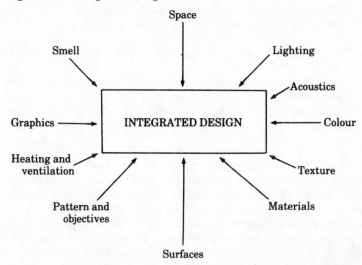

can become accustomed to a certain type of noise. Noise may be airborne, eg external traffic, or resonating, eg door slamming, and different techniques can be applied to reduce each. Some methods of noise reduction are as follows:

1 Isolation of the noise source from other areas.
2 In planning interiors, activities identified as being noise sensitive, can be protected from noisy areas by placing intermediate rooms between them to baffle the noise, eg offices, sanitary areas, circulation areas, will be less noise sensitive than sleeping areas and lounges. Hotel bathrooms, grouped back-to-back, baffle the noise between one bedroom and another.
3 Noisy rooms may be located near noisy exterior areas.
4 Machinery radiating sound may be located in basement areas where the general building structure is likely to be heavier and more sound insulating and vibrations can be absorbed into the earth.
5 The selection of heavier construction materials will enable more noise to be absorbed, eg thick doors.
6 Airborne exterior noise may be reduced by fitting airtight windows.
7 Structural dis-continuity reduces resonance, eg cavity walls and suspended ceilings.
8 Noise may be reduced at source by insulating machines or rooms, eg use of soft furnishings and carpets, double-doors.

Colour Colour is said to induce a sense of comfort, discomfort, activity or calmness. Other psychological effects of colour are to enlarge or reduce apparent space, and to accentuate or disguise certain facets, eg sharp contrasts or bright colours. Whilst colour is a personal matter, good colour schemes can be admired by all and there are various classic schemes:

1 *Complementary* – using colours on opposite sides of the colour wheel
2 *Analogous* – adjoining colours on the colour wheel are used.
3 *Monochromatic* – one colour is used with various tints and shades.
4 *Triad* – contrasting colours are used against a neutral background.

Besides psychological effects, colour selection must be made with practical considerations in mind as well. Apparent soilage will depend on the colours of the soilage matter as well as the colours of the surfaces. Black is rarely the best colour to disguise soilage. With respect to carpets, research has shown that medium range colours, eg gold, generally give best results. Another practical consideration is the lighting type which will affect the perceived colour. It is essential that colours are chosen under the lighting conditions in the area in which it is to be used (this may well mean natural and artificial lighting conditions). Colour used well can have the maximum effect on the ambience level within a room for the minimum capital cost.

Texture   All materials have textural qualities, and tactile reactions in people can be stimulated without surfaces being touched. Variations in textures are required to give balance to a room, but too much variation in texture can be as disturbing and inappropriate as too little. Textural contrasts include warm and cold, soft and hard, shiny and dull, antique and modern. Natural surfaces tend to have more texture than do synthetic. To be used to the best advantage, textural qualities must be enhanced by the lighting design. Practically, rougher or varied textures show soilage less than smooth textures but are more difficult to clean. In certain clinical areas, smooth surfaces are chosen for their low soilage holding capacity.

Materials   The practical considerations of material selection have been discussed earlier; the psychological aspects must be considered in relation to the other design elements in order to create balance and variety. Shapes, forms and dimensions of furniture need to be appropriate to those elements within the space, eg an antique theme would determine furniture styles and influence materials selection.

Pattern   Pattern may be achieved through colours, material variations, textures, lighting, fixtures, pictures, ornaments, etc. Psychological effects of pattern can be similar to the effects of colour, eg enlarging or diminishing space, creating atmosphere. Practical effects of pattern can be to disguise soilage and wear or, in clinical conditions, to reveal soilage.

Heating and ventilation   Many of the practical implications have already been explored. With respect to the psychological effects, again, the systems chosen need to be in keeping with the overall plan. Despite all their practical drawbacks, open fires are still used as focal points or to develop an atmosphere (though, frequently, the heat generated is supplementary to a central heating system, and the ventilation currents created may not always be desirable). In other situations, heating systems may be selected because they are barely visible and do not detract from the décor.

Graphics In public buildings, signs, room numbers, directions and printed stationery are normal practice. The form of these graphics must be considered from both a practical and psychological viewpoint. Practically, they must be understandable to all those to whom they are intended to communicate. Users may be of various nationalities so various national and international symbols may be selected: in some cases they are legally obligatory, eg for fire safety. From an aesthetic point of view, graphics must be considered with the general décor and design of the establishment in mind. Printed notepaper or names on buildings, may be the first impression customers have of the establishment. Braille graphics are becoming more common, as the needs of the disabled are considered.

1.3.3.1 Principles of design

From the above a constant inter-linking and cross-referencing of design elements can be seen; none of the elements can be considered independently. Lighting installations affect colour perception, accentuate pattern and texture, and can enlarge or diminish apparent space.

Colours must be balanced with pattern and texture, and selections made in the lighting conditions of that space. Acoustic properties are affected by texture, materials selection, dimensions of space and situation. In this manner of design, elements intermingle and, to achieve good integration, four overall principles have been identified:

1 Unity, variety and balance should be achieved, eg in line, form, texture, colour. If several colours are used, texture and pattern variations should balance this. A sense of order is required without becoming monotonous
2 One centre of interest or one dominant idea should be identified
3 The design should incorporate rhythm which is a means of leading the eye to the centre of interest
4 There should be good proportions and scale, eg of patterns, furniture and dimensions.

Integrated design must create environments which are, above all, safe to use. They must be practical, and they must achieve the right atmosphere for the planned activities.

Further reading

Architects and Specifiers Guide to: Doors and Windows; Fabrics, Wallcoverings and Furniture

BILLINGHAM, N and ROBERTS, B, *Building Services Engineering*, Pergamon 1982

BORSENIK, FRANK, D, *The Management of Maintenance and Engineering Systems in Hospitality Industries*, Wiley Management Services 1979

BRANSON, J C and LENNOX, H, *Hotel, Hostel and Hospital Housekeeping*, Arnold 1971

BRE DIGEST: *Services and Environmental Engineering*, Constructional Press

BURBERRY, PETER *Mitchell's Building Series: Environment and Services*, Batsford 1983 edition

CLEMENTS and PARKES, editors, *Manual of Maintenance*, Business Publications 1965

EDWARDS, J K P, *Floors and their Maintenance*, Butterworths 1969

END, H, *Interiors: Second Book of Hotels*, Whitney Library of Design 1963

ENGLISH TOURIST BOARD, *Providing for Disabled Visitors*

FABER, OSCAR and KELL, J R, *Heating and Air Conditioning of Buildings*, Architectural Press 1966

GLADWELL, D, *Practical Maintenance and Equipment for Hoteliers, Licencees and Caterers*, Barrie Jenkins 1963

GORDON, J E, *The New Science of Strong Materials*, Pelican 1968

HARPER, DENIS, *The Process and the Product*, Constructional Press 1978

HCIMA, Technical Brief, *Precautions against Legionnaires Disease* 1988

HOPE, PETER, S, editor, *Handbook of Building Security Planning and Design* 1979

HURST, R, *Services and Maintenance for Hostels and Residential Establishments*, Heineman 1971

KUT, D, *Heating and Hot Water Services in Buildings*, Pergamon 1968

LAWSON, F R, *Hotels, Motels and Condominiums*, Architectural Press 1976

LAWSON, F R, *Restaurant Planning and Design*, Architectural Press 1973

LUFF, M G, *Air Conditioning for Students*, Technitrade Journals 1980

McLAUGHLIN, T P, *The Cleaning Hygiene and Maintenance Handbook*, Business Books 1969

RIBA, *Commissioning an Architect*

STANK, D, *Ergonomics of Restaurant Seating*, Catering Education Research Institute 1968

STRAUK, P, *Ergonomics and Functional Design for the Catering Industry*

TOMPSON, T A, *A Guide to Sanitary Engineering Services*, McDonald and Evans 1972

TUCKER AND SCHNEIDER, *Professional Housekeeper*, Cahners 1975

2

Housekeeping Services

Housekeeping is defined here as the cleaning and maintenance of the interior of a building and the provision of tangible client-care services such as beverage, laundry and dry cleaning. A caring concern for the building user (client and personnel) is inherent.

The scope of the housekeeping service is variable, ranging from purely a cleaning service in one operation to cleaning, maintenance and extensive client-care services in another.

Although cleaning may be perceived as an integral part of the total maintenance system of the building (effective cleaning contributing to the overall aim of the maintenance plan, which is to extend the physical life of the building), in reality the cleaning and maintenance services are usually separated. Each service having its own organisational structure and managed by its own departmental head. The head of maintenance often being a professional engineer or surveyor.

It is the intention in this chapter to provide a general overview of the maintenance service and an in-depth study of the housekeeping service, with special emphasis on the management of the cleaning programme.

The success of any housekeeping and maintenance service is influenced by company policy and the attitudes of higher management to their value within the total operation and, hence, whether or not, finance is made available.

The only feasible housekeeping or maintenance sub-system to adopt is one which is planned, involving the analysis of the building users' requirements, the physical needs of the building, and programming the appropriate activities at optimum frequencies.

The alternative, which unfortunately often exists in practice, is a haphazard system where R Lee[2] suggests 'over a period of time a number of unrelated compromises between the physical needs of the building and the available finance occur', usually as a result of crises management where little attention is paid to the inevitable consequences of such *ad hoc* arrangements.

It is vital to consider the benefits of cleaning and maintenance and their cost, in the context of the whole enterprise and the total building needs, bearing in mind that there may be several properties involved over a wide radius.

The benefits to be gained from adopting a planned housekeeping and/or maintenance sub-system can be considered in financial, functional, aesthetic and human terms.

Financial benefits   Over a period of time it should prove more cost effective to provide cleaning and maintenance services on a regular planned basis, so extending the life span of equipment, plant, surfaces, furniture, fittings and furnishings, and deferring the heavy expenditure of frequent replacements or renovation.

A haphazard system does tend to result in more frequent replacement costs and/or high renovation costs.

A planned system involves levelling out costs over the cycle, rather than incurring extreme fluctuations from year to year.The property value might be reduced if little attention has been paid to cleaning and maintenance, and deterioration has occurred.

A building maintained in a good state of repair and décor is easier to clean; occupancy levels can be maintained if not improved; sales increased; and higher productivity is easier to maintain.

Functional benefits   Effective cleaning and maintenance should preserve the physical characteristics of the building and its services, ensuring that everything functions satisfactorily, and preventing rapid deterioration and breakdown. Inconvenience, down-time of equipment and plant, the possibility of accidents and the occurrence of emergency repairs should be reduced, and future cleaning and maintenance costs should be lowered.

Aesthetic benefits   Cleaning is not only essential to retain the appearance of surfaces and total areas, both inside and outside the building, but also, in some cases, can actually improve appearance. For instance, by using initial treatments, such as a pigmented seal, the appearance of a concrete floor can be improved; this action also prevents the dust (worn off bare concrete) from being trodden elsewhere. Appearance and apparent cleanliness do have a psychological effect on the building user, who may make a value judgement of the total experience based on this perception – often the initial perception – of appearance and standards of cleanliness.

In a profit-making operation particularly, first impressions are important. Surveys undertaken in the past have shown that aesthetic standards do affect reputation and repeat business, so aesthetic standards can be regarded as part of the corporate image and marketing strategy.

Human benefits   Clean, attractive, well maintained surroundings are more pleasant, enjoyable and comfortable for clients to use, increase customer satisfaction, affect repeat business and improve public image. They also encourage good working standards, pride in work, personal appearance and morale which not only affect labour turnover and recruitment generally but also are of paramount importance when motivating housekeeping personnel to maintain these building standards.

Cleaning and maintenance also contribute to the removal of fire, health, hygiene and safety hazards. Since the implementation of the

Health and Safety at Work Act 1974, the health, both physical and mental, and the safety of all building users must be maintained.

2.1 MAINTENANCE

Maintenance can extend the physical life of a building almost indefinitely, provided initially the structure of the building is sound. Effective maintenance will delay deterioration and replacement and so defer the expenditure on new construction. If the building can be modified internally to accommodate changing user requirements, maintenance can be regarded as a substitute for new construction, but only if the building remains functionally satisfactory. A relationship does exist between the adaptability of the original building design, building life, maintenance costs and new construction costs. The extent to which maintenance is considered at the design stage is likely to depend on whether the client commissioning the construction of the building is likely to be the subsequent proprietor, manager or user.

Unfortunately, in some cases, maintenance (and cleaning) seem to be the last consideration at the planning and design stage. The British Standards definition (BS 3811, 1964) defines *maintenance* as 'a combination of any actions carried out to retain an item in or restore it to an acceptable condition'. The actions referred to in the definition are those associated with the initiation, organisation and implementation of maintenance activities. *Retaining* is defined as 'carrying out work in anticipation of failure (preventive maintenance)' and *restoring* as 'carrying out work after failure has occurred (corrective maintenance)'. The perception of what is an 'acceptable condition' will vary according to the view point of the client paying for the work, the building user, or an outside authority enforcing minimum standards such as the Fire Authority or Health and Safety Inspector.

2.1.1 Alternative maintenance systems
There is basically only a choice between a well planned system or a haphazard *ad hoc* system, as mentioned earlier. However, BS 3811 does define the following types of maintenance:
— *Planned maintenance*, ie 'maintenance organised and carried out with forethought control and the use of records to a predetermined plan'
— *Preventive maintenance*, ie 'maintenance carried out at predetermined intervals or to other prescribed criteria and intended to reduce the likelihood of an item not meeting an acceptable condition'
— *Running maintenance*, ie 'maintenance which can be carried out whilst an item is in service'.

As preventive maintenance also has to be planned, a combination of a planned and a preventive maintenance system is common, hence the term *planned preventive maintenance*.

2.1.2 Planned preventive maintenance (PPM)

According to R Lee[2] a planned preventive maintenance system must possess at least four essential features:

1 Failures must be anticipated
2 Appropriate procedures must be devised for prevention and rectification
3 A course of action must be planned to deal with the inevitable consequences of deterioration
4 Measures must be devised for even remote possibilities.

This type of system is only worthwhile if:
— it is cost effective
— it meets statutory and other legal requirements
— it reduces the incidence of running maintenance which precipitates user requisition
— it meets operational needs
— there is a higher percentage of actual work for the maintenance craftsmen to undertake rather than purely inspection of items.

The concept of PPM is more applicable to plant and equipment which are subject to mechanical wear, but most building elements walls, windows, roofs, etc, can also justify inclusion in this system.

2.1.3 The benefits of planned maintenance systems

When devising a maintenance policy, it is essential to consider the benefits of adopting a planned maintenance programme, the objectives which would be achieved and the costs involved in the context of the whole enterprise. As the building life covers at least à 60 year span, if not longer, it is vital to consider not only the short-term but also the long-term benefits.

The long-term consequences of maintenance are often brushed aside.

2.1.4 Developing a maintenance policy

BS 3811 defines a *maintenance policy* as 'a strategy within which decisions on maintenance are taken'. The maintenance policy devised will be influenced by company policy, the attitude of higher management, available finance and the number and location of the buildings involved. Operational and cost objectives will have to be formulated which will involve identifying the maintenance activities to be undertaken, the standards to be achieved and the financial framework and budget limits within which to operate. A balance has to be achieved between preventive and corrective maintenance to ensure that preventive measures are not carried out more often than necessary, incurring excessive expenditure. A balance also has to be achieved between maintenance activities which can be programmed and work requisitioned by the building user, either emergency repairs (such as replacing a washer, mending the toilet) or new requirements (such as putting up shelves on a small scale) or modification of space for a new use on a larger scale. In most operations a proportion of maintenance work is put out to contract and a balance must also be achieved between direct and contract labour. The outcome of these considerations will affect the structure and staffing of the maintenance department. Where a number of properties are involved, the extent to which day to day organisation and control of the maintenance function is decentralised will also have to be decided.

2.1.5 Devising a planned preventive maintenance system

When devising a planned preventive maintenance system, the factors to consider are not unlike those involved in devising the cleaning programme discussed in section 2.2. A building survey must be undertaken and the anticipated future state of each building element must be considered in order to decide what maintenance operations have to be performed, and at what stage in the maintenance cycle. The activities then have to be programmed, monitored and controlled. Figure 2.1 identifies the scope of the maintenance system.

Figure 2.1 *Scope of maintenance*

	Internal	External
Plant	Heating, lighting, ventilation centralised vacuuming, lifts and escalators, plumbing	Lighting, fuel stores
Services	Electricity, gas, water	Drainage, sewage
Machinery and equipment	Catering, laundry, cleaning, firefighting, access	Transport, fire fighting, access
Specialised areas	Swimming pools, operating theatres	Swimming pools, gazebos, barbecue areas
Building envelope	Doors, windows, walls, ceilings, paintwork, structural repairs, redecoration	Roof, guttering, fire escapes, masonry, chimneys, paintwork, windows, structural repairs, redecoration
Site		Gardens, pathways, fences, gates, boundary walls

2.2 THE CLEANING PROGRAMME

The cleaning programme requires analysis of the needs of the building and its users to determine what has to be done; how often; how; with what; when; by whom; and how long it should take.

2.2.1 The cleaning process

The main aim of the cleaning process is to remove as much soil as possible from a surface and prevent its redeposition. In order to achieve this aim, it is necessary to identify the nature and characteristics of soil; its source; its transportation into and within the building; and its deposition on various surfaces. Subsequently, this data will influence the method of removal, the equipment and agents to be selected and, to some extent, the frequency of removal.

2.2.1.1 The soil

The nature of the soil present in a given area and its characteristics will influence how it is to be removed from a surface.

In general terms, soil can be classified as dust and dirt.

Dust can be defined as 'loose, dry particles from the air, which eventually settle on a surface'. As can be seen from figure 2.2, dust comprises several types of matter, including inorganic (mineral) and organic (animal and vegetable) matter. Dust can also be contaminated with harmful microbes.

Figure 2.2 *Types of dust*

Types	Examples
Inorganic (mineral) matter	Earth
	Powdered rock, eg sand
Organic (animal and vegetable) matter	Hair and animal fibres
	Skin
Protein	Particles breathed out
	Dried excrement
	Pollen
	Insects
	Micro-organisms – bacteria
	yeast
	moulds
Carbohydrates	Vegetable fibres
Fats	Fats
	Oils

The characteristics of dust, which influence its method of removal and, to some extent, the frequency of removal, are outlined in figure 2.3.

Dirt can be defined as 'an accumulation of dust and other foreign matter, such as stains and spillages, held together by moisture or grease and/or embedded into a rough or porous surface'.

Again, it is useful to highlight the characteristics of dirt and consider the implications as far as the removal of dust is concerned. See figure 2.4.

Figure 2.3 *The characteristics of dust and their implications*

Characteristics	Implications
Floats in air	Easily transported by airborne means
Heavier than air	Settles eventually, particularly, if undisturbed Will settle more readily on horizontal rather than vertical surfaces Therefore, clean horizontal surfaces more frequently
Scatters easily	Easily redispersed, especially by airborne means – consider method of removal carefully
If electrically charged	Use opposite electric charge to attract
If 'gritty'	Effective, frequent removal to prevent excessive abrasive/cutting/scratching action
Attracted to damp surfaces	Use damp method of attraction to remove
Attracted to greasy surfaces	May use 'tackiness' as means of removal eg impregnated mops May need chemical to emulsify grease May need hot water to aid removal Avoid the use of polishes which leave a 'greasy/waxy' film
Caught in rough surfaces or crevices	May need strong force to remove Use non-porous, shiny surfaces Consider design to prevent dust traps

Figure 2.4 *The characteristics of dirt and their implications*

Characteristics	Implications
Build-up, accumulation	More difficult removal/need force, friction, weight, to aid removal
Stains, spillages	Use specific chemicals
Held together by moisture, grease	Need chemicals to breakdown grease, allow penetration and remove build-up use of heat
Engrained	Use of force – weight, friction

Where does soil come from? Tracing the soil's source, helps to identify its type and ways of preventing its transportation. Soil is either brought into a building from the outside or is generated within the building, and then transported from one area to another.

External sources include:
— The earth, ie actual soil
— The beach, eg sand
— Pathways and buildings, eg powdered concrete

— Building works, eg sand, mud
— The weather, eg rain, snow, salt
— The atmosphere, eg smoke, car exhaust fumes, pollutants, salt (seaside).

Internal sources include:
— The building user, eg sewage; shedding skin scales; coughing, sneezing; carelessness/vandalism; smoking; fibre shed from clothing
— Heating and ventilation systems
— Equipment
— Dirty cleaning methods
— Animals, vermin, pests
— Natural decay/deterioration of all surfaces
— Specialist areas, eg chalk boards, kitchens, laboratories.

Measures can be introduced which will prevent transportation or reduce the amount transported into the building from outside. Ideally these measures should be considered during the design and planning process so that measures of a structural nature can be implemented during building construction.

The following measures are worth considering:
— the use of mat wells and grids outside the building to encourage dust and dirt particles to be removed from shoes.
— The use of revolving and double doors at entrances, prevents blasts of air transporting vast amounts of dust into the building.
— Double glazing.
— If the area between the double doors is of sufficient length, a suitable door mat can be laid. This must allow for at least three paces, ie approximately 3 metres so that dust, dirt and grit from shoes can be deposited in this area and not transported further.
— Hot air barriers, sometimes used in departmental stores, prevent blasts of cold, dust-laden air from being carried into the store when the doors are open.

Measures can also be introduced, to prevent transportation of soil from internal sources:
— Dust control or barrier mats may be laid at entrances or exits of, eg operating theatre suites or burns units.
— Air pressure can also be used to prevent dust-laden air from being carried from one area to another, eg higher air pressure in operating theatres generating outward not inward, flowing air currents. Air pressure can be used within the theatre to take air from the immediate operating table environment to the outer theatre perimeter and not vice versa.

In some cases the air must flow from clean area to dirty area. For instance, in a hospital laundry, the air must flow from the area where the laundered items are being temporarily stored to the area where dirty linen is awaiting processing, to avoid cross contamination.

Means of transportation   Soil is transported by some means of energy or vehicle to the place where it lands. This may only be a temporary resting place before it is transported elsewhere.

Soil can be transported by the following vehicles:

— Air – wind, draughts, ventilation systems, hot air, movement of people, equipment, activities
— Humans – shoes, clothing, baggage, hands, hair, nose, mouth
— Equipment – dirty equipment, wheels, cables
— Animals/pests – feet, bodies, bowels
— Water – contaminated cleaning and rinsing water, sanitary appliances, laundry facilities.

Soil may be transported several times by different vehicles. How far it travels will depend on the amount of energy or the type of vehicle used, or even how high it is initially released into the air.

2.2.1.2   Deposition
Soil may actually be deposited on a surface by:

— Impingement, that is when soil strikes or is dashed against a surface and comes to rest. For instance, if the soil has been transported by air, the velocity of which is rapid and there is an object in the midst of the airflow
— Gravity, when the soil sinks or settles under the force of gravity
— Electro-static attraction, when the soil is attracted to a surface carrying an opposite electrical charge. This usually occurs through the generation of static electricity when soil is attracted to the surface carrying static, such as a nylon carpet.

2.2.1.3   Soil removal
Once the nature and source of the soil has been established and the method of transportation to the surface identified, then the method of removal can be determined. If the purpose of cleaning is to produce a 'clean' surface, that is one which is soil free, then the aim must be to *remove* the soil and prevent re-deposition. Soil removal can be achieved in one of two ways, either by dissolving the soil or by using force.

(1) *Dissolving*   Soil can be dissolved in various types of solution such as:

(a) *Water*   Water is a solvent and certain types of soil particles are soluble in water. However, water by itself is not a good wetting agent and normally a chemical surfactant needs to be added to break down the surface tension of the water and allow it to wet the surface, before soil removal can take place.

Water, therefore, is usually used as a medium for detergents, chemicals and some solvents, which are themselves water soluble. Water is used for rinsing purposes to remove the dissolved soil from the surface and transport it to the drain.

(b) *Organic solvents* In this context these include agents which are spirit based or incorporate a grease solvent in their formulation. They are required where oil or fats are present which need emulsifying or where a specific staining material is solvent soluble. They are also specifically required for the removal of a solvent-based floor polish.

(c) *Detergents* Detergents are generally added to water, but in certain circumstances may be added to organic solvents. They are required to break down the surface tension of water (or solvent) to allow it to wet the surface and so allow the soil to be dissolved by the detergent solution. There are different types of detergents for different purposes but basically a neutral detergent, normally formulated from a mixture of ionic and non-ionic detergents, is used for light dust and soil removal, and an alkali detergent is used for the removal of a build-up or accumulation of dirt, particularly if it is greasy in nature. A caustic detergent may be used in very limited circumstances, for instance, drain cleaning, but great care must be taken as it will be damaging to the user's skin and most surfaces. Sometimes a neutral detergent based on cationic detergents may be used where chemical disinfection or anti-static properties are also required.

Usually the application of heat to the water medium will help to dissolve and remove soil, and will particularly aid the emulsification of oils and fats through molecular change. However, some detergents are now designed for use in cold water, in an attempt to save fuel costs.

(d) *Other chemicals* These include acidic cleansers, such as toilet cleansers, stone and window cleaners, and abrasive and 'non'-abrasive cleansers, which are all designed for the removal of specific types of soil on specific types of surfaces. For instance, the acid nature of a toilet cleanser is required to remove the uric acid (inorganic) found in the lavatory pan, whilst the abrasive actions of some metal cleaners is designed to remove tarnish caused by oxidisation which develops on certain metals. In limited circumstances dry powders may be used to absorb spillages, eg salt used for red wine, fuller's earth to absorb grease.

(2) Force is the alternative method of removal and it is convenient to divide it into positive and negative.

(a) *Positive force* is where force is being applied to the surface to aid soil removal. This includes the application of one of the following:

Pressure — application of manual pressure when scrubbing or rubbing a surface

— use of pressurised air to blow soil away

— water under pressure, eg in water injection/extraction carpet shampooers or pressure cleaners

— mechanical pressure, eg use of a scrubbing machine where weight is also of importance

— hydraulic pressure, eg use of a hydraulic water extractor in the laundry

Friction or agitation — dry sweeping, dusting or mopping

— use of abrasive materials, eg pads and agents
— damp dusting, mopping
— scrubbing and spray cleaning
— agitation in laundry processes
— ultrasound, ie the introduction of sound waves to cause vibration which shakes out soil, grit or dust. This method is used to a limited extent in the cleaning of carpets and venetian blinds.

(b) *Negative force* — is where soil is attracted or pulled away from the surface by force. This includes the occurrence of one of the following:

Suction — dry suction, ie vacuuming

— the use of wet suction, eg for the removal of dirty water after floor scrubbing or carpet shampooing
— the use of a plunger for clearing blocked drains
— emptying of syphonic type of lavatory pans.

Centrifugal force — extraction of water during the laundering process

Static electricity — use of static mop sweepers and door mats

— use of cationic detergents to attract soil of opposite charge.

2.2.1.4 Cleaning methods

The methods of soil removal may, more simply, be classified as dry or wet cleaning tasks and generally include the tasks listed in figure 2.5 which form the basis of any cleaning programme. These cleaning tasks are adequately defined in other text books (see end of chapter for titles).

There are benefits in analysing and standardising the exact procedure, equipment and agents used for each cleaning task (see *Task determination* page 83 and section 2.2.3 Planning the cleaning programme). Once the soil has been removed from a surface, using one or a combination of the tasks listed in figure 2.5, it must be entrapped and prevented from resoiling that, or other surfaces, until it can be disposed of either with the general rubbish or through the sewage system.

2.2.1.5 Preventive measures which aid the cleaning process

There is a number of preventive measures which may be implemented to facilitate soil removal or aid the cleaning process. Most of these measures should be considered at the design stage of the building, but some may be introduced later, if considered feasible. They include:

— Designing stream-lined areas without ledges, which act as dust traps. This should be definitely so in the case of high risk hygiene areas

— Curved skirtings to prevent build-up of soil in edges and corners and

Figure 2.5 *Wet and dry cleaning tasks*

Groups	Purpose	Type	Applicable surface	Equipment	Agents
Dry methods	Dust removal	Suction cleaning (vacuuming)	Hard floors Carpets Upholstery and furniture Soft furnishings and curtains Walls	Dry suction cleaner and attachments Vacuum bag	
		Mop sweeping	Hard floors Walls and ceilings	Impregnated mops or static mops	
		Dusting *	Furniture Horizontal surfaces	Dry dusters and cloths of various kinds Impregnated dusters	
		Dry mopping *	Hard floors	Dry mops	
		Dry sweeping *	Hard floors	Brushes and brooms	
	Floor maintenance	Buffing	Hard floors	Scrubber/polisher Buffing brush/drive disc Buff pads Red/white or blue pads	
		Seal removal	Wood or cork floors	Drum sander	
Wet methods	Dust removal	Damp dusting	Furniture Horizontal surfaces	Disposable cloths Sponges Pail	Neutral detergent
		Damp mopping	Hard floors	Damp mopping equipment	Neutral detergent

		Sponge mops (poly/cotton viscose heads)	
Hard floor maintenance	Wet mopping	Hard floors	As above	Neutral detergent
	Scrubbing	Hard floors	Scrubbing machine Scrubbing brush/drive disc Scrubbing pad (green)	Neutral detergent
	Suction drying	Hard floors	Suction drier	
	Spray cleaning/Spray burnishing	Hard floors	High, super or hyper speed burnishing machine Vacuum attachment Drive disc Relevant floor pads (brown, navy, mustard, pink, cream)	Floor gel; Water-based emulsion; Liquid solvent-based polish; Water; or Neutral detergent
	Polish and seal removal (stripping)	Hard floors	Scrubbing machine Scrubbing brush/drive disc Floor pads (black/build-up removal) Suction drier	Alkali detergent; Fortified alkali detergent; or Solvent-based detergent wax remover
	Polish and seal application	Hard floors	Applicators Applicator trays Mops	Water-based emulsion; Solvent-based polish; Water-based seal; or Solvent-based seal and Thinners

	Stain removal		Cloths pail	Stain removal agents
Carpet maintenance	Stain removal	Carpets	Cloths pail	Carpet shampoo
	Bonnet buffing	Carpets	High/super speed machine, Drive disc, Bonnets, Spray	Carpet shampoo
	Shampooing	Carpets	Carpet shampooer eg dry foam machine, water injection	Shampoo, Spot remover
Wall and ceiling maintenance	Wall washing	Walls	Cloths, Sponge mops, Pails, Access equipment	Sugar soap; or Alkali detergent
Window maintenance	Window cleaning	Windows, Mirrors	Cloths, Pails, Squeegees, Access equipment	Neutral detergent; Alkali detergent; Methylated spirits; Vinegar; or Proprietary brands
Sanitary Fittings Maintenance	Cleaning of	Toilets, Baths, Basins, Sinks, Showers, Sluices, Slop sinks	Pails, Toilet brushes & holders, Cloths, Bottle brushes	Toilet cleanser; Neutral detergent; Hard surface cleansers; Scouring creams, pastes, powders

NB Those tasks * do not comply fully with the aim of the cleaning process, *viz a viz* soil removal, as they tend to scatter a higher proportion

aid suction cleaning and damp mopping
— Use of non-porous surfaces to prevent absorbtion of soiling matter (there may be conflict here with insulation requirements)
— Initial treatments of porous surfaces such as sealing a timber floor to prevent soil penetration or the use of silicone or flourochemical treatments for carpets to prevent absorption of dirt and spillages into the pile fibres
— Use of synthetic fibres to prevent absorption of soil
— Effective ventilation or air conditioning, not only to prevent the circulation of contaminated air but also to control the rate of flow to minimise the transportation of dust from one area to another.

2.2.1.6 Standards of cleanliness
In most situations, the standard of cleanliness required is either aesthetic or clinical, depending on the type of area and the risk of infection. In areas with a low infection risk an aesthetic standard only is necessary. The objective is to achieve a clean, pleasant and attractive appearance.

In higher risk areas it is necessary to achieve a clinical standard, where the objective is to remove as much soil and, therefore, micro-organisms as possible, prevent cross infection, and achieve as high a degree of hygiene as deemed necessary for that area. The hygiene risk in specified areas can be identified, and in high risk areas such as operating theatres, infectious diseases units and burns units, the emphasis must be on achieving aseptic conditions.

2.2.2 Infection control and the hygiene policy
The first essential of any infection control plan is to identify areas of potential risk and examine the infection cycle and the degree of danger. Only then can the appropriate control measures be considered.

2.2.2.1 The infection risk
In certain areas within a building, an infection risk may exist. This may be one of two types. It may be created within the area by the nature of the in-patients or the activities undertaken, eg in sanitary areas, infectious diseases units, research and micro-biology units; or in other areas such as operating theatres, baby units or burns units where the in-patient may be particularly vulnerable.

In the first case transmission of infection outwards must be prevented, in the second, transmission inwards must be prevented.

2.2.2.2 The infection cycle
The infection cycle comprises a source, link or intermediate carrier and a potential victim.

SOURCE

LINK

VICTIM

If the potential victim becomes infected, at worst a fatality ensues, at best a new source of infection is created. The aim is to break the link to prevent the occurrence of cross infection, and to remove the source or prevent a source from occurring in the first place.

In the example illustrated below, if the toilet seat and handle are correctly cleaned by the domestic assistant, (who must also use appropriate hygiene precautions), the link is broken and neither the domestic assistant nor the next user will become contaminated.

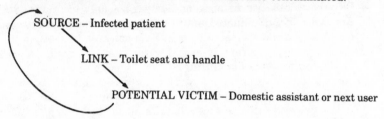

SOURCE – Infected patient

LINK – Toilet seat and handle

POTENTIAL VICTIM – Domestic assistant or next user

2.2.2.3 Cross infection

Cross infection or *cross contamination*, are terms widely used in a hospital situation and can be defined as 'the transmission of harmful bacteria (pathogens) from one medium to another by means of a carrier'. Figure 2.6 outlines possible sources and carriers of infection.

Cross infection, especially in a hospital, must be prevented. Whereas a healthy person can generally build-up a bodily resistance to combat a certain amount of harmful microbes, a hospital patient, generally with reduced resistance, is susceptible to disease and may, therefore, contract a secondary infection.

The risk of cross infection must be minimised by breaking the link and reducing the level of microbes to an acceptable level, recognising that it is impossible to remove all bacteria all of the time, ie to achieve totally aseptic conditions.

2.2.2.4 The role of cleaning

It is recognised that effective cleaning (effective in terms of soil removal, and incorporating means of preventing transmission of bacteria) is one way of reducing the level of bacteria present by removing contaminants and so helping to break the infection cycle. On the other hand, infrequent cleaning, use of unhygienic methods, contaminated equipment and cleaning solutions, and contaminated staff, can contribute to the infection risk by increasing bacteria levels or becoming the source or the link in the infection cycle. For instance, a domestic assistant cleans the toilets, then prepares to serve beverages to the patient without washing his or her hands, or the room attendant washes the early morning tea cups in the en-suite bathroom and dries them with a used towel.

Infection can be spread through the cleaning process in the following ways:

— Use of dirty or contaminated mops, dusters, buckets, scrubbing machines
— Dirty or contaminated water
— Inefficient filters on suction cleaners blowing contaminated air into the atmosphere
— Dry cleaning methods which scatter dust, such as sweeping, mopping, dusting
— Dirty or contaminated towels or tea towels
— Poor waste disposal methods, eg uncovered containers
— Emptying suction cleaners, waste bins in a breeze so rescattering dust
— Transferring equipment from one area to another, eg infectious unit to surgical ward or entrance area to operating theatre.

Domestic or housekeeping personnel may also spread infection:
— Through lack of personal hygiene, eg not washing hands after using the toilet
— Not washing hands after completing a 'dirty' task
— On personal clothing
— On uniforms and protective clothing
— If suffering from coughs, colds, infections, skin lesions
— Washing hands in sinks over crockery
— Smoking, scratching and other bad habits.

Figure 2.6 *Sources and carriers of infection*

Sources

Food stuffs infected at source

Vermin, Pests and Animals

Human beings
— may carry a germ, after being ill and becoming immune
— may carry a germ unknowingly and not even have been ill
— infected wounds
— AIDS and Hepititis B carriers

Other carriers

Foodstuffs contaminated during preparation
Humans pick up infection on hands or feet
Clothing and bedding
Towels
Soap
Surfaces contaminated by hand, faeces, pus
Air
Milk
Water (showers, eg legionnaires disease)

2.2.2.5 *Hygiene precautions*

The following hygiene precautions may have to be considered in conjunction with selecting hygienic cleaning methods, equipment and agents:

— Staff training in personal hygiene, cleaning technology, infection control and precautions against AIDS, etc[4]
— provision of personal hygiene facilities:
— changing areas with locker facilities to prevent contamination of personal clothing or uniforms
— adequate toilet facilities with facilities for handwashing and drying, bearing in mind that tablet soap, nail brushes, textile hand towels are potential carriers of infection
— provision of barrier and hand cream to encourage hand and nail care
— Supervision to ensure equipment is thoroughly cleaned after use and correctly stored (a time allowance must also be given on the work schedule to encourage this practice)
— An organised system for laundering of dusters, cloths, mop heads, tea towels
— Selection of cleaning equipment with its own cleaning, and possibly autoclaving in mind in certain instances
— Equipment allocated to high risk areas and only used there, not transported elsewhere, eg scrubbing machine kept in operating theatre
— Provision of protective clothing, overshoes and mask, waterproof aprons, rubber gloves
— Colour coded equipment to prevent using the same mop and bucket or cloths in wrong areas, for instance in a hospital:
— Blue for ward cleaning
— Red for sanitary areas
— Yellow for ward kitchen
— Barrier cleaning routines in very high risk areas. This involves washing hands in a specified disinfectant solution prior to entering the cubicle such as an infectious diseases, individual cubicle ward. Donning a gown on entry, cleaning the cubicle with equipment located there, taking off the gown on leaving, and washing the hands again. Double barrier cleaning involves washing hands inside and outside the cubicle.

Reverse barrier cleaning occurs in certain areas where infection brought in to the area, such as a burns or baby units, can be critical, therefore, hands are washed and the gown is donned to cover contaminated uniform before entry to the area. The actual barrier cleaning procedure may vary according to hospital policy, therefore clarification must be sought from the Control of Infection Officer.
— Use of disposable items, eg cloths, sheets, gowns to minimise infection risk, although hygienic disposal of these items must also be considered.

Some of the precautions mentioned are required by such laws as the Offices, Shops and Railway Premises Act, 1963, but general standards of health and hygiene are encompassed within the Health and Safety at Work Act, 1974.

2.2.2.6 Hygiene policy

Thus the basis of a hygiene policy has been formulated. It is easy to perceive that a hygiene policy is essential in a hospital situation, but a hygiene policy should be considered in other types of establishments also, to ensure that bad practices do not occur, that lack of up-to-date knowledge in cleaning technology is overcome, and that hygiene precautions are adopted in identified areas of risk.

The formulation and control of a hygiene policy is not purely the responsibility of the domestic services manager or housekeeper. In a hospital, a corporate policy must be formulated, encompassing medical, nursing, paramedical and catering practices. Often a Control of Infection Officer or Committee is commissioned in a hospital to consider the total environment and all building users. An integral part of the hygiene policy must be to consider the use and control of chemical disinfectants.

2.2.2.7 Chemical disinfectants

In a hospital, chemical disinfectants will be used by other departments and the Control of Infection Officer must evaluate all needs and all chemical disinfectants in use, with a view to rationalising and standardising usage, distribution and purchasing.

The intention here is to consider the formulation of a disinfection policy in relation to environmental cleaning. The types of chemical disinfectants and their characteristics are well documented in other publications (see end of chapter for references).

It is essential to realise that no chemical disinfectant is universally effective (see *Control of Hospital Infection*[3]) and that there are many problems associated with the use of chemical disinfectants which have to be controlled. So the first question to ask may well be 'Is a chemical disinfectant required at all?' Before the answer to this question can be given it is necessary to identify the risk areas and analyse the possible sources of infection and the types and levels of microbes likely to be present. Only then can the decision be made either to sterilise, ie destroy all microbes including spores, fungi and viruses, usually by the use of steam under pressure in an autoclave, or to disinfect, ie remove or destroy harmful bacteria, not necessarily spores. Disinfection may be achieved by the use of heat, which is the most reliable method, or chemical disinfectants. It can be argued that cleaning is a method of disinfection, as soil and, therefore, micro-organisms are removed during the cleaning process and disposed of, although not destroyed. Heat treatment, wet or dry, has limited application to the cleaning process and can only be used in some instances, such as laundering or dish washing processes. It may be decided that effective cleaning will suffice, as there is not always reliable scientific evidence to show that the regular use of chemical disinfectants results in a more hygienic result. For instance, there is no evidence to suggest that the regular use of a chemical disinfectant for damp mopping achieves a more hygienic floor, for more than a brief moment in time, than using an effective damp mopping procedure with a neutral detergent. Dust resettles from the atmosphere or is transported into the area in a matter of minutes.

In this example not only is a chemical disinfectant of little value, from an infection control point of view, but it also constitutes an extra item to purchase and an extra labour cost. As many chemical disinfectants are not cleaning agents and, in fact, may be inactivated by dirt, cleaning has to take place prior to disinfection. Hence the floor would have to be cleaned and then chemically disinfected – resulting in two processes, twice as much time and, therefore, additional labour costs. So thought must be given as to whether a chemical disinfectant is essential, and the hygiene benefits must be weighed against the cost and labour implications. It is possible in most types of establishments, even hospitals, that a chemical disinfectant for environmental purposes is not required at all, or only required for use in toilet areas.

If a chemical disinfectant is deemed necessary for specific tasks or areas, then careful selection is important and the following criteria according to B J COLLINS[1] must be considered:
— It should be active against a wide range of microbes
— It should be rapid in action, since once the surface to which it has been applied has dried it is no longer active
— It should be bactericidal in nature, ie kills rather than inhibits growth and prevent multiplication
— It should not be neutralised or inactivated by substances likely to be present on the surface such as organic matter; the medium in which it is used such as very hard water; the equipment with which it will be used, eg cellulosic mop head materials or the materials used for the storage containers, eg cork or certain plastics
— It should cause the minimum possible damage to the surface to which it is to be applied or the personnel using it
— It should be non-toxic, non-corrosive and non-irritating to skin or eyes
— It should be reasonably priced.

If the chemical disinfectant is to be of value it must be used correctly:
— For the intended purpose. It is dangerous to the user to use a caustic coal tar disinfectant, purchased for drains, for general floor cleaning
— At the correct dilution rate. Too weak a solution will not be effective, too strong a solution will not necessarily kill more microbes. It is a good idea to carry out in-use tests in conjunction

with a micro-biologist to determine the optimum dilution rate in a particular area, according to the number of microbes present

— For the specified length of time, a quick dip or application which immediately dries is not sufficient. The solution is only effective whilst wet

— At the correct temperature. Most chemical disinfectants work more efficiently in hot rather than cold water

— Generally after cleaning, unless specifically stated. Some chemical disinfectants are inactivated by organic soil, a chemical disinfectant has to penetrate the bacterial cell before it can kill it and substances such as grease may form a waterproof protection around the cell. Hence cleaning first is necessary to remove soil and to emulsify and remove the grease

— A fresh solution is more effective than one prepared a few days ago. Prepared solutions deteriorate over a period of time, some very rapidly

— Chemical disinfectants must never be mixed with soaps or detergents as both agents may be neutralised. For instance, if an anionic detergent, which contains negative ions, is mixed with a quarternary ammonium compound, based on a cationic detergent which contains positive ions, the result is neutralisation. This solution will not only be inactivated but becomes a potential breeding ground for bacteria.

So it can be seen that the use of chemical disinfectants is complex and, as management have to rely on personnel for their effective usage, it is essential to introduce a number of control measures. Staff training is essential; most personnel do not realise the latent dangers involved. With the use of chemical disinfectants any measure which can be introduced to simplify diluting the solution, to ensure the correct strength is always used, must be worthwhile. Personnel do not necessarily understand ratios (1 to 100 solution) or percentages (a 10% solution) so, for instance, 1 cap to a bucketful, is more meaningful to them. They must be aware of the significance of the correct dilution rate. Caps, proportioners, measured pumps or pre-packed sachets are available options. If solutions are centrally prepared and distributed, sterile, dry containers must be used, and labelled with all product details itemised, including the date of issue and the last date of usage. Effective supervision involves regular checks to ensure solutions are not used after deterioration.

It is also necessary from time to time to carry out microbial tests to ensure that bacteria levels are being controlled; that specified dilution rates are effective; and the correct dilution rate is being maintained.

Generally, the only types of chemical disinfectants which may be seriously considered for environmental disinfection purposes are:

— hypochlorite disinfectants (bleaches)

— phenolic disinfectants, ie clear soluble synthetic phenols (not coal tar).

In the United States, quaternary ammonium compounds seem to be more widely used for environmental disinfection, especially in food areas. B J COLLINS[3] suggests the following acceptable uses of chemical disinfectants for environmental purposes in a hospital:

— For disinfection of known contaminated spillages such as urine, blood, pus, faeces and vomit
— For terminal disinfection of rooms after use by a patient with infectious conditions resulting from organisms not normally present in the environment, gut or on the skin (which may affect other patients or the healthy hospital worker)
— Routine cleaning in areas where patients are highly susceptible to infection and are likely to become infected by normal microbial inhabitants of the environment, eg premature baby units, intensive care units
— Routine cleaning in units where patients with infectious diseases are treated on a regular basis
— Possibly for routine cleaning of operating theatre floors, although the actual value is doubtful.

Finally, aromatic chemical disinfectants, often used indiscriminately, in reality are only active against a very limited range of microbes so their use should be seriously considered against the cost of purchase and application. Smell has absolutely nothing to do with the effectiveness of chemical disinfectants.

2.2.3   Planning the cleaning programme

Planning the cleaning programme will involve determining:

— what tasks have to be undertaken in relation to the needs of the building
— the most effective methods, equipment and agents required for each of these tasks
— the optimum frequency for performing these tasks in each area
— how many man hours are required to complete all scheduled tasks and subsequently how many staff are required.

It is generally accepted by both in-house managers and contractors that the following aspects need to be considered:

2.2.3.1   Terms of reference

When planning the cleaning programme and estimating the optimum manning levels, it is necessary to function within the confines of the departmental objectives or terms of reference. In many situations the terms of reference are not well defined and must be established before progress can be made.

The *terms of reference* are a statement of the boundaries of responsibility within which the department has to operate and any constraints or limitations imposed by a higher authority. It is useful in this context to:

— specify all physical areas of the building
— identify all tasks, activities or services to be performed by departmental personnel such as floor stripping, provision of uniforms, service of early morning tea
— state the standards of cleanliness to be achieved in general terms, ie whether aesthetic or clinical
— state the financial framework within which the department must operate, for instance, break-even at a specific budgeted figure
— state any other constraints or limits to be imposed, eg hours of access for cleaning.

The terms of reference must be approved by a higher authority and be agreed with other departmental heads in order to clarify and formalise responsibility for specific tasks and areas, and to avoid those 'grey areas' occurring in reality. For instance, in an hotel it is often unclear whether food and beverage or housekeeping personnel are responsible for specific cleaning tasks in the banqueting rooms, restaurants and bar areas or whether housekeeping or maintenance departments are responsible for particular tasks, eg sealing and sanding a particular area.

2.2.3.2   Area determination
The next stage is to conduct a detailed physical survey of the building. The purpose of this is to determine the needs and requirements of the building; establish its state of repair, cleanliness and treatments previously used; and to prepare a detailed inventory of each area. The survey can be greatly aided by using the working plans of the building, which should be readily available to housekeeping and maintenance managers. The information to be collected includes details of all room types and the number of each type; the dimensions; a description of the materials used for each surface, eg wall covering, floor covering, furniture, fittings and furnishings, together with details of initial treatments and the state of repair or finish. This data can easily be collated in chart form, with one record per room or room-type, and is commonly referred to as either a *room schedule* or an *accommodation schedule*. See figure 2.7.

Figure 2.7 *A room schedule*

Name of Establishment _____

Room No./Name _____   Use _____

Dimension _____

Object	No./Size	Surface	Object	No./Size	Surface
Floor	60 sq m	80/20 Wilton carpet			
Chairs	20	Polypropylene			

Unless such data is collected, it is impossible to determine, in specific terms, what cleaning and maintenance tasks (ie maintenance tasks performed by cleaning personnel, such as floor maintenance) have to be performed and, consequently, quantify the work to be done. The concept of a room inventory can be useful when implementing any one of the following:

— A planned preventive maintenance programme
— Room control procedure for controlling furniture and furnishing stocks
— A re-decoration and interior design scheme appraisal
— An aide-memoire system together with room photographs for front office personnel responsible for increasing accommodation sales.

At the time of analysing each area, it is opportune to consider two other aspects. Firstly, to identify the standards required in that room type, ie a different standard of hygiene is required in a sanitary area compared with a sleeping area. Secondly, to identify any problems which will be peculiar to that room type, such as barrier cleaning; a permanent equipment supply in an infectious diseases unit; or stringent dust control in a mainframe computer unit.

This database can be computerised.

2.2.3.3 Work load determination

From the data gathered, it is possible to determine the specific cleaning and maintenance tasks and other housekeeping services which have to be completed to produce required results.

In general terms, these tasks can be identified under the following headings:

— *Cleaning tasks*, eg suction cleaning, damp dusting
— *Maintenance tasks*, eg polish stripping, sanding, maintenance checks
— *Services to be provided*, eg early morning teas, dish-washing
— *Special requirements*, eg barrier cleaning, chemical disinfection.

The chart format used for the room inventory can be extended, as shown in figure 2.8, to identify the specific tasks to be carried out on each surface, in each specific area or type of area. Where one room is much like another of the same type it is not necessary to produce separate room inventories.

Figure 2.8 *Task sheet. Work load to be completed in a particular room*

Name of Establishment _____

Room No./Name _____ Use _____

Dimension _____

Object	No./Size	Surface	Task
Floor	60 sq m	80/20 Wilton	Vacuum Spot check Shampoo
Chairs	20	Polypropylene	Damp dust
Wastebins	3	Fibreglass	Empty Damp dust

2.2.3.4 Task determination

Each task must then be examined to determine how it should be carried out; what equipment, agents and supplies should be used; what standards should be achieved by an average competent employee; and how long the task should take to complete. The actual method used will affect the time element to be allocated to the task. This involves a method study or task analysis to be carried out (see Appendix 3) the benefits of which are to:

— establish the method most appropriate for the situation (in terms of the best, most time-saving, the most hygienic, the safest, the simplest)
— set a specific and known standard to aid the training and supervisory processes
— standardise on the method used for a particular task so establishing uniformity and consistency
— standardise on supplies to effect economy of purchase.

It is also essential to identify and state the purpose of the task and break it down into separate stages, highlighting the safety, hygiene and other important key factors to be considered at each stage, and arrange these stages in a logical sequence as shown in figure 2.9. Various terms are used for this kind of documentation, such as Job Breakdown, Work Procedures, Job Procedures, Task Analysis Sheets.

These job breakdowns may be collated into one *Standard Operating Manual*, as is the case in many American hospitals. It is a useful document for use by higher management, and regulatory and inspectory bodies such as the Health and Safety executive.

Job breakdowns also provide a very useful base for the preparation of practical or on-the-job training sessions (see chapter 3).

2.2.3.5 Frequencies

Another crucial aspect to consider is how often each task is to be performed. Frequencies, standards and costs are interlinked. The more often a specific task is performed the more manhours have to be allocated over a period and the higher the cost of cleaning will be. The less often the task is performed the lower the cost and possibly the lower the standard achieved. A too high frequency can result in a lower standard and even higher cost. For instance, too frequent floor polish application can reduce appearance and result in a higher proportion of time and effort to remove the build-up. Frequencies and standards in a given situation have to be correlated to determine the optimum frequency. Some of the following factors will affect the frequency of the tasks to be performed:

— Type of area
— Type and condition of surfaces
— Type and number of people using the area over a period of time, ie user density
— Functions of the area and activities taking place
— How often the area is used and when

Figure 2.9 *Job Breakdown*

.... (Establishment)	Domestic Department

Task	To strip a floor of water-based polish
Purpose	To remove old polish and dirt from the floor in order to repolish, and so prevent a build up
Equipment and supplies	Suction drier Scrubbing machine and drive disc Black thick-line pad Abrasive hand pad Alkaline detergent Rubber gloves Warning signs Mop and bucket Neutral detergent Cloth and plastic bucket Vinegar and pH paper
Special factors	The floor must be in a neutral condition at the end of this operation, in order to easily apply new polish and maintain a good appearance

Procedures	Key points
1 Collect all equipment	To make sure that all equipment is at hand
2 Check all plugs and cables	For frayed edges and cuts, etc. This is a safety precaution Report to supervisor if there are any faults
3 Fill the tank with detergent solution	Read the instructions carefully
4 Prepare the area to be stripped	Remove the furniture Divide into convenient sections to cover Position floor cleaning signs
5 Prepare the machine	Fix the drive disc on the machine and put the stripping pad under the disc
6 Plug the machine in, behind the operator	So the operator works back towards the socket without the cable getting in the way and also is always standing on dry floor
7 Scrub and dry one section at a time	The scubbing machine works from side to side across the section. Also must avoid too much water on the floor Must overlap each lane to avoid missing any floor The drier follows on after 2 or 3 minutes to pick up the water to prevent it staying on the floor for any length of time

	Take care to overlap the lanes at the edges, at each end
	Lift the machine over bottom edge and then pull back to make sure all water is removed
8 If the section has not been stripped properly scrub and dry again	The edges and corners may have to be done by hand with an abrasive pad
	Remember if little polish has been applied this should not be difficult
9 Rinse thoroughly with cold water	This can be done by mopping or scrubbing with cold water and drying
	This is to remove all detergent residue and alkalinity
10 Neutralise the alkalinity with vinegar (mild acid) in water if necessary	Test the floor surface with pH paper
11 Dry with suction drier if necessary or leave to dry	Test again
12 Repeat stages 7–11	Until the whole floor has been thoroughly stripped of old polish
13 The floor should now be ready to retreat	Buff the floor if necessary to produce a sheen and harden the surface, prior to polish application
14 Clean all the equipment thoroughly, wash pads out, and empty the drier.	Use neutral detergent
	The equipment must be put away in a clean condition so bacteria do not breed, so the equipment will work efficiently and last longer and the next person using it, will find it in a clean condition.

NB For scrubbing a floor which has been treated with a water-based polish use this procedure, points 1–7, but use a neutral detergent.

Figure 2.10 *Task sheet to show frequencies*

Name of Establishment	
Room No./Name	Use
	Dimensions

Object	No./Size	Surface	Task	Frequency
Floor	60 sq m	80/20 Wilton	Vacuum Spot check Shampoo	Daily Daily 6 monthly

— What type(s) of soil present
— How much soil is transported to the area and by what means
— How far has soil been transported/location of area
— The degree of infection risk
— The standard which must be achieved
— The amount of money available.

It is normally convenient to establish the frequency for each task on each surface in each area in terms of daily, weekly and periodic tasks, which range from fortnightly, monthly, quarterly, six monthly, annually, and even five yearly in some situations. The chart format of data collection can be further developed as shown in figure 2.10.

For housekeeping purposes an annual cycle is the norm, although redecoration and upgrading schemes may be organised on a two or three year cycle, whereas a maintenance programme may extend over a cycle of 60 years.

2.2.3.6   Calculation of man hours

Calculating the number of man hours required involves multiplying the time it takes to perform a task by the frequency, say over a weekly period, and the adding together of all the tasks in all the areas.

Quantifying the time per task is perhaps the most difficult part as relatively little published data is available, and this is mostly in the form of synthetic time values, ie representative times for various tasks and activities gained from carrying out a number of time studies in a particular organisation, eg 'damp mopping takes ·26 minutes per 100 sq m'. However, this data is usually produced for specific use in one kind of operation and it is not generally recommended to use the data indiscriminately, as different types of problems may exist which have not been accounted for in the figures.

Where published data is not available, three other approaches may have to be considered, namely the use of:
— past experience of the time required to perform cleaning tasks
— experimentation and crude time studies conducted by the departmental manager to establish a time element
— work study personnel to conduct work-studied time studies or use operational research techniques to obtain time elements.

Once a time element has been established for each type of task, the time per task in a given area can be calculated, and if the result is multiplied or divided by the frequency then the time required to perform the task over a given period can be calculated, eg:

TASK	TIME	FREQUENCY	WEEKLY TOTAL
Bed making	5 minutes	Daily $\times 7$	35 minutes
Window cleaning	60 minutes	Monthly $\div 4$	15 minutes

As housekeeping personnel are usually employed on a weekly basis, the man hours required are usually calculated on a weekly basis, although there is no reason why calculations should not be made on a monthly or annual basis. The manpower figure so calculated may or may not include a time element for periodic tasks. In a hospital, for instance, where it is normal policy to undertake a proportion of periodic tasks every week, these tasks would be included in the final manpower figure. Where all periodic work is done at one time, for instance, during the vacation in a hall of residence, then separate figures will be calculated to establish the man hours required for term time and those for the periodic work. Another instance is where all or some periodic work will be undertaken by contractors and so a figure is not required to be included in the normal manning hours.

As the time elements used, particularly work study or synthetic time values, are based on actual time to complete a task only, various allowances must be included in the final calculations. These allowances fall into the following categories:

Contingency – collecting, returning and cleaning equipment, re-doing work

Relaxation – natural breaks, working near the end of a shift, working in hot or cold conditions

Breaks – lunch and tea/coffee breaks

Days off

Holidays and Bank holiday lieu days

Sickness and absence.

All these allowances are not applicable in every situation, for instance, in a hall of residence where only a five day service is provided, an allowance for days off will not be included. In a hospital ward where the workload is consistent seven days a week, an allowance will have to be made to accommodate two days off per person per week. The allowance is usually incorporated on a percentage basis, eg 10% of the total working time for equipment preparation and relaxation purposes. The percentage allowance will fluctuate from one organisation to another depending on company policy and other factors such as variances on holiday entitlements, sickness and absence ratios.

The final calculation is a summation of the total number of hours per area, per week, plus appropriate allowances, eg:

Area A	800 hours	
Area B	1200 hours	
Area C	1000 hours	
		3,000 hours
10% relaxation		300 hours
10% sickness and absence		300 hours
11% holidays		330 hours
		3,930 hours

In some organisations, namely the NHS, this figure is converted to a Full-time Equivalent (FTE or WTE – Whole-time Equivalent), ie a figure used to express the number of staff who would be required if employed on a full-time basis, ie 37.5 hours (at the moment) per week

$$\frac{3930 \ \text{hours required per week}}{37.5 \ \text{hours worked by one full-timer}} = 104.8 \ \text{FTE}$$

This is then referred to as the Establishment Figure for the Domestic Services Department so, in this example, the Domestic Service Department would require 98.25 FTE staff.

It may be more meaningful to express the total in numbers of manhours required per week, as often a number of part-time staff is employed, for instance in the example given 98.25 FTE working 40 hours per week are allowed, therefore 3930 hours per week are available for staff deployment.

2.2.3.7 Scheduling

It is not only necessary to determine the optimum number of manhours but also to plan effectively the allocation of work to members of staff. In practical terms a worker, or small number of workers, will need to be deployed in a specific area of the building, possibly at a specific time, to perform the allocated tasks at the designated frequency in order to achieve the objectives of the department. This involves the scheduling of work to be allocated to staff and the rostering of staff to ensure that all work is covered as and when required. Effective planning at this stage makes it easier for the supervisor to deploy personnel on a day-to-day basis and control performance.

A work schedule can be defined as a timetable of tasks to be undertaken by each individual worker within a certain period of time or shift. The preparation of a work schedule should ensure that an individual member of staff knows exactly what to do, where and when, thus avoiding worry, confusion and fatigue. It also ensures that all tasks, whether daily, weekly and possibly periodic (refer section 2.2.3.6) are covered with none missed out or duplicated.

Each member of staff should have been given a fair and even distribution of work within the number of hours worked, with no overlapping of duties. Time should be saved as, in conjunction with induction and training, staff should not be left waiting for instructions. Supervisors should know where staff are at a particular time and which area or tasks can be checked. Work schedules are also useful:

— where a relief member of staff is covering an area

— as a training aid

— to help set the standard required by ensuring that the necessary amount of time is allowed to perform a task and the tasks are arranged in correct sequence.

Before the work schedules can actually be prepared, the layout of the building, the approach to work allocation, and the grades of staff to be employed, must also be considered. Normally a building will be split into sections of convenient size to be tackled by an individual or a small number of personnel. The type of establishment, its size, design and layout will influence the actual sections or units designated as will the siting of cleaners' cupboards or utility rooms, sockets, water points, large scale equipment stores and lifts, the nature of the work, and the times of usage of the areas. Often a building physically divorced from the rest of the premises is designated a separate unit. In a hospital a section tends to be a ward or block of wards, a department or residence, whereas in an hotel a floor of bedrooms, or a number of public areas, such as restaurants, bars, function rooms, may be regarded as sections. Consideration must also be given to allocating adjoining areas to a member of staff, to avoid unproductive time walking from one area to another. Where areas are not adjoining, an allowance must be added to cover 'walking time'.

When scheduling work, several approaches may be taken. Provision may be made for a member (or members) of staff to be allocated to a specific section, where a range of tasks is carried out in a number of rooms. Alternatively, a small number of tasks may be allocated to a small team of people – team cleaning. This often occurs where certain tasks require a higher degree of skill, or more specialised equipment, and are performed throughout the building. For instance, window cleaning, floor maintenance, curtain rail teams are deployed in many hospitals. Staff may be allocated either on a permanent or a rotation basis to a section or team. Rotation often occurs where some of the workload is boring, repetitive, strenuous, unpleasant or costed at a different rate. In a large on-site hospital laundry, personnel are often rotated from one stage or process to the next on cyclic basis, to relieve boredom and even out wages.

In most establishments, traditionally recognised grades of staff exist with well defined duties and responsibilities, so thought must be given to which grades of staff are required to perform which tasks. This decision will subsequently affect work allocation, work schedules, shift hours and the number of part-time and full-time staff required. Job descriptions (discussed in chapter 3) can then be prepared. See figure 3.2.

It is now possible to draft the actual work schedule for a specific section, using the data already collated. The other data to be considered includes the time span over which that section needs to be covered, the timing of tasks and their sequence.

The routines of other groups of personnel, such as times of bed-making by nursing staff, or times by which rooms should be vacated by holiday makers, will influence the timing and sequences of tasks. Other factors which may influence scheduling of tasks include doctors' ward rounds, visiting times, opening hours and frequency and pattern of usage and therefore availability. For instance, hospital departments and offices only used five days a week and open say 8 am to 6 pm would suggest that cleaning commences after 6 pm on a five day basis. By plotting on a time plan those tasks which can only be performed at certain times; those tasks which have to be completed before a deadline or prior to another task; and meal and break-times; and then fit in all other tasks in sequence, it is possible to highlight the peaks and troughs in activity which will help to determine when periodic tasks can be fitted in and the shift hours when staff are required. This in turn helps to determine the number of part-time and full-time staff required. Sources of recruitment and availability of personnel in the locale will also affect the decision to employ full-time or part-time staff. See figure 2.11.

2.2.3.8 Duty rotas

It is important to plan a system of ensuring that all sections are covered as and when required, at the same time allowing staff to have their off duty allocation on a fair and rational basis. This involves the preparation of a duty rota, indicating on a weekly and/or a monthly basis, which members of staff are on or off duty at any particular time and which sections are to be covered by which named members of staff. When preparing the duty rota the needs of both the personnel and the sections should be considered. It is only reasonable that personnel should know in advance when their off duty will occur and, where a seven day coverage exists – a systematic cycle, for instance, alternate weekends off – will simplify arrangements for all concerned. Where, for instance, a seven day service is provided, a relief allowance to cover days off, will have been included in the manhour calculations. A 'relief' member of staff, covering days off only, may be allocated to a particular section, on a permanent basis. The effects of occupancy trends should be reconsidered at this stage. For instance, if hotel room occupancy is low at the weekend, then less staff are required and days off do not have to be covered as room occupancy determines the work load, or in a hospital where offices are only used from Monday to Friday, provision is made for a five day rather than a seven day service.

In circumstances where enhanced payments are made for shift or weekend coverage, consideration should be given to allocating lower priority tasks and weekly and periodic work at the lower pay rate during the week. For instance, in a hospital if periodic floor maintenance was undertaken on Sunday when double time is paid then the cost of the work is doubled. (See chapter 3.)

Where holiday and Bank Holiday allowances have been made in the calculation, a pool of non-allocated hours must be kept available to employ relief cover for these occurrences, and again a fair and rational system devised for allocating and covering holiday entitlements. It is more difficult to schedule work and roster staff in circumstances where great fluctuations occur daily in the work load, generally due to fluctuations in occupancy. This often necessitates a great deal of

Figure 2.11 *Plotting the work schedule*

7.00	Wash early morning tea pots (20 minutes)	13.00	Lunch break
7.30	Clean Sister's office (10 minutes)	13.30	Clean sanitary areas (1 hour)
		14.00	
		14.30	
8.00	Clean Day Room (20 minutes)	15.00	Serve afternoon tea
8.30	Vacuum ward area (45 minutes)	15.30	Collect dirty pots
		16.00	
9.00	Damp mop (45 minutes)	16.30	
9.30	Break	17.00	Mop/sweep ward floor
10.00	Serve beverages	17.30	Prepare trays
10.30		18.00	Serve beverages
11.00		18.30	Collect trays
11.30	Set up meal trays		Wash up
12.00	Serve beverages	19.00	Check toilet area
12.30	Collect dirty pots		

flexibility in the hotel cleaning programme compared to a static and even seven day or five day coverage of work in hospitals or halls of residence.

2.2.3.9 *Labour costs*

It is now possible to determine the projected labour costs over a period of time as the number of man hours, breakdown of part-time and full-time staff, shift hours and duty rotas have all been determined. As the grades of staff have also been decided, the rates of pay can be determined usually by company policy, and enhanced payments for weekend or shift work must be taken into account. Other costs such as recruitment, training, uniforms, meals on duty and paid breaks must also be taken into account.

It can be seen that the formulation of a well planned cleaning system is an involved and time consuming exercise and, therefore, for this reason a haphazard system is often allowed to happen. This may save management costs in the short term but inevitably, in the long term, management and staff costs will be excessive.

When the cleaning service is to be provided by a contractor the same procedure has to be undertaken but in this case the organisation formulate the specification based on conducting the building survey and specifying the work load, ie the tasks, services, activities to be performed and the areas to be covered, whilst the contractor undertakes the rest of the exercise to formulate the tender bid.

2.3 WASTE DISPOSAL

Waste disposal is an activity often managed by the Accommodation Manager. The waste disposal system involves either collecting up the waste, holding it in suitable containers, moving it to a central collection point and finally arranging for its final removal or

Figure 2.12 *Types of waste materials*

Kitchen waste
 Food; tins; packaging

Litter, dirt and waste paper
 (often referred to as rubbish, garbage or trash)

Soiled dressings and sanitary towels

Operating theatre and pathology waste
 Solid organic waste; human remains and organs

Miscellaneous products
 Aerosols; bottles
*Effluent

Factory/Industrial waste*
 Chemicals; radio-active; nuclear

Fuel emission*

Scrap metal*

---

incineration, or disposing of it at source through disposal units or
sanitary appliances. Initially, waste disposal may seem to be a minor
activity, but waste products do constitute fire, hygiene and safety
hazards. Certainly, in a large operation, where a vast amount of waste
is generated daily, it can be a major problem, especially if an effective
disposal system has not been devised, and waste is allowed to
accumulate. It is unsightly, starts to smell and attracts pests and
vermin. The aim, therefore, is to dispose of all waste materials in a
hygienic and safe manner, as economically as possible, preventing an
unsightly appearance and a fire and health hazard.

2.3.1 Waste collection
Before a satisfactory collection and disposal system can be devised, it is
vital to analyse not only the type of waste produced within the
operation and its characteristics but also its source and the amounts to
be dealt with. Each type of waste may well require different collection,
storage and disposal arrangements and the amount may influence the
most cost-effective disposal option and the decision to buy certain
types of equipment, such as shredders and compactors.
　The types of waste materials which may be identified are listed in
figure 2.12.
　Those asterisked are beyond the scope of this section. Waste
products, such as paper and bottles, which can be recycled, may be
identified separately. Market values and moral conscience may affect
this decision.
　Thought must also be given to two particular problems which occur
at source. Firstly, adequate provision of receptacles must be made in
sanitary areas to contain used paper towels and prevent littering the

floor area. Secondly, adequate provision of ashtrays must be made for two main reasons – not only to ensure cigarette ends are segregated from waste paper bins for fire safety reasons but also to try and prevent damage to floor coverings by smouldering cigarette ends being stubbed out under foot.

2.3.2 Suitable containers

Equipment may be installed so that some waste products may be disposed of at source, eg kitchen waste disposal units for food waste and incinerators for soiled dressings in sanitary areas.

Many types of waste need to be stored in suitable containers to await collection. Containers may be colour coded for easy identification of different types of waste. The suitability of the container depends to some degree on whether the waste is wet or dry in nature but should possess most if not all of the following characteristics:

— be large enough to hold the amount of waste collected from one pick-up to the next – but not too large for handling and transporting
— have a lid or a tie to prevent dust scattering and waste falling out
— have a foot control for the lid to avoid contaminating hands
— be made of a tough durable material which does not burst or split
— be made from a non-absorbent material which does not disintegrate when holding wet waste
— either be disposable or easy to clean or sterilise
— fit on a stand to aid packing and avoid falling over.

Containers may be galvanised iron, rubber, plastic, fibreglass, paper, polythene or polythene lined paper.

2.3.3 Central collection

The first problem to consider here is the transportation from the source to the central collection point.

How – by chute, trolley, motorised trucks
By whom – porters, refuse gang, domestic staff
How often – at least once a day in a busy area to avoid the problems discussed at the end of this section

The second problem is to consider the central collection point itself.

Siting – is it convenient for transporation from all sources?
– is it inside or outside?
– is it camouflaged to prevent building users seeing it?
Size – is it large enough to hold the amount of waste?
Design – does it have easy to clean, non-absorbent surfaces and a water point and drain outlet?
Cleaning – can it be cleaned down regularly, preferably by hosing or high pressure water spraying equipment?
Storage containers – are large storage containers required, if so what type, what characteristics are required? Contractor skips may be used.

Many types of waste may be easily ignited either directly, eg by a smouldering cigarette end or by spontaneous combustion. Waste, therefore, constitutes a fire hazard. It is crucial that refuse porters must not smoke whilst handling waste. If thought is not given to the suitability of this central site, waste may well accumulate and obstruct fire doors, fire fighting equipment and escape routes, so constituting a safety hazard. Some waste, particularly if it is wet in nature also constitutes a hygiene hazard, soon starts to smell and attracts pests and vermin. Frequent removal from this point needs to be arranged to shorten the storage period and reduce the risks.

2.3.4 Disposal

The method of disposal will be determined by the type and amount of waste to be disposed, green policies, costs involved and available finance, market value, if any appertaining to certain types of waste and geographic location.

The following options can be investigated:

Incineration Theatre waste and soiled dressings must be incinerated to meet ethical standards. Other waste products such as general rubbish, sanitary towels and confidential information, such as old records, may also be incinerated. Apart from being a hygienic means of disposal, it also reduces the amount of waste to be disposed of by other means, and in some cases the heat generated can be recycled. It is dangerous to burn certain items, such as aerosols which explode and these must, therefore, be segregated from the general rubbish.

Local Authority Refuse Collection This needs to be arranged on a frequent regular basis and does involve a charge for the operation dependent on local policy and quantity involved.

Contract refuse collection This may be more cost effective than the local authority option. The contractor often leaves a skip which is collected at a prescribed time. At certain periods in time, certain waste products may have a good or bad market value and it may be worth selling them, although transport costs would have to be deducted. This normally applies to waste products like waste paper and fabrics which can be recycled, or food waste which may be used as pig swill, though the latter use has diminished and is subject to strict regulations.

It may be worth investigating the feasibility of purchasing equipment such as shredders, compactors, compressors or baling machines to reduce the volume of the waste, particularly where large amounts of waste paper – some of which contains confidential information – is concerned. Storage space and transport costs may be affected by this purchase.

Chemical disposal This is a useful means of collecting sanitary towels. As it is a contract service, it is convenient to the operation, hygienic and reduces unpleasantness for domestic staff. A disposal unit is usually placed in each female public convenience, and replaced at a pre-arranged frequency.

Bottle bank This may be useful where many non-returnable empty bottles are generated.

If a decision is to be taken to increase the use of disposable items, such as crockery, cutlery, napiery and bedding, thought must be given to the method of disposal and the effect of this decision on the existing disposal system.

2.4 THE LINEN AND LAUNDRY SERVICES

A comprehensive linen system involves providing sufficient quantities of usable items; replacing the dirty linen with clean at the point of usage; processing the dirty linen; repairing or replacing worn linen; storing and redistributing it, and controlling the whole procedure.

Four linen and laundry options are available for consideration, namely:

1 Purchasing linen for the operation and laundering on-site
2 Purchasing linen for the operation and laundering off-site
3 Purchasing easy-care linen and laundering on-site
4 Linen hire.

Sometimes a combination of two systems might be appropriate. An establishment may purchase bed linen and send it to an off-site laundry for processing, and hire staff uniforms and banqueting cloths for a seasonal trade. Disposable linen may even be used in certain circumstances, where hygiene is required, eg disposable sheets for a treatment couch in the doctor's office or disposable gowns in a theatre suite; to prevent cross-infection, eg where sheets from an infectious diseases unit need to be incinerated; for convenience where inadequate laundry arrangements exist, eg table linen or in case of emergency, eg laundry workers' strike.

The linen and laundry system involves two sub-systems: the *linen control system* and *the processing* (laundering or dry cleaning) *system*, each of which will be discussed separately.

the term *linen* in this context does not necessarily refer to the linen fibre produced from flax, but is a generic term encompassing all launderable items used by any operation. If the linen and laundry system is to be truly comprehensive, it should also encompass all fabric items including those items of bedding and soft furnishings which have to be dry cleaned but excluding carpets. As dry cleaning is very expensive it is beneficial to purchase as many items as possible which can be laundered.

2.4.1 The linen control system
The linen control system involves selecting and purchasing items which are suitable for their purpose, in sufficient quantities to

maintain standards and ensure operational ease on an economic basis. Factors to consider when selecting items are discussed in chapter 4. A flow chart of the stages involved in the linen cycle, from the collection of clean linen from a periphery storage area to the redistribution of clean linen from the central store to top up the items used from this periphery store, facilitates explaining the facets of the linen control system – see figure 2.13.

Figure 2.13 *The linen control system*

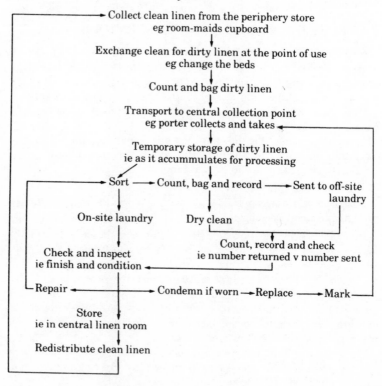

2.4.1.1 Provision of linen

There are alternative ways of providing linen, either to purchase outright or to hire on a rental basis, both having their advantages and disadvantages which are listed in chapter 4, figure 4.7.

A further option involves purchasing only synthetic fibres or fibre combinations such as polyester/cotton which have been specially treated with a 'non-iron' finish. The laundering and tumbling stages must be especially controlled. The wash temperature must be controlled at 40°C and the tumbling cycle must include a cool-down period to avoid creasing.

If items are folded well as they are taken out of the tumble dryer, then no ironing is required. The advantages and disadvantages of this system are:

ADVANTAGES (Easy care)	DISADVANTAGES
Smaller stocks	Initial costs of equipment if not leased
Speedier processing cycle (2 hr)	Repair costs
Cuts out cost of ironing, labour and equipment	Replacement costs
Equipment may be hired or bought	Overloading creates loss of standard
Small area for equipment	Customer acceptance – not quite as crisp a finish
Few staff	
Facilities used for all items and bedding and soft furnishings	
Capital asset	

The stock of linen purchased or hired will have to be stored when not in use. This usually involves bulk storage at a central site and periphery storage near the point of usage, eg linen required for a section of bedrooms is stored in the maids' cupboard. The quantity of stock required plus a contingency to allow for change over and a possible emergency must be estimated and provided. The quantity required will depend on the number of beds in the section, and the frequency of bed changing, with an allowance in case clean linen is not available for some reason from the central storage area, or a bed has to be changed more frequently.

Strict control is required to ensure the optimum amount is stored at each of the points of usage. Too high a stock involves higher capital costs and too little linen may well create stress on staff, affect standards and productivity, and possibly profitability, if a room cannot be let because clean linen is not available to re-make the bed. Control also involves keeping an accurate record of the initial amounts allocated to each point and regular stock-taking to ensure the allocated stock level is maintained and losses or pilfering do not occur.

2.4.1.2 Exchange

The frequency of replacing dirty linen with clean from the periphery storage area will be determined either according to the turnover of the client, eg the table cloth is changed for every new guest group sitting down, or by company policy, eg beds will be changed daily for however long the guest is staying. The exchange creates two problems. Firstly, the dirty linen has to be dealt with and secondly, the stock in the periphery store has to be replenished. The latter problem will be discussed under *Redistribution* on page 100. It is helpful in many cases to provide the employee changing the dirty linen with a trolley to aid productivity and prevent numerous trips backwards and forwards to the storage area. Dirty linen piled high in hotel corridors as rooms are stripped is an eyesore, as well as an obstruction and safety hazard, and departmental policy may dictate that dirty linen should not be left in the corridor. Sorting of dirty linen into like items, or according to its state (eg stained, very dirty), may take place at this point or in the central storage area in a hospital. Infected or fouled linen would be segregated straight away. The number of items may well be recorded so the amount by which the stock has to be replenished is known.

The dirty linen will have to be bagged in some kind of container to facilitate transport, avoid damage and prevent cross-contamination. The containers may be fabric, usually nylon or a non-absorbent synthetic fibre, plastic, fibreglass or even wicker baskets may still be used. Certainly, in the National Health Service bags are colour coded to denote ordinary soiled linen, fouled line, infected linen or theatre and renal linen.

The bags containing fouled and infected linen may be sewn with alginate thread which dissolves with the heat at the pre-wash stage of the laundry process. This avoids contaminating the laundry worker who is sorting the dirty linen.

A decision has to be made as to which grade of staff will collect and transport the dirty linen from each periphery storage area to the central linen area. Room attendants, porters or linen room staff may be involved or a linen chute may be 'in built' to ease transportation.

2.4.1.3 Processing

Dirty linen will be transported, by whatever means to a central site, which will probably be the laundry area, if an on-site laundry operates, or the central storage area, if dirty linen is to be sent to an off-site laundry. A special area should be designated for the accumulation of dirty linen to avoid cross-contaminating clean linen. The accumulated dirty linen will have to be sorted usually into like items, counted, recorded and bagged for transport to the off-site laundry. The containers used will be similar to those already mentioned but, possibly larger and vans or some mechanical type of transport may be required. From a hygiene point of view, clean linen should not be transported by a van which has been used for dirty linen and the inside of the van should be cleaned regularly.

The actual laundry process will be discussed in section 2.4.2 but there are several laundry systems from which to choose. The laundry may be on-site or off-site, but there are two alternatives for each of these options.

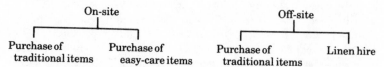

If 'traditional' items of linen made from natural and man-made fibres have been purchased, then processing may take place on-site in a laundry requiring the whole range of laundering equipment, or it may take place off-site at a commercial laundry. If 'easy-care', no-iron items have been purchased, they will be processed on-site in a modified laundry (no ironing equipment is required). If linen has been hired then it is returned to the linen hire company (off-site) for processing. The advantages and disadvantages of each laundry option are highlighted in figure 2.14.

Some items may have to be dry cleaned rather than laundered. The dry cleaning process will be discussed in section 2.4.4.

Control measures must be instituted particularly if processing is off-site. The amounts returned must be counted, recorded and checked against the laundry statement and the amount sent. 'Losses and shorts' must be recorded and the occurrence investigated. The quality of the laundry finish is often checked, although time consuming, and inspection for repairs or the need to condemn is undertaken simultaneously. Items may be rejected and returned to the laundry, sent to the sewing room for repair or condemned. Condemned items are recorded and replacements are issued from new stock if one exists, or ordered from the supplier when sufficient need exists. Repaired items may have to be re-laundered or at least re-ironed. Satisfactory items are then stored.

Figure 2.14 *The advantages and disadvantages of laundry options*

Option	Advantages	Disadvantages
On-site	Can specify treatments	Capital outlay
	Can vary treatments	Higher labour costs
	Can reduce length of total linen and laundry process	Technical expertise or specialised management
	No losses/shorts should occur	Factories Act 1961
	Less stock required as quicker cycle	Repairs, cleaning and maintenance
	Capital asset	Replacement of equipment and premises
	Cover emergency requirements	Opportunity costs
	Can launder bedding and soft furnishings easily	
Off-site	No capital outlay	Limited specification of treatment
	Less, skilled staff on premises	Extra costs for special treatments and stain removal
	Little technical expertise	Losses may occur
		Delivery and collection delays may occur
		Higher stocks required
		Longer time involved in total process

2.4.1.4 *Storage*

All linen should be stored securely to prevent pilferage or loss and to avoid the risk of fire. Processed linen will wear better and last longer if it is allowed to 'rest' before going back into circulation, therefore, good rotation of stock is essential. A well designed storage area will facilitate stock rotation.

It is vital that a stock check is undertaken on a regular basis to audit those stocks in central storage and undergoing processing as well as stocks in the periphery stores. If stocktaking can be undertaken without prior notice, all on the same day, it will be more effective, otherwise items may circulate and be counted more than once.

2.4.1.5 *Redistribution*

As stated earlier, the stock in the periphery stores has to be replaced and this may be undertaken by various means. The distribution options include those discussed in chapter 4, section 4.7 on *stores control*, namely, the clean for dirty, counter exchange, topping-up or imprest, requisition, standard pack or complete trolley systems. Again the decision has to be made as to which staff – linen maids, porters, room maids – are involved in the redistribution system. Effective control requires a record to be kept of amounts of clean linen distributed to each location (periphery store) and any variances against amounts of dirty linen sent for processing. The linen cycle then commences again.

Blankets, soft furnishings, such as bedspreads, valances and curtains, staff uniforms and overalls and residents' (whether personnel or customers) personal linen, are not usually included in the general linen cycle discussed, so alternative arrangements have to be made for each of these. Blankets and soft furnishings are usually laundered or dry cleaned, whichever is applicable, on a less frequent basis. The frequency of cleaning should be specified and a recording and control system devised to ensure that these items are processed at the required frequency. Control and cleaning of staff uniforms can be an enormous problem especially in a large operation and are discussed in section 2.4.5.

The system devised for dealing with residents personal laundry will depend on the type of establishment and whether personnel or customers are involved. The type of customer, their requirements and their average length of stay will influence the arrangements made; for instance, businessmen staying a couple of nights may need a speedy shirt service.

2.4.2 The laundry system

The stages involved in the laundry system are as outlined in figure 2.15. They remain the same except for marking, whether an on-site or an off-site laundry is used, although where easy-care linen is concerned the finishing process is not required.

Figure 2.15 *The laundry system*

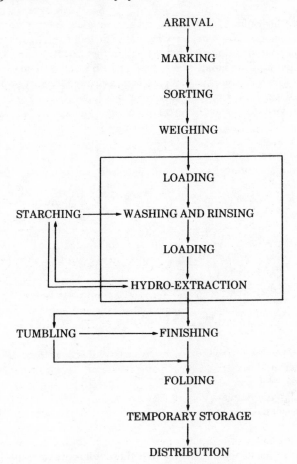

2.4.2.1 Arrival
When the dirty linen arrives at the laundry it has to be unloaded and stored temporarily until processing commences. The dirty linen should be dealt with quickly to avoid growth of infection, mildew and odour problems occurring. Piles of dirty linen are subject to spontaneous combustion and so constitute a fire hazard.

2.4.2.2 Marking
In a commercial laundry the article being laundered must be marked with some kind of code to identify it with the appropriate establishment or individual owner. This mark helps to ensure that the laundered article is returned to the rightful user. In a large operation with an on-site laundry marking may occur only if items have to be

returned to a specific area or department, but generally a pool system operates.

Several methods of applying such marks are available; for instance, embroidering or use of a transfer which is attached to the fabric by pressure and heat; printing by machine with either visible or invisible marks; using pre-printed marks on cotton tape which is sewn on to the item; marking ink or use of safety pins with a printed 'flag' or stamp on the metal shield of the pin. In some cases linen may have been pre-marked with, for example, a company logo during the weaving process.

2.4.2.3 Sorting (classification)

In an on-premise laundry, such as in a hospital, sorting or classification of linen may be the first stage in the operation. Where colour coded bags are used to denote the condition of the dirty linen, eg in a hospital, the dirty linen is sorted according to the colour of the bag, as each type must be processed separately.

The procedure for dealing with infected and fouled linen usually involves pre-washing. The following factors vary according to the type of item being laundered:
— the amount and type of chemicals to use
— the water temperature
— the number and length of wash cycles
— the number of rinses

Therefore, the batches will have to be sorted according to the:
— type of item
— fibre type
— colour and dye fastness
— degree of soilage.

2.4.2.4 Weighing

Each bundle of dirty linen has to be weighed to conform to the capacity of the machine which, in an industrial laundry, may be approximately 45 kg, 225 kg or even 450 kg dry weight of items.

2.4.2.5 Loading

The weighed load of items may then be loaded into the washing machine, either manually or by mechanical means. Manual loading and unloading of a large washing machine involves considerable effort, especially unloading when the work carries with it a great weight of water. Tilting or dumping machines are designed to overcome this difficulty – they tilt backwards so the load can be discharged directly into the machine from an overhead chute or bag. A crane may also be used for loading. Some machines tilt forward in order to tip out, ie dump the washed load on to a conveyor or into trolleys for transfer to the next stage which involves the extraction of the water. Overloading of the machine should be avoided because effective washing may not occur, linen may be damaged and even creasing of crease-resistant items may occur. The weight of loads of bulkier items, such as towels or blankets, should be reduced to ensure washing takes place effectively. For economic reasons machines should not be underloaded.

2.4.2.6 *Washing and rinsing*
(a) Washing
The washing process must be designed to perform three basic operations to:
— remove soil from the fabric
— suspend soil
— discharge the soil from the machine to the drain.

Laundries at present depend mainly on the rotary washing machine, so called because the load to be washed is contained within the inner rotating cylinder (*the cage*).

The cylindrical wall of the cage is perforated with holes to allow wash and rinse liquors to pass in and out. The outer container (*the case*) is not perforated and does not rotate. With the rotation of the cage and the continual tumbling of the work there is a tendency for articles in the load to become entangled (*roping*). To avoid roping, the cage rotates for a period in the order of only 15 seconds before stopping for a moment and then running for the same period in the opposite direction. The number of revolutions in both directions should also be the same.

In the larger rotary machines the inner cage is divided into compartments (*pockets*) with internal partitions (*dividers*). This enables separate loads to be washed together by the same process without the loads becoming mixed. A machine with no dividers is called an *open machine*.

The laundry supplies, such as soap or synthetic detergents and alkalis and bleaches, may be added manually or automatically controlled.

Many machines in use industrially today are automatically operated and controlled, often by the use of metal 'punch' cards, which indicate the number of washes; the number of rinses; the length of each cycle; the temperature of the water; which supplies are to be added and when; or, increasingly, they are controlled by microprocessors or electronic circuits.

Devising an effective wash programme When devising an effective wash programme a number of factors must be borne in mind; such as the:
— fibre and fabric
— type of item
— dye fastness
— amount of soilage
— hardness of the water.

These will influence such things as the:
— number of wash cycles
— number of rinse cycles
— pH value of the wash liquors
— depth of the wash liquors
— temperature
— time needed for soil removal.

(1) *Number of wash cycles* The benefit of several shorter washes rather than one long wash cycle is that more soil can be removed with repeated suds and clean water, than with one solution in which the soil remains in suspension and has a chance to resoil the linen.

(2) *Water hardness* There are many types of soil, all of which have different reactions with various types of water. The best laundering results when both hot and cold water are soft.

Hard water contains salts that mix with soap and synthetic detergents to form a sticky substance called *soap curd*. Soap curd sticks to the items making them stiff and soiled. It will build up between fibres and cause breakdown of fibres, thus greatly reducing the life expectancy of linens. Therefore, the installation of a water softening plant or the introduction of a softener should be considered.

(3) *pH value* The pH of the water is also a critical factor and the pH is usually different for each stage in the washing cycle; for instance, the first washing or suds usually has a pH of 11 to 11.6. This is very alkaline. The excess alkali, called *free alkali*, will combine with fat and oil in the soil to neutralise acid soils and render it free from the fibres to which it is attached. The free alkali is a good wetting agent.

The remaining wash cycles require a pH of 10.6.

(4) *Temperature* Many chemical reactions will not take place unless heat is applied and most can be accelerated by raising the temperature. The higher the temperature of the wash liquor – up to a certain level – the more efficient the soil removal. The highest temperature which can be attained in a typical washing machine is 100°C. However, the highest useful temperature for soil removal for most articles is 65°C.

In a hospital laundry, another reason for raising the temperature during the washing process is to disinfect. It does not follow that every washing process should be operated at high temperatures from start to finish. Certain types of staining substances can be removed easily at low temperatures but become fixed and almost impossible to remove if subjected to higher temperatures. Many fibres will be damaged above certain temperatures.

(5) *Bleaches* If it is desired to use an ordinary bleach during the laundry process, it must be used at a temperature somewhat lower than 65°C. The destructive effect of sodium hypochlorite on certain

certain textile fibres increases as the temperature rises and above 60°C it becomes so severe that it cannot be tolerated. The possible effect of bleach on some dyes and on the heat sensitive character of some of the man-made fibres must also be taken into consideration.

(6) *Depth of liquor* The term 'dip' is used to denote the depth of liquor in the cage of a rotary washing machine. Variation in dip influences firstly, the amount of mechanical action imparted to the load and secondly, the proportion of removed dirt which is discharged.

(7) *Laundry supplies* The essential materials for detergent action in a washing process are water, soap or synthetic detergent, and alkali, the amount of which can be varied between one process and another and between the individual washes of a single process.

Figure 2.16 *Laundry powder components*

Components	Contribution
Active detergent	
Non ionic	Cleansing and suspending powers
	Better detergent properties
	Suitable for poly/cotton
Anionic	Higher foaming for woollens
Non-ionic and anionic	Blend of two is better
Sequestering agent	
Sodium tripolyphosphate	Good suspending properties
(STPP)	Aids preventing redeposition
	Dissolves deposits of lime salts, eg on bath towels
Soap	Increases detergency
Alkali	Neutralises acid dirt
	Increases wetting out
	Emulsifies fats and oils and suspends particles
	Saponifies fatty dirt
	Maintains optimum alkalinity
	Reduces detergent costs
	Must be correct balance
Sour, ie acid powder	Neutralises excessive alkalinity
	Softer finish for ironing
Fabric conditioner	Cationic surface active agents with + recharge
	Fabric has − recharge, therefore, attracted to surface
	Creates softness, bulkiness, springiness, smoothness and antistatic surface

A built powder, such as a proprietary brand, may be purchased based on one of the following:

— Soap and synthetic detergent (tends to be old-fashioned)
— Balanced alkali and synthetic detergent
— Balanced alkali and synthetic detergent plus speciality emulsifiers and other additives.

Or the component parts may be purchased separately and apportioned, as appropriate, to the requirements of a particular wash programme. See figure 2.16 for components and their contribution to the laundering process.

(8) *Duration* Time is needed for soil removal to be achieved. However effective the cleansing properties may be, the dirt is not removed instantly; it is removed gradually over a period of several minutes. The rate at which it is removed is not constant; it is highest at the commencement of the wash and gradually becomes less as time passes until dirt is being removed only very slowly. It has been found that about 7 minutes is the longest time for a wash in most rotary machines but in many processes it is helpful to extend the final wash to 14 minutes, as it is necessary, at this stage, to remove the most resistant dirt. Agitation will of course aid removal.

(9) *Washing formulae* The revised Care Labelling Code conforms to the revised British Standard 'Code of Practice for Textile Care Labelling' and is also in line with care labelling practice in Europe. There are 9 classifications giving different laundering instructions, appropriate to the article to which it is attached. Although designed essentially for home laundering this information can be interpreted to ensure suitable treatments in a commercial laundry.

(b) Rinsing

Once the wash cycles have been completed, then rinsing has to take place. This should:

— Remove the laundry supplies once they have served their purpose
— Remove the small amount of dirt which has been removed from the fabrics but which remains in the 'carry over' liquor, ie the residue which has not escaped from the last cycle, in the load at the end of the final wash.

These requirements are met by adding water to the machine so as to dilute the 'carry over' liquor.

Control of the dip is also important during the rinsing process as the introduction of too much water will result in excessive dilution of the soap carried over from the final wash and hydrolysis could occur, with loss of suspending power and consequent redeposition of the dirt carried over. It is, therefore, necessary to avoid very high dips at the commencement of rinsing.

It is normal practice to use only cold water for rinsing. The load and liquor which is retained carries over heat from the final wash and this warms the rinse water. This procedure is repeated from each rinse to the next, so the temperature falls only gradually, giving conditions which are entirely satisfactory in most circumstances.

A number of rinses may occur, the first being sufficiently alkali to neutralise any soil not removed, the second may be a neutralising rinse, slightly acidic to neutralise the free alkali from the wash cycle and the first rinse. In fact, a sour, ie an acid powder, could be introduced here. A third rinse, slightly acidic again, is recommended for flat work to be ironed. A low pH rinse will leave items soft and relatively wrinkle free and contributes to the ease and speed of ironing. Starching of certain items may take place after the final rinse.

Rinsing leaves the work saturated with water. This has to be removed normally by mechanical means which is much cheaper than the application of heat. This is known as *hydro-extraction*.

2.4.2.7 *Hydro-extraction*

There are two principal types of hydro-extractors:

1 *The centrifugal extractor* This is the most widely used. It has a cylindrical perforated cage (*basket*) which rotates within an outer cylindrical case. Both the basket and the cage are open at the top to permit loading and unloading. They range in size with capacities of up to 225 kg dry weight but most are smaller than these.

Obviously, a centrifugal extractor uses centrifugal force which acts outwards from the centre of the basket, on the load of fabric and on the water which it holds. The load is merely compressed against the cylindrical walls but the water is able to pass through the perforations into the case from which it runs away to the drain.

Man-made fibres and poly-cotton retain less water than natural fibres and should only be hydro-ed briefly, otherwise compression of the fabric produces creases which may be impossible to remove.

Certain precautions are necessary when loading a hydro-extractor. The load should be distributed as uniformly as possible throughout the basket, otherwise the basket is unbalanced. Each article should be bunched up so it is free to move towards the wall of the basket when the hydro runs. If this movement is restricted the article could tear. The risk of either of these faults can be reduced by the use of radial dividers in the basket, usually three, especially in larger machines.

2 *The hydraulic extractor* An hydraulic extractor removes water merely by subjecting the load to a direct external pressure. The only movement which the articles undergo is a small displacement due to the application of pressure.

Even after hydro-extraction, the laundry is still in a damp state, cotton, for instance, retains an amount of water, roughly half its own dry weight. When the work is discharged from the centrifugal or hydraulic extractor it is squeezed tightly into a fairly solid mass known as a *cheese* which needs to be loosened and separated into individual items before further processing can take place.

Washer extractors In the absence of mechanical handling aids, such as cranes, a considerable amount of effort is involved in transferring work from a washing machine to a hydro-extractor. Each 45 kg dry weight of fabric holds at least 135 kg of water when saturated.

This effort can be avoided by using a machine which serves as both washer and extractor. The load remains in the machine at the end of the washing process to undergo the hydro-extraction procedure. The machine is capable of running at two speeds – low speed for washing and rinsing and high speed for extracting. It has to be a robust machine and often requires special foundations to prevent its vibrations being transmitted to the surrounding areas. It does not necessarily remove as much water as a separate extractor. Large scale versions usually have three radial dividers so that there are equal weights of wet work in each pocket which aids extraction. The discharged work tends to be completely loosened because the machine switches back to the slow reversing wash speed for two or three minutes, thereby simulating the action of a shaker tumbler.

2.4.2.8 Starching
It is customary to starch certain articles after they have been washed to impart a degree of stiffness – in some cases only moderate, but in other cases considerable. The starch forms a deposit within and on the surface of the fabric. Starch is applied as a suspension in water, usually in conjunction with other substances which modify the character of the starch deposit. If an article requires only a moderate stiffness, such as sheets and slips, this can be applied in the washing machine following the final rinse. The starch liquor is added to the machine which is run for a few minutes, after which any liquor not taken up is discarded.

It is necessary to provide a separate starching machine for items which need to be stiff. This is because a large amount of starch needs to be used, which is expensive, and any not taken up can be re-used for other loads. The processing may last up to 30 minutes and the items need to be hydro-ed before the starch is applied, to allow penetration of sufficient starch.

2.4.2.9 Tumbling
The complete drying of laundered work by means of hot air tumblers is usually restricted to such articles as bath towels and blankets, which require a 'fluffy' unpressed finish, commonly referred to as *rough* or *fluff* drying. Tumblers are also of use in the processing of items manufactured from fabrics composed totally or partly of polyester fibres where the process has to be carefully controlled; the degree of loading reduced; the load gradually cooled down in the final stage of the cycle; and the item quickly removed and folded.

In other cases tumblers are used merely for heat conditioning which assists in removing extractor wrinkles and moisture so that linen may be ironed without difficulty.

A full load of tightly packed items from the hydro-extractor can be inserted at a single loading operation and in a short time all the individual items are shaken free within the revolving cage. There are two types of tumblers.

Batch tumblers into which a specific weight of damp work is loaded and in which it remains for a predetermined time before being unloaded and passed on for further processing.

Continuous tumblers which are open ended cylinders where the damp work is loaded into one end and discharged piecemeal from the other end. Both types may be used for conditioning work to a suitable state.

Tumblers are constructed in much the same way as a rotary washing machine, except that the inner revolving cage has a greater internal volume for a given load of work. This is necessary to give the work complete freedom to shake out loosely and so allow the free circulation of warm air to assist in rapid drying.

They are generally wasteful and ineffective in their utilisation of heat, since a considerable amount is blown away to the atmosphere, along with the moisture which has been evaporated from the work in process. Whilst the inner cage revolves and reverses to shake free the work and avoid roping, a powerful fan circulates the warm air.

During the process fluff and loose lint will shake off the articles, so a lint trap or screen is fitted prior to the outlet trunking to prevent it blowing into the atmosphere. The trap or screen must be cleaned at regular intervals to prevent the air flow being reduced, resulting in longer drying time. It is usual for the tumbler to be fitted with a damper control which enables the temperature to be varied when necessary and a dial type thermometer is usually mounted on the front of the machine to allow a visual check on working temperature.

2.4.2.10 Finishing

The next stage is known as finishing, ie ironing or pressing according to the size and shape of the item. The quality of finish achieved at this stage depends largely on three things:

1 The moisture content
2 Pressing temperature
3 Pressure.

If an item is too dry before pressing then the resultant finish will be poor, this can, however, be remedied by the use of a spray. Too much moisture will result in an excellent finish but a long (and costly) drying time on the press thus slowing down production. The type of equipment used for ironing or pressing depends on the type of item. Flat items, such as sheets, pillow cases and table cloths are referred to as 'flatwork' and may be calendered or, on a smaller scale, may be ironed by means of a rotary ironer.

Non-flat items, such as uniforms, coats and shirts, are finished on presses of varous forms which have been developed to cater for different types of articles.

In commercial launderies, spreaders and feeders are used to aid the preparation of flat work for ironing, and aid economy of labour and effort to maintain continuous uninterrupted production.

(a) *Flat work* Calenders, with four or five rollers, are used for flatwork and are now designed for once-through operations. The sheets are still moist as they are fed into the calender and so the initial temperature is that of steam 100°C, and one of the problems in the design has been to disperse the steam and moisture dispelled from the damp articles under process. Unless this is effectively done both the quality and the speed of the process suffer. Problems with static can occur during calendering, so the presence of moisture will help to overcome this problem.

The latest type of calender is an upright which has fewer rollers, usually two, and the items pass through the rollers in a figure of eight action at least twice. This type of calendar is designed to be more economical in terms of space.

Folding As the articles of ironed flatwork leave the calender, a flatwork folder may be used which is normally activated either by photo-electrical cells or by micro-switches. A stacking unit at the end of the discharge conveyor is a further refinement. Correct, standardised, folding of each item is important. The folds will aid the operative, for instance, when making a bed or setting a table; they will certainly affect the appearance, and could also aid storage and stocktaking.

(b) *Non-flat work* There are basically three types of presses in commercial use for non-flat work. The jaw or scissor type has a fixed clothed table (*buck*) on which the work is laid, arranged below a hinged heated and polished head which can be brought to bear at considerable pressure to dry off and finish the article. For mass handling of specialised garments, such as overalls and coats, high productivity units are used consisting of a combination of special presses designed to give maximum coverage of the garment in the least number of lays. Units of three or four presses are common, fitted with individual bucks suited to collars, yokes, sleeves and body lays.

The twin rotating table press was developed to be a self-contained one operation unit with the advantage of two bucks or buck assemblies available for the operator at the touch of a foot pedal. These are usually automatically controlled.

There have been a number of finishing machines developed for large quantities of coats and uniforms. One type, resembling a dress makers dummy, allows hot air to be blown through the garment when placed on the form. The hot air dries the garment and removes wrinkles. Another type is a cabinet press where the garment is placed on a similar form (*plate*) as above, but this time it moves into the cabinet for

for finishing, often an operative controls a double unit. Finally, a continuous tunnel can be installed where the garment is placed on a coat hanger on a moving conveyor device which takes the garment through the heated 'tunnel'.

Some items may still need to be finished manually with an iron, but in a large scale operation these are few and far between. These non-flat items will also have to be folded and special folding tables embodying hinged folding plates are available for this task.

2.4.2.11   Temporary storage
When all the work has been finished and folded there still remains the job of arranging the work in the correct order for packing and distribution and so the work is often temporarily stored on fixed or mobile racks for a short period of time.

2.4.2.12   Distribution
The packing operation can be performed in a number of ways. Finished work may be loaded onto mobile racks or into bags, baskets or trucks or even individual boxes for personal work.

Semi-automatic packaging machines are now being used which use sheet polythene or polythene lined paper, which is heat sealed to form instant closure, and so the finished parcel, whether wet or dry, can withstand rough handling and is protected from contamination.

The finished items may then be despatched to the establishment, department, individual or central linen room from whence they came.

The objectives of the laundering process can be summed up as follows:
— To remove dirt and stains
— To prevent damage of the fibre and/or loss of tensile strength
— To 'finish' the item in order to prevent re-entry of dirt for as long as possible and provide a wrinkle and crease free item.

It is important to consider not only the fibre type and its properties, and the characteristics of the finished fabric when initially selecting an item but also the care and maintenance of the item, particularly the effects which the equipment, agents and processes involved have on it.

2.4.3   Infected and fouled linen
In a hospital special thought must be given to the processing of infected and fouled linen. Infected linen sometimes called 'special category' linen, is that which has been in contact with patients suffering from notifiable diseases, such as smallpox, anthrax, typhoid, infective hepatitis and salmonella poisoning. It is generated in isolation and infectious diseases units and usually includes staff uniforms.

Fouled linen is potentially infected because it has come into contact with blood, urine or faeces. Normally it is generated from patient areas and departments such as Accident and Emergency, and includes babies nappies.

Both types are usually put into polythene bags, with secure tops, before placing in the appropriate colour coded bags, which may be stitched with soluble alginate thread. Some infected linen might be incinerated, the rest is laundered. Some of the modern hospital laundries now have a Barrier Washing area, which is physically separated from the rest of the laundry by a wall. The washing machines, which are set in the wall, have two doors, so the dirty linen is placed in the machine in the barrier area and removed after pre-washing and washing at 65°C for 10 minutes from the other door in the clean area, where it then undergoes normal treatment.

2.4.4 Dry cleaning

Some items have to be dry cleaned as laundering processes or agents may cause damage. Generally, fabrics which may shrink, pile fabrics or items which may be subject to fibre distortion or colour (dye) movement, should be dry cleaned even though it is an expensive process. Very large, heavy and bulky curtains may also be dry cleaned to facilitate their cleaning.

Dry cleaning is usually an off-site process but a large hospital district laundry may consider the installation of a dry cleaning plant to be a feasible proposition.

Dry cleaning is a process by which textile items are cleaned by washing in a solvent other than water. The solvent is usually a volatile organic liquid such as perchloreythylene or trichlorotriflouroethane, both of which are extremely expensive to purchase.

The stages involved in dry cleaning are not unlike those already discussed for laundering, see figure 2.17. Spotting or stain removal may take place prior to or after dry cleaning depending on the type of stain involved. Stain removal industrially often involves the use of a pressurised spray gun which sends solvent through the stain in an attempt to loosen it so it can then be blotted out.

Sorting in this context usually involves segregating heavily soiled and lightly soiled items and dark colours and light colours to prevent lint from transferring from one colour to another.

The *batch* process of dry cleaning is the normal process used and it has three distinct stages. The first is known as the *filter run*. Solvent is passed through the load to remove loosely adhering particles of soil and also remove the grease layer which bonds most soil particles to the fabric. The solvent is passed straight out again and the flow of solvent carries away the soil particles removed. The solvent is pumped through a filter and back into the base tank for re-use. Water soluble soil now has to be removed and, therefore, a small amount of water must be added. As water and solvent do not freely mix, a dry cleaning soap must be added to the solvent to allow the water to be carried in the form of an emulsion. This time a dip is allowed to build up and the

Figure 2.17 *The dry cleaning system*

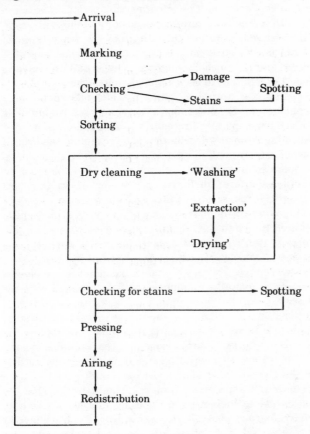

water soluble soil is removed. The solvent is separated and purified for recirculation. One or two rinses using pure distilled solvent may then take place. Centrifugal extraction follows at high speed to remove the solvent, which is once again recovered for re-use. Hot air is circulated so the machine, in effect, becomes a tumbler drier, followed normally by a flow of fresh air to ensure the remaining solvent is evaporated which can be recovered once again. Therefore, washing, extraction and drying have taken place in one machine. The speed of the cage, the capacity, the height of the dip and the degree of loading affect the efficiency of soil removal as with the laundering process.

2.4.5 Uniform control

The provision, issue, laundering and control of staff overalls and uniforms is usually considered to be part of the linen and laundry system. All domestic staff will require some type of protective clothing or uniform which for operational, comfort and psychological purposes should be well designed. Often employees require a change of overalls every day or two depending on the activities they perform and some organisations such as the NHS have a responsibility to provide clean overalls, ie laundered by the health authorities. In other types of operations, uniforms which denote grade, status, theme, say of a restaurant, are required, which are often more like a suit and have to be dry cleaned. A system has to be devised whereby a member of staff receives an appropriate overall or uniform which fits them, with sufficient quantities to exchange for a clean one as required or according to company policy. Procedures for laundering or dry cleaning, controlling issue and distribution and reclaiming the overall on termination of employment all have to be set up. Where an on-site sewing room operates, overalls or uniforms may at best be made to measure or at least altered to fit the person for whom they are intended. Outright purchase of overalls and uniforms can be very costly, especially where a high labour turnover exists and overalls have to be altered time and time again for new employees. For this reason, uniform rental, which works in basically the same way as linen hire may be a feasible alternative. Many rental firms provide a personalised issue service, whereby an individual employee receives a customised supply of overalls or uniforms with a personal code for control purposes.

Some operations are installing a computerised cloakroom system and clean uniform dispenser such as the *Autovalet*. An employee is issued with a computerised card bearing a code number which corresponds to a peg number within the system. When the card is placed in the slot the computer locates the peg, rotates the conveyor belt and dispenses the appropriate uniform. The employee changes into the uniform, places their personal clothing in a polythene bag, fixes a disc on the bag and places it on the conveyor. The bags have to be manually transferred to the appropriate peg and at the end of the shift the personal clothing is reclaimed, the dirty uniform placed in the dirty linen bin and a clean uniform is manually placed on the peg to be claimed on the next shift. The system has many advantages and disadvantages but it aims to improve uniform control, ease issue of clean and collection of dirty uniforms and reduce the number of lockers required, although an individual still needs some locker space for handbags, shoes and valuables.

References

[1] COLLINS, B J, *The Use of Chemical Disinfectants in Hospital Domestic Practice*, Association of Domestic Management Newsletter May 1983

[2] LEE, R, *Building Maintenance Management*, Crosby, Lockwood & Staples 1976

[3] LOWBURY, E J L, AYCLIFFE, G A J, GEDDES, A M and WILLIAMS, J D, *Control of Hospital Infection*; Practical Handbook, Chapman and Hall 1981

[4] HCIMA, Technical Brief Sheet No. 2, *Precautions against AIDS*

Further reading

AMERICAN HOSPITAL ASSOCIATION, *Infection Control in the Hospital* 1970

ALLEN, DAVID M, *Accommodation and Cleaning Services* Vol 1: Operations, Hutchinson 1983

AMERICAN HOSPITAL ASSOCIATION, *Housekeeping Manual for Health Care Facilities* 1966

DHSS, *Laundry Supervisors Manual* 1976

FALES, JOHN T, *Functional Housekeeping in Hotels and Motels*, ITT Educational Services 1971

HCTC, CATERBASE, *Housecraft Accommodation Operations* 1989

JONES, I and PHILLIPS, C, *Commercial Housekeeping and Maintenance*, Thornes 1984

MAURER, ISOBEL, *Hospital Hygiene*, Arnold 1978

NHS HOTEL SERVICES, *Domestic Supervision Training Kit*

3

The Personnel Control System

Housekeeping and maintenance departments are not only labour intensive, but may also be large in terms of numbers of personnel employed. It is generally accepted in a hospital that the domestic services department rates second only to the nursing department in terms of numbers of personnel employed, with the budget comprising 90% expenditure on personnel and only approximately 10% on equipment and agents. In one very large 1000+ bedded district hospital, the domestic service manager controls in excess of 600 'full-time equivalent' staff, contributing to a budget of some three million pounds.

In a medium to large hotel with a 4 or 5 star rating, the number of housekeeping personnel may be large in comparison to other departments.

As personnel frequently constitute such a large resource, both in numerical and financial terms, much of the Accommodation Manager's time is spent dealing with personnel issues. The stages involved in the Personnel Control System are outlined in figure 3.1, the majority of which will be discussed in this chapter. Many operations, particularly large concerns, have a personnel department which will be involved in, if not totally responsible for, some of the issues listed in figure 3.1. Where a separate personnel department exists, close co-operation between departments must occur.

The aspects of the personnel control system, for which each department is responsible, must be clarified. Generally, the personnel department should be responsible for personnel administration – advertising, arranging interviews, dealing with all paperwork, medicals, general induction, sickness arrangements and communicating company personnel policy.

The Accommodation Manager will provide job descriptions, specify personnel requirements, select the most appropriate candidate and arrange departmental induction, training and supervision.

Given the proportional significance of the housekeeping and maintenance labour budget, more scope exists for increasing cost efficiency in this area than many others. Also supervision and quality assurance tend to be difficult issues as housekeeping and maintenance personnel work throughout the building, often singly, in empty areas. This phenomenon can affect the motivation and morale of personnel and create feelings of isolation and insecurity, all of which have to be considered when allocating work and scheduling staff.

Figure 3.1 *The personnel control system*

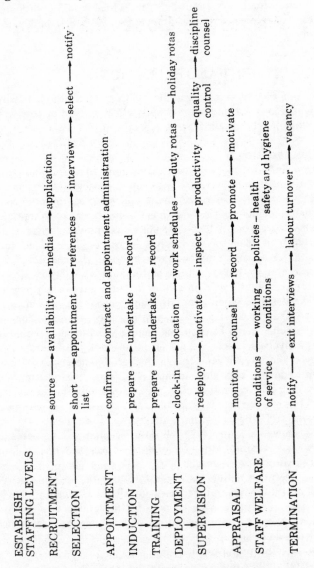

3.1 ESTABLISH OPTIMUM STAFFING LEVELS

Optimum staffing levels contribute to cost efficiency. Too many staff will result in higher than necessary labour costs, with possibly too much time to do too little work or too frequent repetition of work. Too few staff can result in stress, fatigue, low morale and high labour turnover. Both can result in falling standards, user dissatisfaction and high costs.

A method of estimating housekeeping/domestic manning levels, and factors which influence estimating front office and maintenance staffing levels, are discussed in chapter 2, section 2.2, *The cleaning programme*.

3.2 RECRUITMENT AND SELECTION

The aim of this process is to choose the right person for the job, using methods which are cost and operationally effective, and at the same time acceptable to the candidates.

3.2.1 The vacancy

The Accommodation Manager is very rarely going to recruit and select the whole team at once unless a completely new venture is being undertaken. Normally the recruitment and selection process commences when a member of the team has terminated employment and hence created a vacancy. All specific details of the vacancy must be identified, such as place of work, shift hours, grade, and off-duty arrangements. A decision may be taken not to fill the vacancy.

A Job Description, which is a broad statement of the purpose, scope, duties and responsibilities of a particular job, may have been prepared at the relevant stage, when estimating manpower requirements, as discussed in chapter 2. If a job description does not exist for the vacancy, then one should be prepared using a job analysis technique. Job analysis involves direct observation of the employee, interviewing the employee and interviewing the supervisor. Job descriptions must be kept up to date to take into account changes in organisation and technology. The job description may describe not only the duties and responsibilities of a particular grade of staff, but also the environment of the work and lines of communication and responsibility. An example is shown in figure 3.2. Job descriptions are invaluable at interviews for explaining the job and can form the basis of an individual's training programme.

It is also useful to define, as accurately as possible, the desired attributes of the individual required to fill the vacancy. These individual requirements can be collated in the form of a personnel specification, covering the following set of headings, against which candidates can be assessed:
— Age and physical requirements
— Educational qualifications and special skills
— Experience pattern
— Personality requirements for proper integration within the team or organisation
— Special considerations, eg need for a language
— Potential for individual development in line with planned growth of responsibilities
— Interests.

The specification is intended to describe the person who is capable of doing the job adequately, not an impossible ideal.

Figure 3.2 Sample of Job Description form

Domestic Assistants

Job summary
Cleans buildings
Vacuums and mops rooms, wards, waiting areas, stairways
Periodically buffs floors
Cleans all sanitary fittings and surfaces
Washes walls and windows within reaching distance and blinds
Vacuums high ledges
Fills toilet supply containers
Keeps utility area in good order
Helps serve meals
Takes trolley of dirty crockery to the kitchen

Performance requirements
Responsibility for — cleanliness of assigned area
— care of assigned tools and materials
— economical use of all detergents, polishes and other cleaning materials
— clean and neat personal appearance

Physical demands — stands
walks } most of working day
climbs stairs
turns
stoops } in such tasks as { cleaning
crouches scouring
reaches polishing
lifts
carries } cleaning equipment and materials
pushes } vacuum
pulls mop and water

Special demands — willingness to perform routine, repetitive tasks on a continuous basis
— accept supervision
— perform tasks despite frequent interruptions
— ability to perform tasks with due consideration for patients in vicinity
— some initiative involved in determining cleaning to be done
— work under close supervision performing simple, standardized tasks

Qualifications
Education — ability to follow simple oral directions
Training and — some experience is desirable but not essential
 experience worker to learn duties in brief induction training
Job knowledge — must know how to use common housekeeping devices
must be familiar with physical arrangements of building
must be familiar with standard procedures

Working environment

Works in a clean
        well-heated
        lighted   } building
        ventilated

Job relationships

Source of workers   :
Promotion from   : this is an entry job
Promotion to   : no formal line of promotion
Supervised by   : domestic supervisor
Workers supervised : none
Inter-relationship   : some aspects of job are similar to those of:
                                  ward orderly
                                  wall washer
                                  window cleaner

Work performed

See job summary

3.2.2 Sources of recruitment

Consideration must be given to the source(s) of recruitment most appropriate to the type of vacancy to be filled. Candidates may be recruited internally by recommendation, internal advertising or even from an on-going waiting list of possible candidates. Internal recruitment can boost morale, create a promotional structure and ensure that existing talent is not overlooked. Employment agencies may be considered as an external means of recruitment. Advertising in the national or local press; trade or professional journals; magazines; shop windows or any other appropriate media is another external option. When external recruitment is necessary, the most appropriate media and times to attack the labour market required should be selected. Good advertising copy must be created in order to gain attention, through say a distinctive title and layout; hold interest with information about the company; create desire by describing the job, the type of person required and the benefits, and promote action with a simple application procedure.

Cost must be considered, some organisations have an advertising budget and measure the effectiveness of advertising by the number of respondents, the cost per application, per interview or per vacancy filled.

3.2.3 Selection

Interview costs can be reduced by considering an initial screening of the application letter and/or standard application form (see figure 3.3) to eliminate unsuitable candidates or, conversely, select the most suitable candidates to be called for interview. It is courteous to acknowledge receipt of all requests and inform the candidates of success or failure to attain an interview. References may then be taken up for those candidates to be called for interview.

There are basically three alternative methods of procuring a reference, each with its own particular advantages and disadvantages:
— By letter asking for a reference
— By postal questionnaire, asking specific questions
— By telephone.

Individual, ie one to one, interviews are effective for operative and supervisory levels to speed-up the decision-making process and attain consistent judgement from the specialist, in this case the Accommodation Manager, whereas, multi-individual or panel interviews are more appropriate for managerial levels, particularly to give a cross-section of opinions.

3.2.3.1 Interview structure and techniques

It is best to structure an interview to ensure that all relevant areas are covered, but the structure itself should not be too apparent or inflexible. In order to maintain rapport the discussion should be informal but the interviewer must ensure that all the following areas are covered and assessments made:

Impact	Motivation
Education	Adjustment/Compatability
Intellectual capacity	Personal background
Experience	

Despite the failings of the selection interview, if it is properly conducted it can be a potent tool and every manager should be skilled in its use.

The following aspects should be considered:

— *Application forms* Wherever possible these should have been completed prior to the interview and are a valuable aid as a means of comparison against the personnel specification; as a basis for screening and, during the interview, as a basis for question formulation.

— *Appointments* Consideration should be given as to when the interviews are to take place, if all candidates are to be expected at the same time, or appointments are to be staggered on one day or over a few days.

— *Waiting area* Candidates will need a designated area in which to wait until called for interview. The area must be well sign-posted, have enough chairs and be near to toilet facilities. Candidates should not be kept waiting for any longer than necessary as it only increases anxiety and apprehension. An apology and explanation for any delay is only courteous.

— *Venue for the interview* It is essential to consider where the interview is to take place and how the seating and furniture is to be arranged to encourage an informal and relaxed interview. An uncluttered desk aids this objective and telephone calls and other interruptions should be stopped whilst interviewing is in progress.

Figure 3.3 *Application form*

Position applied for			Advertised in	
Surname			Forenames	
Address			Marital Status	Maiden Name
			Date of Birth	Number & Ages of Children
			Nationality	Place of Birth
Telephone Number				

School (Secondary)	From	To	Examination Results Please give grades	

Name of University or Institute of Further Education attended	Academic, Professional and other qualifications obtained or being taken. Membership of Professional Bodies	Year Obtained

REFERENCES Please give details of two persons who may be approached for reference. Where possible these should be your present and previous employer. If shortlisted references will be taken up prior to interview.

Name	Occupation	Address and Telephone Number

Details of Present or most recent employer

Name and Address	From	To	Reason for leaving

Job Title/Grade (where applicable) and duties in brief

Current Salary	Length of Notice required

Details of Previous Employment beginning with the most recent

Names and addresses	Job Title/Grade	From	To	Reason for leaving

MEDICAL HISTORY   Please indicate any serious illness or disability (stating if registered as disabled person).

If there is any further information you consider relevant to your application please give on a separate sheet.

SIGNATURE ....   DATE ....

— *Structure* A definite time plan is useful for each type of interview, especially if several occur one after another. For instance, 20 to 25 minutes is sufficient time for a domestic assistant interview allowing:

   5 minutes for the introduction
   5 minutes for giving information about the post
  10 minutes for fact finding and discussion, and
   5 minutes for drawing the interview to a close.

The candidate will be nervous and anxious so the interviewer should try and put him or her at ease and create a rapport to achieve a relaxed person who will talk freely. The interview should be constructed in a chronological sequence; for instance, working through the application form to the present day and re-tracing steps where inconsistency or disagreement with the application form occurs. Any references received (refer 3.2.3 selection) may also be used to highlight inconsistencies. Questions, soliciting a 'yes/no' answer should be avoided and comment and expansion should be encouraged. The interviewer's role is to prompt, record and listen, and the interviewer should try not to be flippant, off-hand or offensive.

A conducted tour prior to or after the 'formal' interview may be required. Thought should always be given to whether candidates should be informed of their success or failure verbally at the conclusion of the interview (or series of interviews) or by letter within a few days. Whichever option is chosen, the interviewer should be consistent and ensure the procedure indicated to the candidate is carried out. The candidates should be treated as the interviewer would wish to be treated himself under such circumstances, and the interviewer should remember that candidates will take away an impression of the interviewer and the organisation, which could be favourable or otherwise.

— *Assessment* Brief comments under the main headings for assessment already stated should be recorded immediately after each interview as the memory is fickle. Alternatively, simpler headings such as appearance, personality, mental capacity, experience may be used. Some kind of rating scale may be required, a convenient one being: A exceptional; B good; C satisfactory; D below standard; E unsuitable.

Candidates not meeting essential qualifications and experience as set out in the Job Description and Personnel Specification will be unsuitable (E). Compatibility with others in the team or organisation must be considered, potential for growth and career development may well be required attributes.

3.2.3.2 Administration

It is essential, particularly with regard to public relations, to inform both successful and unsuccessful candidates by the date stated at the interview.

A starting date will have to be confirmed with the successful candidate and arrangements will then proceed for uniform provision, medicals, induction, notification of all relevant departments, provision of a Contract of Employment and preparation of a personal file.

The personnel department may have made all the arrangements and the Accommodation Manager purely interviewed and selected the most suitable candidate.

3.3 INDUCTION AND TRAINING

3.3.1 Induction

Induction is the introduction of a new employee to the working environment, the existing members of staff and the purposes, practices and policies of the organisation. It can be seen as a continuous process, as existing staff have to be introduced to new environments when they are moved.

The purpose of the induction process is to relieve anxiety and provide the new employee with a better understanding of the organisation. It should be designed to help the new employee settle in and quickly feel part of the organisation, enabling him to develop confidence and contribute to the organisation more speedily. Induction is beneficial to both the employee and the employer, not only as a basis for formulating relationships and communication links but also as a means of potentially reducing labour turnover which, in the long-term, can be very costly. Many staff leave their employment after a relatively short period – a few days to a few weeks, but a good, well planned induction programme should help to alleviate this occurrence as it tends to create a good first impression, which often encourages staff to stay longer.

In a large organisation, particularly where a Personnel Department exists, induction can be split into two stages:

Stage 1 Immediate (psychological) induction to the work environment, colleagues, the actual work to be undertaken and performance standards, all of which are psychologically important.

Stage 2 Background induction to the wider organisation, its objectives, structure and policies.

Stage 1 is usually organised by the Departmental Manager, immediately the new employee commences, whereas *Stage 2* may be undertaken some time later by the Personnel Department, when the new employee has settled in, and often consists of an admixture of personnel from the whole organisation. The latter is not within the scope of this section. When planning the induction programme, the departmental manager should consider several questions.

(1) *When will the induction commence?* The beginning of the normal shift is often inconvenient to the organiser, and the employee may be asked to start later or earlier than the normal shift time. For instance, in a hospital, a new employee may be asked to start at 8.30 or 9.00 am

instead of 7 am on his first morning, to allow the supervisor to ensure coverage of all work areas before giving undivided attention to the new employee. On the other hand, if a new evening domestic assistant commences who will only work a three hour shift and the evening supervisor has a high ratio of personnel to supervise, it is feasable for the new employee to start an hour earlier than the rest of the employees.

(2) *How long will the programme last?* It may be two hours; the first day; or split over a two or three day period. A balance has to be reached, with time to cover the essential material, but not so long that the employees, especially manual staff, feel that they will never actually perform any work.

(3) *Who will be involved?* Departmental managers, assistants, supervisors, or a mixture, may be involved.

(4) *Where will it occur?* The manager's office, a training room, the work environment may be selected. A tour may be incorporated.

(5) *What will the content be?* There are certain essential areas which have to be covered and a well organised department may produce a checklist to ensure that nothing is missed out.

The following items should be considered, with the order of priority or sequence varying according to the situation and the level of personnel involved:

Reception	Welcome and introduction
Administration	Completion of appointment forms, contracts, confidentiality/bribery forms, P45s
Essential places	Canteen, toilets, locker areas, time clock, wages department
Conditions of services	Working week, rates of pay, period of notice, absence, sickness, holidays, time-keeping, security, fire procedure, grievance and disciplinary procedures
Departmental information	Organisation structure, who's who, objectives, role within organisation, liaison
Introduction to the job	Job Description, hours of work, duty rotas, expected performance standards, check skill level, check familiarity with equipment, training arrangements
Health and safety	Health and safety arrangements, fire procedures, personal hygiene, infection controls, legal implications

Welfare arrangements	Canteen, toilets, lockers, protective clothing, occupational health, medicals, pension scheme, social clubs
Remuneration	Rates of pay, calculations, payment arrangements

General tour

The programme should stimulate interest and provide information in an efficient and systematic manner. Many organisations develop Staff Handbooks as an initial aid to conveying the information, and as a source of reference for the new employee.

3.3.2 Training

Once the induction programme has been completed, training can commence. Under favourable conditions, training allows management to make more effective use of manpower – the most costly resource. Training not only provides the means for enhancing performance of personnel working at less than their best, but also for making better use of personnel already working well. The training process should aim to develop good working methods, habits and skills together with a better understanding of the purpose of the job, the objectives of the various tasks and the expected results or performance level. This provides the employee with a feeling of mastery over the work and increased confidence and job satisfaction, besides eliminating confusion, stress and fatigue.

Other benefits of training include:
— Increased production
— Higher quality output
— Lower wastage
— Reduced labour turnover and increased morale
— Lower accident levels
— Fewer complaints
— Reduced absenteeism, sickness and lateness
— Greater manpower flexibility
— Better talent identification
— Improved labour relations
— Improved safety and hygiene.

3.3.2.1 The approach to training

A systematic and systemic approach to training can ensure that it is carefully planned and supervised and the costs involved are commensurate with the benefits achieved.

The following approach is recommended:

(1) *Identify the need for training* Training is usually required in response to some event such as:
— The appointment of a new employee

— The installation of new equipment or the introduction of a new product, both requiring new or improved skills, eg computer, super-speed floor maintenance machine, sanding machine, or floor gel

— A change in working methods or practices, eg computerisation, spray burnishing, bonnet buffing

— An increasing number of complaints or accidents, eg standards of cleanliness or maintenance, breakages, spillages, poor quality laundry

— A desire to improve quality of inadequate performance, eg hygiene control or equipment care

— The introduction of new legislation or codes of practices, eg health and safety, fire.

Thus a training need has been created. Any training which occurs as a matter of routine, such as the training of new employees, must be reviewed frequently to ensure that the purpose, methods and standards are always relevant.

(2) *Analyse the training need* It is possible, having identified a problem which seems to suggest a training need, that on further investigation the problem is a management or organisational one, and training is not actually the solution. For instance, the recruitment and selection policy may need revising; the ratio of supervisors to personnel may need improving; large scale equipment may require more effective scheduling or maintenance; or stores selection may be inadequate.

If training is considered to be the solution, then it is necessary to consider the overall aims of the training required. The aim or aims may be to develop an understanding of information and ideas and show how these can be applied to different situations; to develop a skill or series of skills or procedures in order to carry out a regular pattern of sequential activities; to change existing attitudes and ideas or develop new ones; and/or to remember facts, figures or technical terms; or often a combination of all these.

(3) *Setting training objectives* For each section of the training programme, clear objectives, in terms of what the trainee should be able to accomplish at the end of the training programme, ie terminal behaviour, should be set. For instance, the trainee will be able to:

— use a specified make of high speed burnishing machine

— spray burnish any floor in the establishment to the specified standard

— clean the equipment down after use.

An acceptable minimum standard of achievement or performance in terms of quality, speed, safety, and cost must be established which can then be conveyed to the trainee during the training process.

(4) *Devising the training programme* The training programme devised will be as simple or as complex as required, according to the

Figure 3.4 *An example of the content of a training programme for a new room attendant*

Room cleaning
— Constituent task — Bedmaking; vacuuming; dusting; ledges; paintwork; walls; telephones; bins and ashtrays; stains
  Washing the teapots
  Replenishing room stocks, soft furnishings and bedding
  Frequencies
  Standards expected – appearance, hygiene, layout when completed
  Time allowed per room.

Bathroom cleaning
— Constituent tasks — Cleaning bath; shower and curtain; basin; mirrors; bidet; toilet; floor
  Replenishing stocks
  Frequencies
  Standards expected
  Time allowances

Services – eg how to serve early morning tea
Laundry arrangements
Waste disposal
Care and usage of equipment
Hygiene
Health and safety
Fire and security
Social skills and attitudes to customers

---

training needs. For instance, it may comprise a single session, such as how to use the new high speed burnishing machine or it may comprise a larger number of sessions for, say, a new Room Maid covering the range of tasks and duties included in the job description (see figure 3.4). In the latter case especially, consideration will have to be given to other issues such as:

— How many sessions are to be undertaken?
— How long will each session last?
— Will the programme be an intensive continuous course, eg a one week course or will it be spread over a number of weeks, eg one session a week for several weeks?
— When will the sessions take place? Before, after or during normal work time; at the quietest time of the day or week?
— Where will the sessions take place? On-the-job; in a quiet/empty area, or in a specially designated training room?
— Who will be involved in training? The Manager; an outside speaker; a company representative; the supervisor?

(5) *Carrying out the training programme* For each session within the training programme to be successful, careful planning should be undertaken. The objectives for each session should also be defined, as discussed in (3) above and not only the actual content but also the format, duration and training techniques should be considered.

Content The content should be relevant for the level of intelligence of the trainees, being neither too simple nor too complex. It should be broken down into logical divisions of knowledge to be conveyed to the trainee by the most appropriate instructional method and for the trainee to master. Key points affecting quality, safety, and costs should be stressed.

Format Thought should be given to the introduction to the session in order to gain attention, to put the trainee at ease and motivate him to want to learn. It is a good idea to state the job or subject and explain the format of the session so the trainee will initially have an idea of what to expect.

A logical sequence of events should follow at a suitable pace, with a range of varied activities wherever possible, to promote participation, stimulate interest and maintain concentration. Information should be summarised at appropriate stages. It is important to aid understanding and retention at the end of the session to recap, test understanding of knowledge or skills required and draw the session to a conclusion. The following maxim is worth remembering: *Tell them what you are going to tell them, tell them, and tell them what you have told them.*

Where a practical skill has been included, some time should be allowed for practise and correction of errors.

The duration of the session should be given careful thought, particularly where manual staff such as Room Maids are concerned, as they are not used to sitting and concentrating for long periods of time, so 20 to 30 minutes only is preferable.

Training techniques Before deciding on which one or more of the alternative instructional techniques or activities to use, the following adage should be considered:

> *I hear and I forget,*
> *I see and I remember,*
> *I do and I understand.*

The alternative instructional techniques and activities include:

Telling	Quizzes
Showing or demonstrating	Case studies
Question and answer	Exercises/problems
Discussion groups	Practical.

To facilitate the transference of information and ideas, visual aids may be used, such as charts, handouts, pamphlets, overhead transparencies, slides, films, videos or photographs. Teaching equipment, such as overhead projectors, slides and 35 mm film projectors, videos, computers, episcopes, flip-charts, chalk boards, magnetic boards and wall mounted clip boards may then be required. The content of the session will, to some extent, dictate the techniques, aids and equipment appropriate, but a variety of techniques and a variation in activities will contribute to the training process. All equipment must be in good working order, and the trainer must be able to operate it correctly.

(6) *Methods of training* Training may be *on-the-job*, which is given by the trainer in the normal working situation with the trainee using the actual tools, equipment, materials or documents that will be used when fully trained. However, the trainee might find this stressful in a very busy, noisy area and learning may well be inhibited, equipment could be damaged, and an amount of spoilt work could occur. An alternative system, not highly favoured but not uncommon, is the method known as 'Sitting with Nellie', where a member of the peer group will train a new employee. This type of training is often used when there are staff shortages. This may be satisfactory if the 'trainer', who may in fact receive a training allowance, is trained to train. On the other hand, this 'trainer' may be a poor trainer and the trainee may be exposed to poor practices and pick up bad habits.

Off-the-job training takes place away from the normal work situation in a specially designated training room, within the establishment. The trainee in this case, is not regarded as a productive worker during the training process. Specialist training of a higher quality should occur and as the trainee can learn in planned stages, higher standards of quality and speed could well ensue. Difficulties may, however, be experienced when changing from the training environment to the production environment. Off-the-job training may also take place at a company training centre or a college but higher costs will be incurred to cover travelling and subsistence expenses.

An allowance for training may have to be made where a bonus scheme is in operation.

(7) *The trainee* The trainee must also be considered when preparing the training programme:

— the number of trainees will influence the format of the session, the range and type of activities, the number of handouts and the layout of the area. The latter in turn influencing the effectiveness of the training process.
— the background of the trainees is also important. The application form and personnel specification can be used to identify the extent of prior knowledge and experience and the age and sex of the trainee which again may affect the approach and training technique used.

3.3.2.3 Training records

During the training period it is necessary for training records to be kept up to date, as a management control and aide-memoire to record what took place, and provide information on staff and their progress. Records are especially useful to record illness or absence; for health and safety purposes, or in the occurrence of accidents. See figure 3.5.

Figure 3.5 *Training record*

NAME	GLADYS SMITH		DEPT	DOMESTIC			
ORGANISATION							

TRAINING RECORD CARD

NATURE OF TRAINING	DATE & DURATION	EMPLOYEES SIGNATURE	DATE & DURATION	EMPLOYEES SIGNATURE	REMARKS	TRAINING COMPLETED SUPERVISOR
To clean toilet	4/7/85 30 min	G Smith	5/7/85 10 min.		Well organised	J V P
To clean handbasin	5/7/85 10 min.	G Smith			No further instr. needed	J V P

3.3.2.4 Assessing the effectiveness of the training programme

Once the training programme has been completed it is necessary to evaluate it. Sometimes this is possible in practical terms but intangible results, such as better co-operation or changes in attitude, should also be noted. In the short term, it is necessary and possible to monitor the trainee to see if the instructions given are being carried out. This ensures that the instructional methods being used are correct. It is possible, in the mid term, to see that standards are being maintained and, in the longer term, to monitor any benefits to the business, effects on other departments, workers or the customer, and changes in the number of complaints, absence, sickness and lateness, labour turnover, productivity, reduced costs or increased revenue. It is necessary to ask 'was it worthwhile?', of the individual, the department, the unit and/or whole organisation, and the customer to establish that the training achieved its objectives and satisfied the originally identified need. This is particularly important when comparing it with such alternatives as:

— Carrying out no training
— Sending the trainee away for training by another body
— Improving recruitment and selection policies by recruiting already trained staff at a higher cost.

During the review and evaluation stage, strengths and weaknesses in the programme or techniques used will be highlighted which can be remedied in the future so that training can be improved.

3.3.2.5 Calculating the cost of training

It is often difficult to establish where training commences and finishes and as many of the costs involved are tangible, it is somewhat difficult to calculate the cost of training. If attempting to calculate the cost of training the following must be considered:

Labour costs
— trainer's salary
— wages of staff whilst training
— outside speakers' fees and expenses
— preparation time
— technician help

Equipment costs — audio-visual equipment and associated costs

Accommodation costs
— training room
— hiring of accommodation
— overnight costs
— loss of revenue if area is taken out of commission

Administrative costs
— duplicating/printing
— stationery

Subsistence — food and beverage costs

Trainees may leave during or after the training programme hence other organisations may benefit from your investment.

3.4 SUPERVISION

'Business success or failure is dependent upon good, bad or indifferent supervision. Supervision is the keystone of any enterprise. There is no substitute for it'.[2]

No matter how well methods and procedures are developed, results cannot be satisfactory unless management makes sure that work is performed as it should be, at the time it should be done, and to the standard required. Management cannot, personally, ensure quantity and quality especially where a large number of personnel are working in all parts of the building. So management's responsibility for quality, quantity and cost must be largely met through proper direction of the supervisory level.

The fact that housekeeping and often maintenance personnel are scattered, individually or in small groups, throughout the premises to perform their duties makes constant, direct supervision impossible. It also means that a high proportion of a supervisor's time may be spent in travelling from one area to another. Management must, therefore, consider two issues in particular. Firstly, the ratio of staff to supervisor. This is an attempt to achieve the optimum number of people that a supervisor can adequately train, supervise and monitor – in the National Health Service, the ratio is 1:25 domestic services personnel. Secondly, management must consider dividing the premises into physical sections (but with the optimum number of staff) in an attempt to reduce travelling time. These problems do not apply to supervising front office personnel who are confined to a comparatively small area of the building.

Even though attempts may have been made to allocate a particular number of personnel, in a specified section of the building, to a supervisor, the very nature of housekeeping activities means that the supervisor has to rely very heavily on the individual employee to ensure that the work is performed as it should be, at the right time and to the required standards. The supervisor's responsibility for quality, quantity and costs are, therefore, met through the direction of personnel and the control of other essentials of production such as equipment, agents, methods and time. The success of the supervisor will be measured largely in terms of his ability to lead and motivate his personnel to meet the required standards.

Management must recognise that the supervisor plays a somewhat invidious role as a mediator between management and the work force and, where applicable, their union representatives. Adequate training and management support is vital if the supervisor is to function effectively and with confidence.

Supervisory training may be in-house or externally conducted, according to the type and size of the operation. If externally conducted, it may be college-based, eg day release City and Guilds Course, organised by the company on a group basis, eg domestic supervisory training within the local health authorities or organised by outside agencies such as the HCTC – 'Training the trainers' certificate or suppliers of equipment, agents or systems. Ideally the training should not only include developing technical skills and competency but also the following list of topics may be included:
— Human relations and personnel control
— Effective communications
— Monitoring quality (and where applicable, Incentive Bonus Schemes)
— How to train
— Health and safety and other appropriate legislation
— Hygiene and infection control
— Cost efficiency
— Dealing with day-to-day problems and situations and customer complaints.

The NHS has developed a 'Training Kit for Domestic Supervisors' comprising extensive guides for both the Domestic Managers and the trainees (in this case the supervisors) on some 11 modules. A similar training package exists for laundry supervisors (see Appendix 2). Some hotel groups devise similar training packages.

3.5 PRODUCTIVITY

Productivity can be defined as 'the ratio between input and output' or more explicitly as 'the arithmetical ratio between the amount produced and the amount of any resources used in the course of production'.

In reality, labour is often the only resource considered, particularly where labour costs are high and materials costs are low. Management must be concerned with productivity in operations where labour costs constitute a high proportion of the budget; which are labour intensive; where ever-increasing financial constraints are imposed or where competition from outside agencies is a threat such as the possibility of introducing contract labour to replace directly employed labour. Where management are concerned with productivity, emphasis must be placed on seeking ways to improve output either by increasing the amount of work performed for the same manhours, materials and money spent or, more usually, producing the same amount at a reduced cost. AXLER[1] suggests that recognising the cost of any product or activity, ie *Work cost awareness*, may well be sufficient to spur action to increasing productivity or reducing costs.

As the supervisor is directly concerned with controlling resources and the quantity and quality of work produced, productivity is also an important supervisory concern.

3.5.1 Evaluating productivity

Productivity cannot be improved unless existing productivity is evaluated and issues for subsequent examination and improvement are identified. In some situations, productivity can actually be measured, for instance in work study terms it is possible to measure the productivity of workers or machines using the 'standard minute' as the basis of calculation.

$$\frac{\text{Output of work in Standard Minutes}}{\text{Input of labour time or machine time in Clock Minutes}}$$

This aspect of work study is beyond the scope of this book (see end of chapter for references). In some situations, productivity may be relatively easy to calculate using the definition of productivity given at the beginning of this section. In a laundry, for instance, it is easy to calculate the amount of work produced in terms of weight of dirty linen processed or number of pieces of linen processed. In other situations it is not so easy to identify a unit of production by which to calculate the amount of work produced, for instance in housekeeping or the front office (although it could be argued that occupancy levels might be the yardstick, see chapter 5).

Costs of resources will also have to be evaluated especially labour, where existing manpower levels, scheduling arrangements and work allocation may also provide pertinent data. In a revenue producing concern such as an hotel, these costs may be viewed in relation to volume of sales achieved or amount of revenue produced. When evaluating productivity, it is also useful to consider those issues which influence, or are influenced by, the level of productivity or performance.

These issues include labour turnover; absenteeism, lateness and staff complaints with regard to inefficient procedures. In a service industry there may be times when personnel are required 'to cover' for health, safety or security purposes or in case any chance guests arrive or a guest needs something, even though periods of idle or non-productive time exist. This obviously affects productivity and the manager must aim to minimise these occurrences.

As a result of the evaluation process, it may be found that part of the answer is to invest capital in new equipment, for instance, it might be decided that the purchase of an automatic spreader and feeder unit will save time in the laundry. It might be decided that the introduction of a computerised front office system will rationalise the number of grades of front office personnel and, therefore, the number of staff required on duty at any one time (see chapter 5). In fact, sales may be increased as the new multi-purpose receptionist now has more time to devote to selling accommodation and in-house facilities and services.

The cost of automation must be offset against the expected cost of savings, which may be a limiting factor in a small operation. The cost of automation must not exceed anticipated savings.

3.5.2 Work study
When evaluating and improving productivity, not only is a work study approach to investigation effective, but also work study techniques, such as method study and work measurement, may be used when devising improvements or remedies. The basic work study procedure can be adopted firstly, to diagnose what is happening, what is wrong and how time is spent, secondly, to devise solutions or remedies by examining the design and organisation of work, the efficiency of the individual worker or the utilisation of the labour force (each of which will be discussed in detail) and thirdly, to construct 'standards' of procedure and performance.

The British Standards definition of work study is 'a management service comprising those techniques, particularly method study and work measurement, which are used in the examination of human work in all its contexts and which lead systematically to the investigation of all the factors which affect efficiency and economy of the situation being reviewed, in order to effect improvement'.

GULLEN and RHODES suggest the primary aim of work study is to make the optimum use of present resources.

The International Labour Office suggests that: 'work study succeeds because it is systematic both in the investigation of the problem being considered and in the development of a solution' and 'that as a management "tool" it can be applied everywhere'.

This includes all aspects of accommodation management. Management services or work study personnel may be commissioned in some cases to undertake an objective investigation, on the other hand, the accommodation manager may well conduct an investigation using a work study approach. (See Appendix 3, for further details.)

3.5.3 Improving productivity
In the system of Accommodation Management, the greatest impact on productivity will probably be achieved through improving the design and management of work, the efficiency of individual personnel and the utilisation of the labour force.

3.5.3.1 The design and management of work
(1) *Method improvement* One remedy may be to improve processes, procedures or methods of work, by adopting *Method Study* techniques.

Once the new process, procedure or method has been devised, it is probable that a defined time allowance has to be calculated using

Work Measurement techniques. (See Appendix 3 for further details.)

(2) *Improving the work system*   The aim here is to improve the work system of personnel, methods and equipment which maximises the productivity of the unit.

Personnel should be working productively for as much time as possible throughout their working day. A well organised work programme should ensure that personnel are not idle due to lack of work or forced into periods of non-productivity. It should also lead to improved performance and productivity.

Ratio-delay, which is a form of activity sampling, is a useful technique to deploy. It involves observing personnel, equipment and work at random and at irregular intervals in order to study the relative activity of individual personnel and equipment. It also helps to identify the proportion of the working day during which personnel and equipment are producing and which is used up by delays. The reasons to be analysed (the ratio of the delay time to total working time can be calculated).

Therefore, time spent in waiting for supplies; waiting to start one phase of an operation whilst another employee is completing a prior phase, or waiting for equipment to become available is highlighted. It can also reveal that a high proportion of an individual employees time is unproductive, ie not actually performing tasks, but collecting supplies, preparing for work, walking from one work area to another, transporting equipment or cleaning it down after use. These unproductive tasks can occupy a significant amount of an individual employee's time in one work day, say 1½ hours in an eight hour work day, as may be the case with a domestic assistant in a hospital. This can be translated into financial terms to realise the enormity of the problem. Therefore, more effective planning of work to reduce idle time and improve the organisation of the work system to reduce unproductive activity must be considered.

(3) *Effective planning*   When programming work and devising work schedules the sequences of tasks must be plotted and allocated a realistic amount of time. Some tasks have to precede others, some have to be performed at a specific time, some at the same time as others, and some after others. The application of *Net Work Analysis Techniques* such as PERT (*Program Evaluation and Review Technique*) and *Critical Path Analysis* is particularly relevant in this context.

Although it is virtually impossible to consider the functioning of the whole department in such detail, it is possible to isolate and identify those tasks which are critical and affect other activities, and to schedule accordingly. Adequate time must be allowed for the completion of these tasks before the activities, which are dependent on them, are scheduled to commence. Activities that can be performed concurrently may be scheduled in the same time period if the overall completion time needs to be reduced. Low priority or non-critical activities can be used to fill slack periods of a work schedule. The production of an operational plan, such as a Work Schedule, as already discussed in chapter 2, is extremely beneficial to management, to ensure that the sequence of activities performed by different employees has been effectively plotted and a realistic amount of time allotted to eliminate problems.

(4) *Equipment scheduling* In order to utilize equipment, particularly expensive 'capital' equipment, effectively, its use should be planned and scheduled. This should ensure that personnel are not unproductive or delayed whilst waiting for its availability when someone else is still using it or it is being transported from one work area to another. It should also ensure that the equipment is not overloaded or unproductive.

The scheduling of equipment may affect the sequence of activities or an individual employee's activities. For instance, if a scrubbing machine and suction dryer are to be shared by say several hospital wards, then weekly floor maintenance must be scheduled at different times of the week on the different wards. On the other hand where two employees are allocated to undertake all activities on one ward area, and only one vacuum and one set of mopping equipment is available, the work has to be scheduled so that one employee vacuums and one follows on a few minutes later and damp mops.

Effective planning and utilization of equipment can also affect capital expenditure and purchasing policy. It may be more cost effective to purchase one set of floor maintenance equipment to be shared by several work areas thus reducing initial expenditure. However, if maximum utilization is scheduled, maintenance costs over a period may be increased, the risk of down time (ie out of commission) may be higher and the length of life of the equipment shorter. On the other hand, with planned preventive equipment maintenance and an in-built replacement cycle, up-to-date equipment can be purchased more often. It may be false economy to skimp on equipment when it is a comparatively small proportion of the budget, and when lack of equipment could decrease productivity.

(5) *Improving the work flow* According to AXLER[1], a work system consists of personnel, equipment and materials functionally interacting. When designing a work system, the flow of work should be scrutinized with a view to speeding up activities and increasing productivity by limiting delays within the system, particularly transportation and storage, all of which ultimately affect the total cost.

Delays or obstacles which restrict or impede work flow within phases or between phases must be examined with a view to eliminating them.

AXLER suggests the following remedies or guidelines which may be considered:

— Keep work moving in one direction, in a short straight line
— Design the work area to be self-sufficient, for instance, consider the siting and design of utility areas within the work area, to avoid

unproductive time spent in obtaining supplies and preparing for work. If there is no convenient utility area or much time is wasted in walking to and fro, provide the chambermaid with a housemaids trolley.

— Plan the work system around the human element, ie consider the capabilities of personnel and speeds at which it is possible to work.

— Where appropriate, consider bulk processing. It is more effective for the book-keeper to post a number of charges onto a number of guest accounts at one time rather than post one here and one there. The preparation time is spread over a greater number of units.

— Consider the team approach to scheduling where a high degree of skills and/or knowledge is required – for instance floor maintenance; where an activity must be completed in a short time or where proportionally less energy is expended by a number of personnel undertaking an activity over a shorter period compared to one individual undertaking the same activity over a much longer period.

— Assign unavoidable non-productive work to cheaper labour or where enhanced payments exist for weekend work, schedule less frequent, low priority activities during the week.

— Consider the layout or the venue of elements of the system, so that the process sequence can be practically maintained avoiding criss-crossing, back-tracking or unnecessary movement of personnel or work.

— Build flexibility into the system to allow for instance, for different configurations or different activities with different purposes to take place. Mobile equipment which can be immobilised can be re-positioned, the customer and the chambermaid carry out different activities with different objectives in the same area, bed configurations can be changed to suit occupancy trends.

3.5.3.2 *Improving the efficiency of personnel – individually and collectively*

(1) *Improving the performance of the individual employee* The performance of an individual can be rated by assessing the rate at which an employee works relative to the observer's (usually the trained Work Study Officer) concept of the rate corresponding to standard rate of performance. Standard or normal performance (or pace) is defined by British Standards as: 'the rate of output which qualified workers will naturally achieve without over-exertion as an average over the working day or shift provided they are motivated to apply themselves to their work. This performance is denoted as 100 on the standard rating and performance scales.'

Performance can be affected by:
— Functional efficiency of equipment
— Deviations from specified methods
— Variations in concentration and motivation
— Changes in environmental conditions.

It is not the intention here to discuss motivation, which obviously has a great influence on an employees performance, but to consider more practical issues over which the manager has some control and which may promote or reduce employee productivity.

(a) *Planning time* Once again the Work Schedule is an invaluable aid. This time to the employees, particularly those who are unable to plan their own time effectively. The work is plotted in a logical sequence, sufficient time allowed for completion of tasks, and work areas in close proximity to each other are allocated, thus minimising walking time and aiding individual productivity.

(b) *Motion economy* This involves designing work and methods which enable the employee to perform tasks in the shortest possible time, with the greatest ease and satisfaction, expending as little energy as possible. It involves one element of ergonomics – *kinetics* which in turn involves using the muscles in the way they were intended and obviously has to be considered when devising standard methods of work. It also involves the training of personnel in the correct ways of lifting, carrying and using equipment in order to reduce fatigue.

If a domestic assistant is not trained to use say a long-tailed mop correctly for damp mopping, then much unnecessary time and energy can be expended, especially when a very large area is involved, resulting in rapid fatigue, slowing down of activity and taking too much time on subsequent tasks. Thus some activities remain uncompleted or reduced standards result. It is often a difficult aspect to promote as old habits are hard to change.

The design and layout of the work environment can affect the amount of movement and the way in which the employee uses the body. Improvements in design and layout can economize on movement and reduce fatigue. String and flow diagrams may be useful means of analysing movement.

(c) *Equipment and agents usage* Productivity may be improved not only if improved methods and motion economy are considered but also if equipment and agents are used correctly. First of all, personnel should be encouraged to collect all equipment and supplies initially to save on repeated trips to the utility room and, secondly, should be trained to use equipment and agents correctly for their intended purpose. Correct use of equipment and agents will prevent overloading, overusage, damage to surfaces and equipment and reduce effort and energy expended by the employee, thus reducing fatigue. Personnel should be encouraged to treat equipment with respect, clean it after use and report any failures. A messy worker can create work in many ways, eg slopping buckets; 'parking' wet machines on clean floors; walking over wet polish; and bumping trolleys round corners.

Not only will effective training and supervision aid efficiency but also management must select equipment which is appropriate for the task, well constructed, easy to use and appropriate for the operative –

whether male or female. Adequate supplies which have been well stored must be provided in conveniently situated storage areas.

(d) *The physical environment* An employee who is physically comfortable in the work environment, will be more productive and maintain a productive pace for a longer period of time. Ergonomics, especially anthropometry and applied human physiology (see chapter 1) are relevant in this context. Considerable improvements which encourage efficiency and productivity are possible in every environment in relation to:

Furniture — is there sufficient?
— is it the right size, height, shape?
— is there a correct relationship between items used in conjunction with each other like tables and chairs?
Noise — is it too loud or too quiet?
Heat — is it too hot or too cold?
Humidity — is the atmosphere too dry creating static or too moist?
Ventilation — is it too draughty or stuffy; are there too many air changes thus affecting temperature?
Lighting — is it inadequate, insufficient, too bright?
Structure — are there deficiencies in the structure (which could also constitute safety hazards) such as slippery floors, bumpy floors, narrow aisles, sloping surfaces?
Colour — does the environment appear too hot or too cold; is the colour appealing or drab?

Where environmental conditions cannot be improved, alternative methods of reducing fatigue must be considered. These may include:
— More frequent rest periods
— Designing the pace of work relative to the environmental conditions – slower pace in hot conditions
— Specific protective clothing
— Provision of comfortable rest areas
— Provision of good catering facilities, serving well balanced, nutritious meals.

Finally, it is worth noting that even the provision of uniforms can have some effect on efficiency both psychologically – providing an attractive, smart, comfortable uniform, and practically – designing a uniform which is comfortable, does not restrict movement and is styled to suit the activities which the wearer has to perform.

(2) *Utilizing the labour force effectively* After assessing the productivity, it may be found that the unit is overstaffed. In labour intensive units, such as Domestic Services and maintenance, this means excessive labour costs. The manager must be constantly aware of the true cost of labour. An operating statement received regularly will be invaluable but only if it reflects the costs of the labour under review.

In order to determine why and where overstaffing is occurring or why labour costs are excessive, the staffing structure, scheduling arrangements and labour turnover, absenteeism and lateness problems must be appraised.

(a) *Staffing structure* When appraising the staffing structure, consideration should be given to any jobs which could be eliminated or combined and if any jobs could be down-graded and performed by a lower paid grade of staff. Job Descriptions might be too inflexible and demarcation of duties too rigid to allow other grades of staff to help out at peak periods or in emergencies.

(b) *Scheduling* When appraising the pattern of work over a full day, peaks and troughs in activity and periods of inactivity can be identified as previously discussed. Where possible, staff should not be scheduled over periods of inactivity and the feasibility and cost implications of the following measures should be considered.

— Employ part-time staff working less than 15 hours or earning less than £34 a week resulting in reduced employment costs

— Employ more part-time rather than less full-time staff to avoid the inactive or idle times

— Reduce (where Contracts of Employment, personnel and/or unions allow) the shift hours of staff already employed to avoid paying staff for being inactive

— Re-schedule low priority, infrequent or periodic work to fill inactive periods

— Schedule employees to cover several sections to fill inactive periods or create shifts which are acceptable to potential employees. For instance, a potential employee will not be interested in working an hour a day to cover dust control and washing-up on one ward in the evening, but a two hour shift covering two wards is a different proposition. It may be cost effective overall to pay for walking time from one ward to the next.

— Employ part timers to assist full timers at peak periods rather than appoint full-timers who are then inactive

— Pay 'overtime' to a full timer where just an odd hour is involved instead of appointing another employee for a very short shift

— Schedule low priority, infrequent or periodic work currently being carried out when enhanced payments are made, to cheaper time periods during the week.

(c) *Labour turnover, absenteeism and lateness* Labour turnover, absenteeism and lateness, can all affect productivity. Ways of avoiding excesses or dealing with these occurrences must be considered.

Labour turnover This subsequently increases labour costs, as selection, recruitment, personnel administration, induction and training costs will increase. Costs may also be incurred in the initial period of employment as a new employee is more prone to a higher percentage of errors, wastage and breakages.

(d) *Absenteeism* Productivity is affected when personnel are absent as other personnel have often to cover extra work. Absenteeism can be planned for if accurate records are maintained, as an appropriate allowance can be made when estimating man-hours. There may be a tendency to over-compensate resulting in overstaffing. Where compensation is made, a relief pool of personnel may exist to cover days off, holidays, sickness and unforeseen absence. It may be more appropriate to have a pool of hours rather than employed personnel, so that casual staff or overtime are paid only when required, and relief staff are not idle.

(e) *Lateness* This obviously affects the individual's productivity and the performance of the whole unit, besides standards. Thought should be given to disciplinary procedures to prevent its occurrence or re-occurrence. It also raises the issue of whether personnel should clock-in at a central point before proceeding to their place of work.

Whenever potential changes which affect personnel, either individually or as a whole, are deemed necessary, great thought must be given to their acceptability, both to personnel and the Trade Unions, in appropriate situations.

3.6 INCENTIVE BONUS SCHEMES

Incentive bonus schemes have been introduced into some sectors of accommodation management in the past, namely domestic and laundry services in the National Health Service.

3.6.1 Reasons for introduction

Incentive bonus schemes were introduced into the National Health Service in the late 1960s, in an attempt to solve some of the following problems, highlighted by the Prices and Incomes Board Report No. 69, 1967:

— Large concentration of low paid workers
— Low productivity resulting from low pay and poor motivation
— Little pay differential existing between grades
— Lack of opportunity to earn overtime
— Poor financial control
— Poor supervision
— Poor management structure
— Poor utilization of the labour force.

3.6.2 Types of incentive bonus schemes

Three types of incentive options were considered for implementation within the ancillary services of the National Health Service, and the second option was adopted for domestic services and for laundry services. These three types are:

1 Variable incentive schemes directly relating earnings to performance
2 Measured day work schemes – where a fixed addition to the weekly or hourly rate is paid if a set target is reached
3 Productivity agreements based on the acceptance of improved methods.

Other types include: piece work and profit sharing.

3.6.3 The implementation of an incentive bonus scheme

The introduction of an incentive bonus scheme should not cause standards to fall or be detrimental in any way to the building user. Before an incentive bonus scheme can be introduced, or extended if one already operates, a work study investigation including a full method study must be conducted. The scheme will be based and then maintained on the work study basis, if it is considered to be a feasible proposition. In the case of a Domestic Services scheme the work study investigation involves surveying the whole building, preparing accommodation schedules, determining methods, frequencies, standard times; the very approach discussed in chapter 2.

Before the work study investigation commences, consultation with employees and Trade Unions, where appropriate, must occur, to outline the purpose and scope of the investigation and the way in which consequential staff adjustments will be handled. In fact, staff and trade union representatives may be invited to join the work study team after receiving some basic training. Appreciation courses could be arranged for all personnel.

If a scheme is deemed feasible, the estimated gains and costs must be calculated to show the estimated:

— increase in productivity
— aggregate increase in earnings of employees directly involved
— increase in total costs of all kinds resulting from the scheme including management consultant fees, work study fees, additional supervisory and other costs. This may well be apportioned over the first few years of the scheme.
— gross savings.

The calculations must show that all costs are more than offset by the savings and there will be a clear and substantial benefit.

The scheme should specify the performance level below which bonus will not be paid (75 on the BS rating scale, 1–100 for a domestic service bonus scheme) the normal rate of bonus for standard performance (100) and the measures to maintain the agreed quality standards of output. Bonus is not usually paid in respect of absence, holidays and sickness.

Supervisors and managers are often paid a flat rate for managing a scheme. The scheme has to be presented to staff and Trade Unions and agreed with management before being installed. In the National Health Service personnel can (technically) withdraw from a scheme at any time.

3.6.4 Installation

This obviously involves discussions, training with regard to the new methods, frequencies and work schedules, plus the administrative arrangements for calculating and paying the bonus.

Sometimes a practice period of say one week's duration is undertaken to overcome some of the teething problems.

Figure 3.6 *Task sheet*

Week Ending _____

LOCATION WARD F

JOB	M	T	W	TH	F	S	S	Week Creds	Deduct	Day Creds	Deduct	FULL CREDITS
Entrance/Corridor								14		31		231
Pantry								7		2		21
Sisters Office								4		11		81
Single Cubicle								-		13		91
Single Cubicle								-		13		91
Main Ward (left)								28		57		427
Bathroom								3		22		157
Sluice/Toilets								4		18		130
Single Cubicle								-		13		91
Single Cubicle								-		13		91
Side Ward/Mother Baby								4		15		109
Kitchen								38		30		248
Treatment Room								-		16		112
Small Ward (right)								12		41		299
Large Ward (right)								31		85		626
Sluice/Toilets								4		18		130
Bathroom								3		24		171
Doctors Office								2		9		65
Cleaners Room	0	0	0	0	0	0	0	5		-		5
Half Way House								-		8		56
Patient Services								-		116		812
Verander - Steps	0	0	0	0	0	0	0	5		-		5
High Dusting	0	0	0	0	0	0	0	60		-		60
Carbalise	0	0	0	0	0	0	0	70		-		70

Supervisor's Initials

Not done weekly (B)
Add daily deductions (A)

Total Deductions (C)

Not done daily (A)

TOTAL FULL CREDITS   4179
Deduct Total (C)
TOTAL PAY CREDITS

D.S.M. _____

LOCATION WARD F

3.6.5 Maintenance

As the scheme is based on work study, the work study officers are usually responsible in the first place to ensure that installation proceeds smoothly. They will also be responsible for closely monitoring the scheme for an initial period, usually six months and reviewing and amending it annually.

However, the day to day running of the scheme will be the responsibility of the Accommodation Manager and the standards achieved and maintained depend very much on effective supervision. The scheme may (in theory) increase the number of supervisors. The supervisor normally completes a daily task sheet (see figure 3.6) as a record that quantity and quality of output have been satisfactorily achieved. A procedure for rectifying poor standards is written in to the scheme; for instance, in the National Health Service, a ward sister or departmental head can send a written complaint to the hospital administrator which has to be signed by the assessing supervisor and domestic services manager. The staff concerned can become ineligible for productivity payment and be taken out of the scheme to undergo re-training.

A clerk is often employed to calculate the bonus weekly, but a monthly average is normally paid to hospital domestic staff and a group, rather than an individual scheme, operates.

The basis for calculation is:

$$\frac{\text{Standard Hours of authorised work}}{\text{Total Clock Hours}} \times 100$$

3.6.6 Problems
The following problems have been encountered with the domestic service scheme, although the efficiency of the scheme does depend, to some extent, on its management:
— The Daily Task Sheets are time consuming to complete and subject to abuse. Supervisors do not always check thoroughly and in some cases allow personnel to complete them
— Calcualtion of the bonus is time consuming and the employment cost of a clerk has to be covered
— Standards fall if staff cannot achieve targets and supervision slips
— Holidays, absence, sickness, trainees and employment of disabled personnel upset the scheme
— Sometimes personnel do not like the scheme
— Work study officers and the domestic services manager do not always agree on methods, frequencies, equipment, etc. Co-operation and joint agreement at this level is imperative
— The bonus payment becomes an accepted addition to the weekly wage and after a period is no longer perceived as a bonus.

3.6.7 Alternatives
There are other ways in which productivity can be improved, other types of incentive schemes and other areas of Accommodation Management besides cleaning and maintenance where incentives may be considered; for instance, incentives may be offered for:
— Lack of absence, sickness, lateness
— Constantly maintaining high levels of good work
— Increasing sales (see *Front Office* chapter 5)
— Safety and lack of accidents

Sometimes competitions, for example, 'the best employee of the month' may be effective.

3.7 QUALITY ASSURANCE

BS5750, the UK national standard for quality systems, has emphasised the need for total quality management in all spheres, including that of accommodation services. Quality assurance can only be achieved if required standards have been set, procedures specified and effective controls implemented and monitored.

The quality of the building structure and the internal environment was discussed in chapter 1. In this context we are particularly concerned with controlling the standards of building care and maintenance, including standards of cleanliness, hygiene, maintenance and safety. Before any standard can be effectively controlled, it must be set, defined and communicated to those concerned with the achievement.

3.7.1 Setting the standard

Setting the standard involves:
— Knowing the aims and objectives (terms of reference) of the department
— Defining the work load (what tasks/activities have to be carried out)
— Establishing standard methods (if this task is to be completed in this sequence using these techniques, this equipment and these products then this finish is the expected outcome)
— Setting time standards (if this task is completed in the standard way within this amount of time then this is the expected outcome)
— Determining frequencies (see chapter 2)
— Planning and programming work effectively
— Selecting the right type and amount of equipment and agents (see chapter 4)
— Selecting the right staff (see chapter 3).

3.7.2 Defining standards

Standards should be defined, particularly when method study has occurred, in order to communicate them to those concerned with their achievement. After all it is unfair to expect employees automatically to know, or worse to discipline them for achieving poor results, when they were not told what standards they were expected to achieve in the first place. Attempting to define 'a standard of cleanliness' or decide 'how clean is clean' is difficult, as we are dealing with an intangible product and one which is subject to varying interpretations from one person to another, and this easily leads to misinterpretation and misunderstanding.

Through the development of standard methods for instance, the standard to be achieved is really being defined. However, it may be considered necessary to define specific outcomes, for example:
'When this bath has been cleaned it must have:
— no grease line
— no hairs in the plug hole

— no water spots on the tap
— no traces of cleaning agent
— a dry internal surface
— shiny taps
— plug chain hung over the tap
— new soap in the soap tray
— clean bathmat over the side

It is essential that the information is communicated during the training process to the persons undertaking this task. The supervisor must also be fully aware of the standards to be reached.

3.7.3 Controlling standards

As discussed in section 3.4, it is impossible to continually monitor individual performance, and individual employees do ultimately control the standards achieved. Personnel must be highly motivated to work on their own initiative, even with the guidance of work schedules. Training, therefore, is an essential control to ensure that personnel know how to perform their activities and the specific standards or results which have to be achieved. Even though continuous supervision is impossible, the supervisor still has to ensure that:

— All work is completed
— All tasks are carried out in the correct manner
— Safety and hygiene precautions are enforced
— Standards are achieved
— Poor standards are rectified and good standards recognised
— Equipment is kept in good working order
— Surfaces are in good repair
— There are effective feed-back mechanisms.

Supervision of the supervisors and regular inspections to evaluate standards being achieved are also other control measures to be considered.

3.7.4 Evaluation of standards

The most usual method of evaluation is a visual inspection of the work area, to check that work is being completed and to the correct standard. This visual inspection tends to be subjective if not organised and well controlled. Inspections must be carried out on a regular basis to be of value, but as they can be very time consuming, it may not be necessary to check the finished result of every item every day.

It may be more feasible to 'spot check' certain items. For instance, in a hospital ward, a couple of washbasins can be thoroughly checked or one toilet in a sanitary area, rather than all. Whether a full inspection or a spot checking system is thought more appropriate, it must not be predictable. Consideration must also be given:

— to the frequency of inspection, eg daily, weekly
— by whom the inspection is to be undertaken. Normally the

supervisor will conduct the regular inspection, although the departmental manager may periodically inspect and the Accommodation Manager or even general manager may conduct occasional inspections

— with whom the inspection is to be undertaken. Is it with the supervisor only or the supervisor with either the departmental manager, the member of staff concerned, or the user of the service, eg ward sister or the contractor's client, in the case of a contract service?

It is effective to develop a systematic approach when inspecting an area to restrict time, movement and energy, and ensure all items to be inspected are included. A checklist is a useful aid.

Attention to detail often means the difference between a high and a mediocre standard, and inspection of less obvious areas like under doors, in corners, behind open doors, backs of wardrobe tops, under basins, behind toilet pedestals, may encourage higher standards of performance.

If poor workmanship is found, it should be rectified straight away, not tomorrow; and re-training must be given where necessary. Remember that praise for good workmanship is vital, although often ignored. Difficulties can be encountered when evaluating standards of cleanliness, as straight after cleaning the toilet may be used again, a spillage may occur and the dust re-settle. Perhaps the criteria, therefore, is not purely the finished result, but whether cleaning has occurred.

3.7.4.1 Inspection checklist
A checklist is useful, if well designed, to:
— encourage a systematic approach
— introduce some degree of objectivity
— ensure that nothing is forgotten
— focus attention and aid concentration.

It is very easy, when inspecting several 'like' areas, to lose concentration, forget items and let standards slip. The checklist can be designed for each room type, the Accommodation Schedule being used as a basis, bearing in mind the tasks which have to be completed and their frequencies. Thought should be given to the means of measurement to be used when completing the checklist. The simplest means are a good, bad or inferior indication, or a tick or a cross indicator (with specific defects recorded as necssary). See figure 3.7.

In the circumstances, when inspections are conducted with the client or service user, eg ward sister, the checklist can be dated and signed by those involved and kept as a record of the standard achieved at that time, in case of future complaint. It may be useful to have a checklist for inspecting cleaning standards and a separate one for inspecting the fabric of the building.

Other types of inspections or evaluations may be appropriate in certain circumstances:

Figure 3.7 *Inspection checklist – for an hotel bathroom*

YES   NO

* Does the door open easily?
* Do all lights work?
* Does the air conditioning work?
  Is the waste bin empty and clean?

Wash hand basin
  Is the wash hand basin clean?
  Is the overflow clean?
  Is the plug clean and attached?
  Are the taps spotless?
  Are the bases of the taps clean?
  Is the underneath of the basin clean?
  Is the pedestal clean?
  Is the mirror spotless?
  Are the required supplies present — soap
                                    — shampoo sachet
                                    — tissues
                                    — tooth mug
                                    — face cloths
* Are the taps dripping?
* Are the washers in good condition?

Bath and shower
  Is the bath clean inside?
  Is the bath clean outside?
  Is the overflow clean?
  Are the taps and shower head spotless?
* Do the taps and shower head drip?
  Is the shower curtain/door — clean?
                            — in good repair?
* Does the shower spray correctly?
* Does the tnermostat work effectively?
* Is the grouting in good condition?
  Are the required supplies present — bathmat
                                    — soap
                                    — shower cap
  Is the splash back clean?

Toilet
  Is the toilet clean inside?
  Is the toilet bowl outside and pedestal clean?
  Is the cistern clean?
  Is the lid clean – top and bottom?
  Is the seat clean – top and bottom?
  Is the top of the toilet bowl clean?
  Is the toilet clean under the rim? (mirror test)
  Are the hinges clean and in good repair?
* Does the toilet flush properly?
  Are the toilet brush and holder clean?

Is there sufficient toilet paper?
Are there sufficient ST bags?

Floor
Is the floor clean?
Are the corners clean?
Is the area under the door clean?

Linens
Are the correct towels supplied?

* Are there any other faults or problems to report?
List _____

_____

Date: Signature:

_____

* Maintenance tasks as opposed to cleaning tasks.

— Bacterial counts can be undertaken in high risk areas or where clinical standards of hygiene are required. Air counts can be taken to determine bacterial levels in the atmosphere; swab tests can be undertaken on equipment, in cleaning water, toilets, washing-up water, etc or a 'slit sampler' can be used to evaluate the effect of air disturbance caused by using equipment which raises the dust, such as vacuum cleaners, mops and brushes.
— Checking equipment frequently should ensure it is in good working order, cleaned and emptied.
— Safety checks should also be conducted on access and fire fighting and detection equipment.

3.8 CONTRACT LABOUR

There may be occasions when a full contract labour service is a more feasible alternative to a direct service. Company policy might also impose the consideration of contract services on Accommodation Management.

The advantages and disadvantages of contract services in general, and the types of services available are discussed in chapter 4. In this section we discuss briefly the occasions when a full contract service may be feasible and the problems encountered in changing from direct labour to contract labour.

3.8.1 The occasions when a full contract service may be considered

A full contract service may be considered as an alternative to a direct service on the following types of occasions when:
— Economic or accounting advantages may be achieved
— Reduction of administrative work load is sought
— Staff availability is difficult

— High levels of sickness, absence, labour turnover are occurring
— Capital equipment, involving a large amount of money, needs replacing
— A new unit is being opened
— Testing of the competitiveness of in-house services is required.

When the cost of monitoring and controlling a full contract service are higher than the resultant savings, it is not a feasible proposition.

3.8.2 Changing from direct labour to a full contract service

When contemplating changing from a direct labour force to a full contract service, the following factors need to be considered:
— What happens to the departmental manager?
— What redundancy arrangements will be made?
— Will the contractor re-employ the existing labour force?
— What will happen to all equipment and agents in stock?

3.9 PERSONNEL CONTROL

Personnel control encompasses all the issues discussed in this chapter and outlined in figure 3.1 but, as yet, reference has not been made to Appraisal, Counselling and Termination.

3.9.1 Appraisal

Appraisal is the judgement of an employee's performance in the appointed job, not necessarily based on productivity alone. Appraisal is of particular value when monitoring the progress of a new employee or when determining the future of an employee in terms of whether to promote, demote, dismiss or leave in the present job. If a policy of staff development exists, or promotion is a potential outcome, then appraisal is also useful to analyse an individual's strengths and weaknesses, and to determine future training and experiential needs.

Appraisal may be by observation and discussion with supervisors or other personnel or departmental heads, or alternatively, by conducting one or a series of appraisal interviews with the individual concerned. The purpose of the interview is to encourage a self-evaluation in an objective and impartial manner and mutually agree the future course of action. It is possibly more appropriate above operative level and may also serve to encourage further motivation amongst supervisors and assistants.

3.9.2 Counselling

The Accommodation Manager or indeed the supervisor may have to counsel personnel either during appraisal, grievance or disciplinary interviews, or because an employee seeks assistance with work or over a personal problem. The immediate supervisor, in some cases, may not be asked or may not be capable of assisting. As with any interview (see section 3.2) thought must be given to its format, venue, seating, etc, and the policy to be adopted, such as an open door policy – where an employee can call any time; a 'limited' open door policy – where the employee can call between certain hours each day or week; or an appointment policy either through the supervisor or the secretary. Listening is an attribute to be developed on the interviewer's part and any positive help which can be given to the employee in terms of advice; where to get further information, actions to take to solve the problem, or even just sympathy, may not only help the employee but also develop a better relationship between manager and employee. The Accommodation Manager should be careful not to 'gossip' about the employee as confidentiality is also an important factor.

3.9.3 Termination
The Accommodation Manager must clarify the extent of their authority with regard to the termination of an employees employment for whatever reason. In some organisations only the personnel manager or general manager can terminate employment.

If an employee terminates his own employment, it is useful to know the real reason which is often different to the reason actually given. Usually, the employee has to complete a termination form or submit a letter, but an exit interview is invaluable if an attempt is being made to establish the real reason for termination. This may highlight a particular or a recurring problem which may be affecting labour turnover and hence labour costs. It can only be rectified if it is identified.

3.9.4 Retention
The cost of recruiting, selecting, inducting and training a member of staff is high, particularly if that member of staff subsequently leaves. High labour turnover obviously increases the cost of employing personnel. The Accommodation Manager must consider ways to retain staff and reduce labour turnover, especially in light of the changing demographic trends.

3.9.5 Staff records
Another control measure, whether undertaken by the Personnel or the Accommodation Department, is to keep effective personnel records. To be of value these records must be relevant, accurate, up-to-date, in a useful format and summarised, often in statistical form on a regular basis. Labour turnover, sickness and absence ratios lend themselves to statistical analysis.

Figure 3.8 suggests the personnel records which need to be kept either by the Personnel or the Accommodation Department.

Figure 3.8 *Personnel records*

Staffing requirements —	Number required*; vacancies*; grades*; shifts*; location*; job description*; work schedules*
Recruitment	— Adverts; response statistics; applications*
Selection	— Shortlist*; application forms*; personnel specification*; interview form; confirmation/ rejection letters
Appointment	— Personal file – appointment form, contract of employment; references; medical
Induction	— Induction programme; record and progress*
Training	— Training programme, record and progress*
Deployment	— Clock-cards/register*; work schedules*; duty rotas*; holiday, Bank holiday records
Supervision	— Quality control*; disciplinary
Appraisal	— Interview records; absence and sickness*; progress*; disciplinary*; problems*
Staff welfare	— Conditions of service; policies; sickness, occupational health
Termination	— Reasons*; labour turnover*

* Indicates those to which the Accommodation Manager must keep or have easy access.

References
[1] AXLER, BRUCE H, *Management of Hospitality Operations*, Bobbs-Merrill 1976
[2] SYSKA and HENNESSY, *The Housekeeping Supervisor – Keystone to Success*, American Training Manual

Further reading
A.D.M. Guidance Series Book 5, *A Quality System For Domestic Services* 1990
DHSS, *Domestic Supervisors Manual* 2nd edition 1983
HCITB, *A guide to Systematic Training* 1982
INTERNATIONAL LABOUR OFFICE, *Introduction to work Study* 1968
GULLEN, H V and RHODES, G E, *Management in the Hotel and Catering Industry*, Batsford 1983
PIB, Report No. 29 March 1967

4

Purchasing and Supplies

The next sub-system to consider, in the system for the Management of Accommodation is that of Purchasing and Supplies. It is not difficult to appreciate the systemic role of supplies and purchases, whether they be for the purpose of replenishing stocks or extending plant. Figure 4.1 shows the significance of the 'needs of the users'. (The user could be the domestic assistant's requirements of a detergent, the squash player's requirements of a floor finish, or indeed the needs of any building user who will be affected by the purchase.)

Figure 4.1 *The purchasing and supplies sub-system*

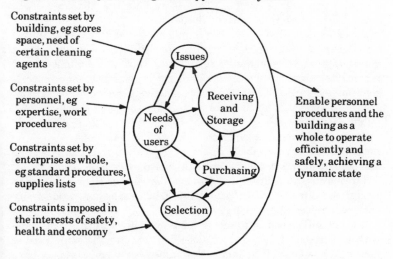

Constraints set by building, eg stores space, need of certain cleaning agents

Constraints set by personnel, eg expertise, work procedures

Constraints set by enterprise as whole, eg standard procedures, supplies lists

Constraints imposed in the interests of safety, health and economy

Issues

Receiving and Storage

Needs of users

Purchasing

Selection

Enable personnel procedures and the building as a whole to operate efficiently and safely, achieving a dynamic state

4.1   ITEMS TO BE PURCHASED

As the specific role of the Accommodation Manager varies from one establishment to another, so the items purchased under his authority will vary also. They might include such a diverse range as:

Cleaning agents and equipment
Surfaces and fittings, eg floors, light fittings
Furniture
Furnishings and linen
Uniforms

Computer systems or components
Front Office equipment and materials
Capital items, eg expensive equipment items
Services, eg consultancy, pest control.

Such items may broadly be categorised into:
1 Consumables, eg stationery, cleaning materials
2 Service contracts, eg equipment and maintenance
3 Capital items, ranging from small buildings to larger items of equipment.

The specific categorisation will depend on the particular establishment and its accountancy system, eg *consumables* might be any item costing up to a certain fixed amount, *capital* items may be sub-divided into: (a) new and (b) replacements.

4.2 THE SELECTION PROCESS

Monies spent by the Accommodation Manager on items other than personnel, may only represent a small percentage, say around 5% to 10%, of the overall budget. This is not to say that any such expenditure should be entered into without due thought. It has been estimated that over £750 million is spent in the United Kingdom every year on cleaning. The domestic services manager in a hospital, may be spending £25,000 per year on equipment and material alone. Careful selection here can be as important as careful selection of staff. Selection cannot effectively be made by a non-specialist. Indeed, a good choice of cleaning equipment, for instance, might reap some of the benefits shown in figure 4.2. The domestic services department in any establishment is, and must be, by the nature of its service, labour intensive. By selecting cleaning agents and equipment wisely, some direct savings may well be achieved, but of far more significance is the possible man-power saving. It can be seen from figure 4.2 that, if attention is paid to selection, productivity may be increased by various routes.

It is not sufficient just to replace automatically a worn out machine with a new model, nor a worn floor with exactly the same type of flooring. Technology is dynamic. Newer, better alternatives may have emerged since the last purchase was made. It is not always justifiable to go for the lowest price. A low tender for a laundry contract might indicate fewer deliveries or poorer quality materials. A low list price for front office equiment might result in inferior back-up services being available.

It is rarely prudent to purchase items simply because they are marketed effectively, or because they happen to be those stocked locally, (though this might be a determining feature at the end of the selection process). A good manager should carry out the selection process personally, not allow a supplier do it for him or her, (though the

Figure 4.2 *Possible benefits achieved through a good choice of cleaning equipment*

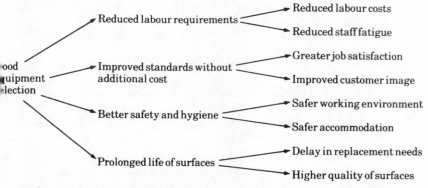

supplier might be a valuable source of advice). The buyer must not let the manufacturer 'blind him with science'.

Irrespective of what is being purchased, whether a piece of laundry equipment costing thousands of pounds, or a new stock of cleaning cloths, selection decisions should be made purposefully and a systematic approach taken.

4.2.1 Stages in selection

Step one – problem analysis

The selection process commences with the analysis of a problem. The problem might be any of the following: low stocks of neutral detergent; hotel guest complaints regarding inaccurate billing; or repeated accidents involving slipping. When a problem has been identified, the manager should not immediately prescribe a solution, but, rather, investigate the matter, looking at such factors as frequency of occurrences of the problem, severity of occurrences, possible causes, and effects of the problem. This will enable the manager to put the problem in perspective, and is the first stage in the selection process.

In some instances, as in the case of the neutral detergent, the problem might be immediately diagnosed as a 'supplies need', ie simply that stocks need replenishing. This diagnosis may or may not be justified. Any manager would be advised to investigate problems before classifying them and making assumptions as to their causes. In some instances a detailed investigation may be virtually automatic; in others, the idea that there might be an alternative solution to the obvious is not considered. Probably a certain amount of self-discipline on the part of the manager is required here to make more than superficial enquiries when attempting to solve any problem, no matter how trivial it might appear. By no means all problems can be solved by making further purchases.

Thus the first stage of selection is to identify, not just that a problem exists but, specifically, what the problem is. The true problem is not always apparent. The specific problem, in the case of low stocks of neutral detergent, could be any of a number of root problems, such as:

1 The results of normal usage and the stocks being correctly identified as minimal
2 Excessive usage due to inadequate training, pilferage, exceptional work loads
3 A poor stores control system, perhaps a standing order is not being honoured
4 A poor stores issuing system where excessive stocks have been issued, and are being stock piled at the point of use
5 That particular brand of detergent may no longer be in use and stocks are being run down.

Many alternative root problems might exist and, when the matter is investigated, probably a combination of factors will be seen to be acting.

Step two – solutions identification
It is not until the root problem has been identified that the search for a solution can begin, otherwise the wrong problem may be tackled. This may at best only reduce the symptoms, and, at worst, prolong and aggravate the difficulties. Reordering detergent when stocks are low does not solve a pilfering problem. When the true root problem has been identified, the manager must again restrain himself from immediately dictating the solution. There may well be many possible solutions to the problem, and the second stage in the selection process is to identify these alternatives. At first sight, many of these solutions might appear inappropriate, but the application of some lateral thinking here may well pay off.

To take the example again of the neutral detergent, if the root problem has been identified as one of inadequate training of staff, leading to excessive usage, there are several possible solutions such as:

(a) Directly controlling dilutions of the product·
(b) Selecting a detergent which is more difficult to use in excess
(c) Improving the training programme
(d) Stopping staff from using the product.

At this stage in the selection process, the aim is not yet to choose a solution, just to identify possibilities.

Step three – solution selection
Step three of the selection process is to choose the most appropriate solution. In some instances, this decision may be outside the authority of the Accommodation Manager; in other instances, there may only be one possible solution. If none of the solutions seems appropriate, there must be a process of reiteration, either to seek an appropriate solution or to investigate the root problem further.

Step four – solution requirements

When a solution (or combination of solutions) has been chosen, the requirements of this solution must be identified. In the example of the neutral detergent, to take the first listed solution, ie 'directly controlling dilution of the product', the requirements here would include:

(a) The appropriate neutral detergent

(b) Some means of directly controlling dilution, eg supervisory staff, automatic or mechanical method of proportioning.

Step five – performance specification

The final stage in the selection process is to develop specifications of performance or 'performance attributes', for the requirements listed in stage four. This may well be the most difficult part of the selection process, and has similarities with Job Descriptions and Job Analyses of staff; it calls for analysis, where other stages have called for enlargement and development.

In the example sited, two performance specifications are needed; one for the detergent itself and one for the method of dilution control. The specification for the detergent might include elements such as:

pH level	Available in 4 litre containers
Ability to remove grease, water soluble soilage and carbon stains	Minimum shelf life of 3 months
	Non-irritating
	Biodegradable
Low foam	Effective in cold water
Low odour	Non-streaking
Within in-use cost limit	Non-corrosive.

The specification for the dilution control might include:

Not involving additional labour

Cost effective

Useable in domestic staffs' peripheral stores

Maintained by manufacturer or supplier, and durable

Give variable, regulated dilutions

Not specific to one detergent type

Hygienic in use.

The list of performance attributes can then be compiled as a performance specification and, to assist in the final selection of a product, the attributes can be ranked, eg essential; highly desirable; or desirable.

Performance specifications may be relatively simple, such as in the example given, or extremely complex such as might be prepared prior to the invitation to tender for a complete cleaning service. The process of preparing performance specifications is sometimes referred to as 'Value Analysis', ie not 'over specifying' qualities required. Unnecessary luxuries can be omitted from specifications, so hopefully, reducing costs. For example, noise suppression of some cleaning equipment is often desirable but if the equipment is to be used in a noisy boiler room, this requirement becomes unnecessary.

4.2.2 Selecting cleaning and maintenance agents and equipment

In preparing specifications, consideration must be given, not just to the efficiency of the product but its suitability for that particular situation. Some general aspects to consider in preparing specifications for cleaning and maintenance agents and equipment might include:

(a) Site characteristics, eg floor coverings and their conditions, soilage types and rates, furniture densities, service points, and power sources available, storage facilities, access facilities (ramps and lifts), geographical layout of site, use of building and special requirements (low noise, electrical suppression, vacuum filtration, etc).

(b) Labour considerations, eg numbers sharing one machine, training aspects, size and strength of operatives, working hours, supervisory cover, effects on productivity levels and agreements, health and safety.

In chapter 2, performance attributes of cleaning agents and equipment have been considered with respect to the characteristics of soilage. Cleaning and maintenance agents and equipment selected would include various items from the list in figure 4.3.

4.2.3 Selecting computers

Within the general sphere of Accommodation Management, significant use of computers is seen in the Front Office departments, particularly of hotels, but other uses include stores control, design work, personnel records and indeed any use where quantities of data are to be collected, stored and manipulated. Due particularly to the developing technology associated with computers and the vastness of their 'memories', it is probable that the Accommodation Department will not buy a computer independently of other departments. A central computer may be purchased with remote 'terminals' for general use, or a number of personal computers may be purchased within an establishment with the aim of them being compatible.

In preparing a specification for a computer, assistance will eventually have to be sought from specialists, but if a general outline of requirements can be established at an early stage the manager will have identified his basic needs and will perhaps recognise, for instance, when he is being guided towards something which is in excess of his requirements or unsuitable in some other way.

When the manager has identified the main functions which he wishes the computer to fulfil, some criteria will determine hardware requirements of the computer system (processors, primary and backup data storage devices, printers, Visual Display Units and keyboards) and some the software requirements (operating system, computer language and prepared programmes). These two facets of the computer system must be planned together. Computer suppliers will frequently have available computer 'packages' comprising certain basic items of hardware and standard software programmes. These components of the computer system would come from one manufacturer or from several,

Figure 4.3 *Cleaning and maintenance agents and equipment from which selection must be made*

Cleaning agents
Detergents
Seals and polishes – for floors, furniture and metals
Abrasives
De-odourisers
Chemical disinfectants
Specialised soilage removers, eg chewing gum remover; acid cleaners; stain
 removers; graffiti removers; window cleaners
Slip retardant treatments
Soilage repellants
Bleaches
Fabric conditioner
Laundry 'sour'
Starches and laundry finishing agents
Dry cleaning agents

Floor maintenance equipment
Brushes and dustpans
Dry and wet mops
Buckets, wringers and trolleys
Floor maintenance machines
High speed and hyper-speed spray burnishing machines
Suction dryers
Suction cleaners
Carpet shampooing machines

Accessories
Floor pads
Seal and polish applicators and trays
Access equipment, waste collectors

Wall and fittings cleaning equipment
Upholstery cleaners
Wall washing machines
Pressure washers

Laundry equipment
Scales
Trolleys
Washers/Washer-extractors
Hydro-extractors
Tumble driers
Callenders

the items must, however, be compatible.

Some of the requirements which the manager would need to identify are shown in figure 4.4, and the influence these would have on computer selection is also shown.

Figure 4.4 *Computer selection: management decision and their influence in the selection process*

Manager would need to determine:	Influences on computer selection
1 Specific functions for which the computer will be required. Quantities of data involved, types of data manipulation involved and frequency of data access	This will determine capacity requirements of the computer and also influence software selection
2 Who will use the computer, when and where would they ideally like to use it. Will calculation of results and computer access be required at once	These will influence software selection and hardware requirements, eg number of terminals and capacity
3 What are the physical constraints imposed by room dimensions and layout	These will affect hardware selection and layout

Other factors which would need to be considered in the selection process include:

1 Past records on reliability of hardware
2 Maintenance contracts available and speed of service in case of breakdown
3 Installation procedures and timescale
4 Software availability and expertise availability
5 Training of staff and acceptance of system by clients as well as users
6 Cost of the system and expected lifespan of its components before becoming obsolete; upgrading as developed by the manufacturer.

One of the main advantages which computers offer the manager is speed of operation. Once appropriate programmes have been developed and operatives have become proficient, vast quantities of data can be entered into the computer. This data is stored and can be accessed in various formats and for various applications, almost instantaneously. In the hotel Front Office, for example, advanced reservation data (including cancellations and amendments) can be fed into the computer, which, at a later date, can be retrieved as an arrivals and departures list, room allocation list, VIP list or room status report. With other programmes and additional data, the original information can be used to print out confirmation letters, compile guest histories and keep guest accounts, prepare occupancy statistics, carry out auditing routines and calculate trading figures.

Training of all users is, of course, necessary, though this is not a particularly long process when compared with the traditional training involved with the use of electro-mechanical billing machines, for example. Management can become more sensitive to deviations from the 'norm' of trading figures, due to an increased volume of management information and the reduction in mistakes. Another attraction of computers, again associated with the hotel situation and with the speed of response, is that, with terminals sited at all points of sale within an hotel, late charges are virtually eliminated. Customer's bills are up-to-date at the time of presentation and much revenue is saved.

There are also disadvantages associated with computers, such as installation inconvenience, initial 'teething' problems and computer fraud. The establishment must also make registration of the computer's use as required by the Data Protection Act. Also, in a service industry, the personal touch must not be devalued, and it is unfortunately a fact that a degree of deskilling can be a result of computerisation. These social problems call for all the skills of the manager if they are to be minimised and, where necessary, resolved.

Thus, in selecting a computer system, not only must technical facets be analysed, and physical and financial constituents identified, but also social aspects must be given adequate attention. Further consideration of computers is made in chapter 5.

4.2.4 Selecting surfaces, linens, fittings and furniture
In chapter 1, consideration has been given to the performance attributes required of items such as floors, windows, soft furnishings, heating and lighting installations. In general terms three aspects must be considered:
1 The purpose and overall function of the establishment, eg non-profit orientated, health care facilities, commercially orientated leisure centre or rapid turnover fast food operation
2 The standards aimed for within the organisation
3 The integrative nature of design.

4.2.5 Selecting contract labour
Selecting contract labour or selecting services, as opposed to supplies, is a complex operation but, basically, it will follow the same pattern. A selection process must be followed, and a performance specification prepared before tenders are invited. Contracting of labour is discussed more fully later in this chapter.

With the development of a performance specification, the manager is part way to solving the problem. The selection process may seem time-consuming and involved but, in the long run, may save valuable management and staff time. The true problem has been isolated and the best solution identified. The next stage is to endeavour to purchase that solution (or the nearest fit).

4.3 PURCHASING PROCESS

The purchasing process commences with investigations as to what is available on the market, which appears broadly similar to the products required. This information may be gathered from trade literature, manufacturers' leaflets, trade exhibitions, manufacturers and suppliers. When the market has been surveyed in this way, a limited number of the most appropriate products may be considered further, until the choice has been narrowed down to perhaps two or three. At this stage, depending on the products to be purchased, it may well be valuable to approach manufacturers or suppliers with a view to the demonstration of equipment or materials, or to the viewing of samples of fixtures, fittings, furniture, furnishings, linens and similar items.

4.3.1 Demonstrations

Demonstrations, or the examination of samples, should be viewed as serious undertakings if they are to be of true value. It may well be useful, if not obligatory, to seek other opinions from within the buying organisation, eg when buying staff uniforms in a hospital, people who might be invited to see and comment on samples include:

Supervisory grades and representatives from staff
Unit Manager
A member of the Health and Safety Committee
A member of the staffs trade union
Control of Infection Officer
Linen Services Manager

Inviting such varied opinions may well be constructive and highlight aspects which the Accommodation Manager may otherwise have overlooked or underestimated. It can also promote goodwill between the Accommodation and other departments, and between management and staff. Conversely, of course, inviting comments and apparently encouraging participative management on the one hand, then, apparently, ignoring comments made, could also create staff difficulties. The balance is aimed for.

When equipment, particularly cleaning equipment, is being purchased, competitive demonstrations may be set up. Two or three manufacturers are invited to demonstrate their products simultaneously. Direct comparisons can be made, eg noise levels, ease of handling, efficiency. Care must be taken not to be influenced by the quality of 'salesmanship'.

To be of full value demonstrations, competitive or otherwise, must be well planned. Planning should include:

1 Site of demonstration. Somewhere which will be uninterrupted to create minimum inconvenience to other building users and yet to provide suitable and representative conditions, eg when testing floor maintenance machines, a variety of floor coverings may be required

2 Decisions must be made as to whom to invite to the demonstration
3 Adequate notice, both to suppliers and to the other interested parties, must be given.
4 A checklist should be prepared of criteria to be measured and some scale must be attached. This scale may simply have two values, satisfactory and unsatisfactory or, alternatively, criteria might be measured on a scale of 1 to 10.

Following the demonstration or viewing of samples, prices and in-use costs of products must be determined. Hidden costs, as well as quoted prices, must be considered, eg prices of accessories, service costs, delivery charges, life expectancy, dilution rates of cleaning agents, must all be considered.

4.3.2 Field trials

In some instances, the value of demonstrations is fairly limited. Much more information regarding the suitability of a product can be gained by testing the product on site by the operatives who will be using it. It is not sufficient, however, to acquire a piece of equipment for a week or two, or a small quantity of a new polish and give it to the staff to 'see what they think'.

To be safe, as well as efficient, field trials need to be carefully set up and monitored. Before a final decision is made, and following any demonstrations, the product may be tested or perhaps two or three may be used on site, so that comparisons can be made. Some of the planning to be done, and decisions to be made when setting up field trials, are as follows:

1 In which areas of the building are the products to be tested, eg if a trial was to be conducted to compare duvets with conventional bedding, double, as well as single, beds must be included in the trial
2 Which staff are to be involved? Are these staff representative of the others who will be using the product?
3 Is training needed before staff can use the product? If so, will this be given by the supplier?
4 For how long are trials to last?
5 Who else, besides those carrying out the test, need to be informed of the trials?
6 A means of evaluation must be prepared, eg checklists, comments from supervisors and others who have been affected. In the case of some cleaning products, bacteriological tests may have to be set up. In the case of linens, certain in-house testing may be valuable.

The format of the evaluation checklist might be as shown in figure 4.5.

In carrying out field trials, as with any scientific testing, it is important to ensure that only one variable changes at a time. In testing floor maintenance machines, for example, measures need to be taken to ensure that similar pads and floor maintenance products are

Figure 4.5 *Check list for suction cleaner field trials*

Machine manufacturer: ....

Model: ....

Area/s tested: ....

Floor types and soilage: ....

Product characteristics	**Rating**		
Ease of use	*Good*	*Satisfactory*	*Poor*
Training needs			
Ease of assembly			
Manoeuverability			
Weight for carrying			
Cable length			
Stability in use			
Ease of emptying			
Ease of adding attachments			
Storage of attachments			
Capacity of collection bag			
Ease of cleaning			
Variety and effectiveness of attachments			
Efficiency			
Apparent soilage removal — on pile carpet			
— on low pile carpet			
— on hard floors			
Real soilage removal — on pile carpet			
— on low pile carpet			
— on hard floors			
Efficiency on other surfaces			
Environmental factors			
Air disturbance			
Air filtration			
Noise level			
Acceptability by users of area			
Appearance of machine			

Acceptability by user

Safety aspects

Durability expected

Users name ....   Other comments:

Supervisor ....

used. It is the efficiency of the cleaning machine which is being measured, and all other variables should remain constant. In the case of detergent testing, dilution rates must be carefully monitored, manufacturer's instructions must be followed and in-use costs calculated. When testing fabrics, usage, laundering or other cleaning processes and cleaning agents must all be controlled.

Before a final decision is made, and an order placed, the manager must also discover details of deliveries, and customer services he may require, such as training and installation.

In this purchasing process, the buyer is choosing from the market the product most suited to his requirements, as documented in his performance specification. It is unlikely, in fact, that he will find a product which exactly meets his criteria; he will usually have to settle for the best compromise (hence the importance of prioritising elements in the specification). In the case of very large organisations, due to their 'purchasing power' or volume of trade, products may be custom made by specification (manufacturers make up products to meet the actual specification). Regardless of the size of the organisation, drawing up a specification is not a once-and-for-all exercise. Circumstances are always changing and thus specifications need updating.

Where services, as opposed to supplies, are to be purchased, field trials are of course difficult. Even if one small unit could be isolated and the services completed there to give a sample of standards, running two systems, ie direct and contract labour, in harness within the same organisation, is almost bound to cause labour unrest and in any case may not give a true picture. The best chance of 'sampling' work is to visit other establishments already serviced by interested firms.

4.3.3 Sources of advice

There are many sources of advice from which valuable information is available, guidelines set, and, in some cases, strict rules laid down with respect to purchasing supplies. Particularly on safety, where data is available, the manager is well advised to seek this information. Some of the relevant bodies include the following:

British Standards British Standards prepared and published by the British Standards Institution (B S I) are technical agreements on such matters as safety, comfort, efficiency and dimensions on all manner of aspects. With respect to purchases the Accommodation Manager might make, there are British Standards for some items of cleaning equipment, some detergents, furnishings, wallpaper, colours, chairs, and many others. The Standards describe criteria needed to ensure that items are fit for the purpose for which they are intended. Products which are made to BS will be marked with the relevant BS number, and this is the manufacturer's claim that it is made according to the documented standard. In addition, the BSI licence some manufacturers to use the BSI kitemark (mark of safety) indicating that BSI inspectors have inspected the manufacturer's quality control system as well as testing sample products.

British Electrotechnical Approvals Board The British Electrotechnical Approvals Board is related to the BSI, but specialises in electrical items. Again, the BEAB mark on products, given under licence, is a sign of safety (design, construction and endurance).

The Design Council The Design Council is government sponsored, and aims to promote good design within British Industry. It assists in many ways, including the provision of direct advice and assistance to manufacturers. The Design Advisory Service has been established by the Design Council, to assist in the diffusion of knowledge, with respect to technological development and design skills. Member companies subscribe to this service.

The Council's design index is an illustrated record of modern products which have been selected by the Council from British products, as being of above average design. Products are checked, where the relevant BS exists, and Design Centre labels can be bought by the manufacturers of items selected. (The object of these labels is to promote the product and so aid marketing.)

Public Authority and Private Organisations Standards Local Authorities, Government bodies, and large organisations, take advantage of their large purchasing powers, and set up central purchasing supplies departments which can buy largely by specification. To prove that specifications are met, manufacturers may need to submit samples to independent testing houses before tenders are considered. (These testing houses include such bodies as the Building Research Association (BRE), WIRA and the Shirley Institute for textiles.) When products are accepted, they are included in the products information circulated to member organisations of the purchasing body. The products are then known to be of a certain standard, specifications can be viewed, and probably a reduced price will have been negotiated.

Other Associations Other organisations from whom advice may be available, with respect to purchases, include the manufacturers' own associations, eg Contract Cleaning and Maintenance Association, Contract Furnishings Association. These are professional bodies with agreed Codes of Practice for members. They may provide valuable information in the area of their own expertise.

4.4 HIRE OR BUY

After a formal selection has been made, a further choice of hire or buy may be open in the case of services, eg labour, and many supplies, eg machinery, linen and, in some cases, furniture items.

4.4.1 Supplies

Some of the occasions, when hiring or buying may be appropriate, are shown in figure 4.6. In addition to these factors, the policy of the purchasing organisation and its accounting system, may well determine whether items are bought or hired.

Figure 4.6 *Occasions where hiring or buying may be appropriate*

Hiring appropriate	Buying appropriate
1 Infrequent use is likely, storage difficult/expensive	Daily or very frequent use
2 Maintenance, laundering, etc, likely to cause problems	Own maintenance department/ laundry or service contract taken out
3 Equipment is unreliable, linen or furniture usages highly variable and hirer may have alternatives available in case of breakdown or back-up stock	Suppliers or servicing company may make short term loans to cover breakdowns or shortages
4 Short term cost advantages	Long term cost advantages
5 Short life expectancy. Many factors may speed up obsolesence	Technological advances or fashion trends expected only gradually

4.4.2 Equipment hire or buy

The types of equipment, which may be hired in preference to buying, include larger items of cleaning equipment, particularly those used periodically, high cost laundry equipment and office equipment.

4.4.3 Linen hire or buy

Whether linen is hired or bought will be closely linked with the laundry process planned. A decision to buy linen, rather than hiring it, cannot be made independently of the choice of laundry and repair system, nor of the type of linen service overall which is to be established. The main types of linen systems have been considered in chapter 2, and a comparison of the main characteristics of these systems is given in Appendix 4. Figure 4.7 shows some of the advantages and disadvantages of hiring or buying linen.

A decision to hire or buy linen stock must be considered closely with respect to the servicing of that stock.

4.4.4 Furniture hire or buy

Furniture hire is becoming increasingly popular, particularly:
1 Where replacement cycles are planned to be short
2 Where circumstances, eg conferences, exhibitions make abnormal demands
3 Where labour problems, associated with maintenance are experienced, and the hiring firm can offer a maintenance contract, along with the furniture.

4.4.5 Services

The Accommodation Manager has open to him a very wide range of contract services. These include:

Carpet shampooing
Cleaning services

Laundering
Management services

Decorating	Night security
Degreasing	Pest control
Drain cleaning	Telephone cleaning
Dust control mats and mops hire	Uniform hire
Equipment maintenance	Upholstery cleaning
Floral arrangements	Wall washing
Hand towel provision and laundering	Window cleaning

Recent years have seen a growth in contract services. Occasions where contract labour may be appropriate are as follows:

1 When staff availability of direct labour is low; perhaps through sickness, holidays or vacancies
2 When infrequent tasks occur which would require expensive equipment and/or expertise in the completion of that task. (These might in any case be outside the job description of existing staff.)
3 When a reduction of administrative work is sought to enable an organisation to concentrate on its primary function.
4 When economic or accounting advantages can be achieved.

In any of these circumstances, contract labour may well be preferable to direct labour. Contract labour can, nevertheless, have its drawbacks. Problems may be encountered with contract staff due to difficulties of their split loyalties to their employer on the one hand, and the establishment on the other. Difficulties may be encountered with a low standard of work which arouses complaint from other building users. This in turn necessitates management communicating the problem to the contractor. This all takes time. Other difficulties may be the inflexibility of the service, concern over safety

Figure 4.7 *The advantages and disadvantages associated with purchase or hiring of linen stock*

	Advantages	Disadvantages
Purchase	Freedom of selection of fibre, fabric, colour, quality, cost, manufacturer. Capital asset	Require storage space High capital outlay Strict control required Repair costs Replacement costs
Linen hire	No heavy initial cost No replacement costs No repairs No staff Short term loan arrangements Charges may be no greater than depreciation and laundering costs No repair or replacement costs Easier budgeting	Limited choice of style, quality and colour Still have to purchase bedding and soft furnishings Constant control Pay for excessive loss and damage Subject to contract price rising Pay monthly charge even if less numbers May be delivery problems

standards, confidentiality of staff, security lapses. Employment contract labour is not justified when the cost of monitoring contract is excessive.

One means by which the risk of many of the above difficulties can be minimised is by the preparation of a tight specification before tenders are invited.

The specification should include:

1 A definition of terms and exact details of the work to be done, eg in window cleaning, pest control and similar contracts which might be drawn up to include the entire building, it must be made clear, whether ancillary buildings, or remote parts, are to be included in the contract
2 It may be appropriate to include details of frequencies of service, eg equipment maintenance, in other cases this may be left to the contractor's discretion, eg visits to deal with pest infestation will largely be determined by the methods of eradication being applied. Frequency of visits must, therefore, be left to the discretion of the contractor.
3 Provision of supervisors may be a requirement laid down in a specification, also details of how the contract is to be monitored, what the channels of communication will be, eg in case of complaints or for regular briefing meetings
4 Details of provisions which will be made by the client, eg stores areas, changing facilities, sluices, restaurant facilities, and those which must be made by the contractor, eg uniforms, security, waste, disposal, access equipment, must be identified.
5 Any restrictions imposed on the contractor must be made clear, eg working hours, restrictions on chemicals used, staffing restrictions, such as minimum wage rates, union membership, building access restrictions, requirements in emergencies and to meet unusual circumstances
6 Insurance requirements of contractors must be covered in the specification
7 Duration of the contract, breach of contract and termination arrangements must be covered.

4.5 SOURCES OF SUPPLY FOR PURCHASE

There are various sources of supply for purchases open to the Accommodation Manager, and the choice of supplier should be the result of a conscious decision process. Although a low quote, particularly in the case of a one-off item, may well be the chief criteria, it is not the only one. Sources of supply include retail, cash and carry, wholesale purchasing organisations, central purchasing departments, and manufacturers. A comparison of these is shown in figure 4.8.

4.5.1 Retail

This includes shops and supermarkets and is really only a suitable

Figure 4.8 A comparison of the sources of supply

	Retail	Cash and Carry	Wholesale	Central Purchasing	Manufacturers
Choice of goods	Wide	Wide	Selected choice (though special orders may be arranged)	Selected choice (as Wholesale)	Widest choice
Suitability of goods for large scale use	Usually unsuitable	Often unsuitable	Suitable	Suitable	Suitable
Relative cost of supplies	Expensive	Less than retail	Less than retail or cash and carry	Usually relatively cheap	Much depends on quantity
Quantities available	Small	Large	Large	Large	Large
Amount of notice needed	None (except for special orders)	None (except for special orders)	Order must be placed	Order must be placed. Delivery may be quicker than wholesale	Order must be placed
Delivery	Rare	None	Normally made	Normally made	Normally made
Customer service, eg training	None	None	Possibly some and manufacturers may be contacted	May be some and manufacturers often involved	Usually offered

source of supply to solve unforeseen situations or, in an hotel situation, for purchasing goods on behalf of guests. Stocks available are limited in quantity, unsuitable for large scale use and expensive. Usually cash must be paid, and money from petty cash is used.

3.5.2 Cash and carry

The main advantages that cash and carry suppliers have over retailers are that goods are available in large quantities and generally cheaper. Generally the stocks are designed for the domestic market rather than for large scale use, and usually, they do not offer the same convenience as the retailer due to their, frequently, more remote locations.

4.5.3 Wholesale

This usually involves buying from some agency warehouse, or purchasing body, which stock a range of products suitable for large scale use. The supplier may specialise in the products of just one or two manufacturers, or may have a more varied range. Often deliveries can be made more quickly than by placing an order with a manufacturer whose factory or base is some distance away. In addition, the purchasing organisation buys in bulk, and may pass on some of the discount achieved to customers. This may be an advantage, particularly to customers placing smaller orders involving, for example, a standard pack being split.

4.5.4 Purchasing departments

Many large organisations, such as the example of the N H S already discussed, set up their own central purchasing departments which, to the individual units of the organisation, act almost as a wholesaler, but with further advantages:

1 The central purchasing departments are not profit orientated. They provide a service within their organisation and therefore users may gain the advantages of lower prices
2 Products stocked are specifically selected for use in that particular type of organisation.

Restrictions may be placed by the central purchasing departments in that individual managers loose freedom in the choice of products. They may be required to buy only those products named on the department's supplies lists. In such instances savings are probably being made through standardisation but, to an individual manager, the restrictions may in fact be costly. The manager may otherwise have the opportunity to take advantage of a special offer or a superior product.

4.5.5 Manufacturers

Buying products direct from manufacturers can give the manager the maximum freedom of choice in one sense, the restrictions, however, are on the manager of the small organisation. Without sufficient purchasing power, list prices on some items can be relatively expensive, and the manager may not be able to buy much in bulk if storage space is limited, and, in any case, this does not make for good stores control or cash flow. Conversely, a very large organisation may be purchasing by specification direct from the manufacturers. In this case, the revenue involved makes it worthwhile for manufacturers to produce a product specifically for one customer.

Other advantages of buying direct from the manufacturers are that customer services of various forms may be available and, if goods are faulty, there is a direct line between user and manufacturer.

In most instances, more than one source of supply may be used. In some organisations, policy decision may limit the choice of supplier. To achieve effective purchasing, the buyer must develop an effective stores, ordering, and control procedure. A balance must be achieved with respect to quantities purchased, bearing in mind the administrative costs of placing an order, storage costs and quantity discounts.

4.6 HOW TO BUY

In making purchases for large organisations, there are various methods which may be adopted, and usually more than one will be employed by an organisation depending on:

The products or services
The expected frequency of subsequent orders (if any)
Policy decisions.

Frequently, there are at least two levels of buying goods and supplies:

1 Minor items (consumables)
2 More expensive items (capital purchases)

In addition to this, as has already been seen, the Accommodation Manager is likely to be purchasing services. These may be restricted to window cleaning or equipment maintenance, or may run to complete cleaning systems.

Minor items
The actual cut off price, which would determine whether an item was minor or capital expense, varies considerably from one establishment to another. In one establishment, the figure could be £20, while, in another, £500. Products within this category – at whatever the price range is set – can usually be bought on the open market, ie from whomever the manager decides. If the goods are ones which will be frequently replenished, ie stock items, a contract may be drawn up with a supplier and a more favourable price negotiated.

In the case of minor items, the manager having gone through the selection process, decides on the supplier and purchases are made appropriately.

Capital items

More expensive items, ie items costing more than the upper limit for minor items, could be bought on the open market, or on contract but, usually, the manager will be required to justify his or her choice of supplier by submitting, with the requisition, more than one quotation (usually 3). In some cases, specific approval for the purchase may be needed, possibly when the budget proposals were submitted in the previous financial year.

4.6.1 Buying supplies by contract

When products are to be reordered frequently, and substantial amounts bought in a year, often more favourable prices can be arranged if a contract is drawn up between supplier and buyer. The buyer agrees to purchase certain quantities over a period of time, and the supplier agrees a fixed price for that period. Contracts might be drawn up by an individual unit, eg an hotel; a number of units or a central purchasing organisation. When a contract has been drawn up at a level higher than unit level, individual managers may or may not have that individual product imposed on them. To maintain the purchasing power of their contract negotiating body, officers will be encouraged to a greater or lesser degree to buy from the contract list.

Services

The purchasing of services involves the drawing up of a contract which, when signed by both parties, is legally binding. The stages involved, prior to the signing of a contract are as follows:

1 The Accommodation Manager must prepare a specification of his or her exact requirements, any constraints that will be imposed and the exact duration of the contract
2 Tendering will be invited. Tendering may be open, ie advertisements will be posted locally, nationally, and even internationally, or 'selective', where a few firms are directly contacted and invited to tender
3 Interested contractors will be provided with specifications and any other relevant information, for example a floor plan may be issued for cleaning and pest control contracts. Opportunities to visit the site may be provided. They will also be given a final time and date for the submission of their tenders
4 As tenders are submitted, they must be kept by the client in tight security until the deadline. In many instances they will remain unopened until that time. If competitors were aware of other quotes, undercutting may occur, as a result of which low quality standards may be seen at a later date.
5 At the deadline, usually a team will be involved in viewing the tenders and if specification has been sufficiently tight, the client would automatically select the lowest quote. In some instances, it may be possible to compare the contractors' quotes with past contracts, or costs when the work has been done by direct labour. It is vital, when comparing quotes, that the selection team is

confident that like is compared with like, eg in cleaning contracts, actual proposed methods of cleaning may vary, as may proposed frequencies of cleaning. Valid comparison is only possible with a tight specification.

6 An interview may then ensue with the contractor(s), offering the most favourable tender(s), before a final decision is made, and the contract drawn up between the winning contractor and the client.

Once a contract has been made, the Accommodation Manager will still need to monitor the work being carried out. It may not be necessary to consider too much how the work is being done. This might, in any case, be outside the manager's field of expertise, eg selection of chemicals for pest control. He or she will, however, need to monitor standards. Waiting for complaints or accidents is not sufficient. Whilst the Accommodation Manager may have passed many routine and mundane matters on to a contractor, standards must still be monitored.

Monitoring a contract will involve physically viewing standards – and, perhaps, work in progress – on a regular basis and receiving regular reports from the contractor. It should not involve supervision of the work.

4.7 STORES CONTROL

The aim of any stores control system must surely be to have, at a minimal cost, goods available in sufficient quantities, and of the correct type and quality for staff to carry out their work. As has already been discussed, equipment, materials and linen do not represent a very large portion of the housekeeping budget. Labour is the costly element and if labour is available and unable to work, due to failures in the stores control system, much money will be wasted. Other reasons for developing an efficient and effective stores control system are as follows:

1 Shortages, or poor stock rotation or storage will reduce standards. Linen shortages may mean reduced room availability and, therefore, directly reduce revenue

2 When supplies are lacking, items may need to be borrowed from other sections (or staff may even bring items from home). This may well constitute a safety risk, eg borrowing inferior equipment, and, in a hospital, could constitute an infection risk

3 Excessive stock may constitute a safety risk, a fire risk, be costly in storage space (through lost opportunity costs), be time consuming to operate and reduce cash flow

4 'Losses' may occur which must be identified, causes established, and controls implemented

5 Good store control is necessary to implement Health and Safety procedures, eg maintenance of equipment

6 Monitoring of use and product evaluation is better achieved

7 Budgetary control is facilitated
8 Standardisation of quality is facilitated.

4.7.1 Storage requirements

Some items should not be kept in stock at all for safety reasons, eg plastic floor seals, or solvent based detergent wax removers, which may well constitute a fire hazard. Their use is infrequent, and purchases can be made for a specific operation. Other items should not be stocked in any quantity due to their limited shelf life, eg some chemical disinfectants.

Many products need to be kept in stock if an efficient accommodation service is to operate. The levels of this stock, needed to provide an efficient system, will vary with circumstances from one establishment to another, eg reliability and proximity of supplier, degree of variance in work patterns, and levels of staff, eg are annual spring cleaning programmes operated, or a more regular process of periodic maintenance?

The stores area required will depend on the overall stores system of the organisation, eg is a central store operated, or does each department have its own stock room? Frequently, a combination of systems operate. The advantage of having different levels of stores areas within the establishment is that goods are available at close proximity to the point of use. Operatives do not waste time in requisitioning or collecting stores when, perhaps, the storekeeper is not available, or perhaps they themselves would be involved in some productive work which must be interrupted. Conversely, too many peripheral stores areas will increase administrative and control procedures in other ways, and the stores themselves may be utilising potentially valuable revenue earning space. A balance between too many and too few stores areas must be reached which is economical with respect to space and man hours.

In general terms, the requirements of domestic stores are similar to those of most other stores areas. They include:

1 A good situation, which facilitates the delivery of goods throughout the establishment. Ground floor sites, with close proximity to service lifts are common
2 Stores need to be easily and effectively secured
3 Space and fittings need to be adequate to enable safe storage, ease of stock taking and effective stock rotation, eg island shelves
4 Environmental conditions must be suitable to work in, (though, usually, for only short periods), and also for storage, eg controlled heating, adequate lighting (though not necessarily daylight), suitable ventilation
5 Surfaces need to be easy to maintain to appropriate hygiene and safety standards
6 Clerical equipment will be needed though the types will vary
7 Stores areas are particularly vulnerable to fire outbreaks, and must meet the appropriate fire precaution standards

8 Hand washing and drying facilities will probably be required.

Other requirements of domestic stores areas vary with the different commodities stocked, eg cleaning and maintenance stores, linen stores, furniture and equipment stores.

4.7.1.1 Requirements peculiar to cleaning and maintaining stores

1 Non porous surfaces to facilitate cleaning of spillages
2 Some chemical disinfectants may need to be protected from sunlight, eg closed cupboard
3 No excessive temperature variations as this will cause deterioration of some chemical products, eg water based emulsion polishes
4 Electric sockets needed for some equipment
5 Sink, slop sink or sluice
6 Hanging space for storing vacuum hoses and other items
7 Drying space for cleaning cloths, floor pads, etc may be required
8 Dispensing aids may be needed for issuing chemicals, eg detergent proportioners or drum stands
9 Flame proof cabinets for flammable and highly flammable materials, eg chewing gum remover, solvent based polishes, as directed by the Fire Authority
10 Slatted shelves to aid air circulation around certain items, eg impregnated mops and mats to minimise the chance of spontaneous combustion.

4.7.1.2 Requirements peculiar to linen stores

1 Slatted shelves to assist air circulation around linen and prevent dampness
2 Strict pest control to prevent damage by moths and rodents.
3 Protection from sunlight for some items, eg linen
4 Use of colours and textures in the area, such that they are easy to maintain in a hygienic condition but do not cause excessive glare for storekeepers working in the area. (Glare is a fairly common problem in linen stores, where much of the stock is white and surfaces are chosen for hygiene and hygienic appearance)
5 Sewing and fitting rooms may adjoin the linen stores
6 Separate areas for clean and dirty linen may be required, depending on the linen system
7 Large working surfaces for sorting and folding, etc.

4.7.1.3 Requirements peculiar to furniture and equipment stores

Furniture stored in these areas will be items not in constant use, eg in hotels, cots may be stored to meet customers requests, seminar tables may be stored for temporary conversion of bedrooms to meeting rooms, banqueting tables and chairs may be stored. Equipment stored may be just items used infrequently, eg carpet shampooing machines, or a central room may be used for all equipment storage. (This greatly assists planned servicing of that equipment, also security can be tighter, though, the disadvantage is that equipment is less accessible to staff.)

Furniture stores, in particular, rarely receive the same frequency or amount of use as the previous stores areas. Apart from periodic cleaning and maintenance, the working involvement of staff in these areas is usually restricted to the collection and return of stocks. Conditions, therefore, do not have to provide a working environment. Such stores must not be subjected to excessive temperatures; they must be dry and ventilated, clean and well protected from fire outbreaks and damage from pests.

4.7.2 Stores administration

To enable good stores administration, the physical requirements of the storage area must be satisfactory and, in addition, systems for the monitoring and control of incoming and outgoing stock must be devised. The first decision to be taken is to determine which items should be stocked. This information can be collated from work procedures. The next decision is with regard to quantities to be kept. This decision is much more difficult to determine, and is reached on the basis of:

(a) Quantities required for one operator
(b) Frequencies of operation
(c) Degree of variance between peaks and troughs in the work load
(d) Minimum quantities supplied at one time
(e) Reliability of supply
(f) Storage space available
(g) Issuing system
(h) Shelf life of product and any associated storage problems
(i) Economics related to bulk purchase.

When the stock and stock levels have been determined, systems must be developed for:

1 Ordering of stock
2 Filing correspondence
3 Receiving, checking and receipting deliveries
4 Authorising payment
5 Recording stock levels
6 Recording batch numbers, model numbers or other identifying data
7 Checking and monitoring requirements
8 Recording and monitoring issues
9 Recording usages, defective stock and any product evaluation data
10 Recording details of stock returned to supplies
11 Recording details of replacements
12 Stock taking.

Figure 4.9 *Flow chart showing a stores cycle*

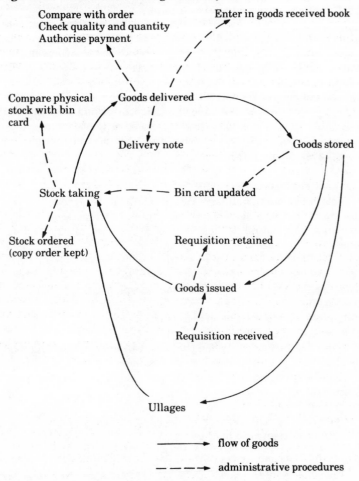

A flow chart of the stores cycle is shown in figure 4.9, together with the clerical and administrative implications.

As can be seen from the chart, official orders are frequently sent by an administrative section, rather than from the stores themselves. These orders are, however, initiated by stores and details of goods, supplier, quantities required, and any other relevant information is shown on the requisition. When goods are delivered, they are accompanied by a delivery note, a signed copy of which is generally returned to the supplier, so initiating their invoice; another copy is sent to the finance department, as an authority to pay. Ideally, goods should be checked for quality and quantity when they are delivered, so that any defective items can be returned at once, and discrepancies in quantities can also be dealt with.

Financial dealings are not often the responsibility of the Accommodation Manager, stores invoices are often sent to administrative sections and payment dealt with by a financial department. A point worth noting here is that the Accommodation Manager, as budget holder, must be kept informed of expenses incurred. In some cases, invoice totals will vary from the expected value, eg annual price increases, periodic reduction price offers, discounts for quantity.

When goods have been accepted by the storekeeper, the details are entered in the goods received book, and the stock is stored appropriately. Stores areas are of particular fire risk, due to their infrequent occupancy. Goods must not be stored against hot pipes, against light fittings and so on. They must be stored in a manner which will facilitate retrieval for use, and also enable stock rotation.

Bin cards are frequently used as a means of keeping a quick check on current stock. A sample bin card is shown in figure 4.10.

In domestic cleaning stores, larger items of equipment, eg suction cleaners, carpet shampooers, laundry equipment, must be controlled. Information regarding these items cannot be effectively recorded on bin cards and equipment cards may be used (see figure 4.11). By the use of equipment cards, one particular vacuum cleaner may be identified from an identical one, and useful information gathered on breakdown frequencies, spare parts required, etc. Such information is vital in the process of equipment evaluation when cost efficiencies can be measured and depreciation of future items assessed.

When periodic stock taking takes place, quantities counted on shelves should, in all cases, equal balances on the bin cards. Any discrepancies should be investigated.

4.7.3 Issue systems
A variety of issue systems and their advantages and disadvantages are shown in figure 4.12. Often a combination of systems is used, depending on the goods and the situation. The main aims of distribution systems are to facilitate stores control by:

1 Ensuring sufficient goods are available for operatives at all times, and to minimise time wasted, due to insufficient supplies, broken equipment or any other reason
2 Minimising labour time spent on stores matters
3 Recovery and control of the use of stores such that deviations from the norm are quickly identified, and can be investigated. Such investigation might identify training needs, particular operational problems, wastage or pilfering
4 Provision of information for budgetary control
5 Provision of information on product evaluation.

Stores control can be a complex matter, but an efficient system is crucial to the effective running of the department. Good stores control can have a significant effect on wasted man-hours. It must be remembered that the system of stock control must, itself, be cost

Figure 4.10 A bin card

Item: Water based emulsion polish
Product and manufacturer: 'Floor brite' by Sel
Units: 5 litre
Minimum stock: 2 × 5 litre
Maximum stock 12 × 5 litre

Date	In	Out	Balance

Figure 4.11 Equipment card

Machine: .... Model: .... Serial No: ....

Manufacturer: ....

Date purchased: .... Purchase price: ....

Date commissioned: .... Date condemned: ....

Accessories: .... Price: ....
....

Usual location of machine: ....

Date	Service details	Date	Service details

Figure 4.12 Methods of stores issue

System	Operation	Advantages	Disadvantages	Comments
New for old (or counter exchange)	The user must return the old mop head, empty bottle, etc before a replacement is given	Tight control is achieved over usage	Time consuming for each member of staff to go to the store room. Not a hygienic method collecting in dirty items	Need specified time for stores collections
Topping up/imprest	Each domestic assistant's store has a predetermined stock level. Items are topped up to this level on a weekly basis by a supervisory grade	One person can be made responsible for stores distributions. Excessive variations in usage can be identified and investigated. There should always be sufficient stores. There is some flexibility	Setting the level can be difficult to allow for justifiable variations in use	Commonly used for linen as well as cleaning stores
Set amount	A set quantity of stores is determined for each cleaner's store and that amount is issued weekly	Stores distribution is simplified and record keeping minimised	Excesses can build up and encourage mis-use. Alternatively, if the level is set too low problems will occur	Periodic stock checks in each point of issue are necessary. A variation is to collect leftovers from a previous delivery
Requisition	Users complete requisition slips for goods required. The requisitions are recorded by the storekeeper	Usage is recorded and excess easily identified. Some restriction in use though to some extent staff set own limit	Time consuming. Level not controlled normally by supervisory grade. Generally more paperwork	Need specified time for requisition to be handed in and items collected

effective. Control must be directed towards cost efficiency. For example, a system which causes staff to reduce neutral detergent needs by 10%, may save tens of pounds over a year, but, to achieve this, stores administrative costs could be much higher, and goodwill might be lost. Control must be kept in perspective, and labour costs, incurred by stores control, must be accounted.

One means of reducing labour costs in stores control, and a system, which can also be highly efficient, is by the use of a computer. With a basic input and output unit (ie keyboard input and visual display unit) installed in the stores area, orders, bin cards, product specifications, goods received, goods issued, usages, can all be recorded on the computer. A computer can readily be programmed to keep current balances.

Further reading

BRITISH STANDARDS

    5415 (1985 and 1986) Safety of electrical motor operated industrial and commercial cleaning appliances

    3762 (1986) Analysis of formulated detergents

    808 Chick Martin Test

BROOKS, N S, *Hospital Safety a British Point of View*, Professional Housekeeper Journal October 1979

GULLEN, H V and RHODES, G E, *Management in the Hotel and Catering Industry* Batsford 1983

JONES, DR W T, *The Health and Safety at Work Act: A Practical Point of View*, Graham and Trotham

KASAVANA, M L, *Hotel Information Systems* CBI Publishing Company 1978

TUCKER, C and SCHNEIDER, M, *Professional Housekeeper* Cahners 1975

WALKER, D and CROSS, N, *The Man-Made World* Open University Press 1976

5

The Client and the Front Office

Terms, such as *Front Office* and *Reception* have traditionally been related only to the hotel industry. This is probably because a well defined Front Office organisational structure exists in an hotel covering the whole range of customer activities and transactions, from the initial request for accommodation, to the actual reception of the customer on arrival, to guest accounting and departure. Also, a physical reception area exists which is the focal point of contact for the in-house customer.

The traditional front office functions associated with hotel operations do operate in other types of organisations such as hospitals or halls of residence although they may be difficult to identify; are often fragmented, and may only occur on a very small scale, such as the reception in a factory or office block. The front office system is therefore not purely the domain of the hotel sector.

The term *Front Office* is used throughout this chapter in preference to Reception as the latter is only one function of the total front office operations. A number of excellent front office textbooks are available which describe the variety of accepted front office procedures (see end of chapter for titles) and it is assumed that the reader is familiar with such.

5.1 THE GUEST CYCLE CONCEPT

The activities of the front office, indeed of the total operation, revolve around the activities of the client, whether hotel guest, hospital patient or sports hall user. (As the client in the hotel sector is referred to as the 'guest' this term will be used throughout this chapter).

It is possible to plot the sequence of the guests' activities by using a flow chart, commencing from when the potential guest first makes contact with the establishment until the final transaction is completed. This concept is referred to as the *Guest Cycle*, which M L KASAVANA[2] suggests is 'an effective means for enabling management to better monitor, chart and control the guests' transactions'.

It means that the activities which must be conducted by the front office at the time appropriate to the guests' activities and the flow of information can be readily determined.

In simple terms, the guest cycle activities tend to fall into three sections, with a number of activities occurring in each section.

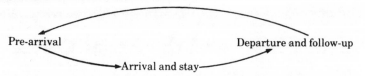

Figure 5.1 is a more detailed flow chart showing the guest activities which occur in each section.

Although the guest cycle outlined refers to a typical hotel flow chart, the concept can be amended and used in other types of establishments, such as hospitals, particularly private hospitals; halls of residence or conference centres.

Figure 5.1 *Flow chart to show guest activities*

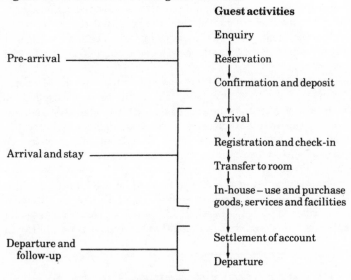

5.2 FUNCTIONS OF THE FRONT OFFICE

The front office activities to be undertaken to satisfy the guests' requirements have been highlighted in figure 5.2. These front office activities tend to be grouped under the following headings which so define the basic functions of the front office system:

Advance reservations
Reception and check-in
Accounting (and check-out)
Sales and selling
Information and communication services
Security

These functions may be carried out in other types of operations but often by personnel in unrelated departments, which are controlled by different managers. Most of these activities are carried out in a hall of

Figure 5.2 *Flow chart to show the front office activities which must coincide with the guest activities*

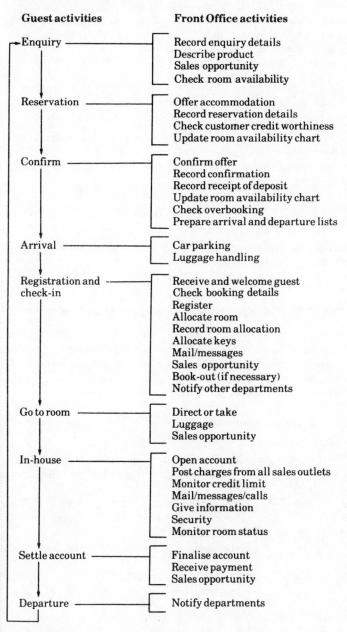

Guest activities	Front Office activities
Enquiry	Record enquiry details Describe product Sales opportunity Check room availability
Reservation	Offer accommodation Record reservation details Check customer credit worthiness Update room availability chart
Confirm	Confirm offer Record confirmation Record receipt of deposit Update room availability chart Check overbooking Prepare arrival and departure lists
Arrival	Car parking Luggage handling
Registration and check-in	Receive and welcome guest Check booking details Register Allocate room Record room allocation Allocate keys Mail/messages Sales opportunity Book-out (if necessary) Notify other departments
Go to room	Direct or take Luggage Sales opportunity
In-house	Open account Post charges from all sales outlets Monitor credit limit Mail/messages/calls Give information Security Monitor room status
Settle account	Finalise account Receive payment Sales opportunity
Departure	Notify departments

residence, a private hospital as well as a National Health Service hospital.

In a National Health Service hospital a patient:
— has to be Registered, whether to out-patients, admissions or the accident and emergency unit
— has to be allocated a bed, which involves
    — making enquiries
    — checking documentation
    — allocating a specific bed to a specific patient
    — recording bed status
    — controlling bed occupancy
— has to have a 'file' opened, recording details of services (treatment, etc, received)
— has to receive services and facilities besides physical accommodation and medical treatments
— will incur costs which have to be monitored and paid by someone, whether the patient (private patient in an NHS hospital or patient in a private hospital) or the DOH.

Nursing and medical personnel who are resident have to request accommodation which has to be allocated; register on arrival; receive keys; be shown the way; and pay their account on a regular basis.

5.3 DESIGN OF FRONT OFFICE ACTIVITIES

The intention here is to pose a series of questions, under the function headings, which require consideration when either setting up a front office system or evaluating or redesigning an existing system. The sales function will be discussed in detail in section 5.5. The following questions will therefore be of value:

5.3.1 Advance reservations

Enquiries
How do the general public communicate with the establishment? – by letter; telephone; telex; computer terminal; personally or through an intermediary?
What characteristics does each means of communication possess which has to be accommodated by the system? (See figure 5.3)
What does the enquirer wish to know?
Who enquires – an individual; a personal secretary; conference organiser?
How long in advance will enquiries be made?
What data must be recorded and how?

Room availability
Which means of checking room availability is most appropriate? – hotel diary; traditional reservation chart; density chart; room rack/whitney system; computerised system. (See figure 5.4)

Does room availability need to be summarised at regular intervals to aid speed and efficiency and highlight heavy demand periods?

How will the room availability system be kept up-to-date and monitored?

Is an overbooking facility required in the room availability system adopted?

Reservations

Will the product require selling to the enquirer? – if so, will the personnel involved need to possess product knowledge and be trained in salesmanship?

Will special needs be ascertained, eg disabled facilities required; baby minding, etc?

What reservation details will be recorded and how?

Will accommodation be reserved by room number or room type?

If the potential customer does not accept the offer are reservation records still to be retained?

Will it be necessary to analyse why enquiries are not converted to sales?

If accommodation of the type requested is not available will an alternative offer be made, will a waiting list be opened or will overbooking occur?

Must an overbooking policy be adopted?

Is a time release for accommodation to operate, to create the opportunity to achieve full potential? If so how is the potential guest to be informed?

Will the potential customer wish to guarantee a room reservation by credit card?

Credit worthiness

How is customer credit worthiness to be evaluated? Is it necessary to know how the potential account will be paid? – cash, credit card, cheque, direct debit (eg switch), euro-cheque, travellers cheque, foreign currency, charge account.

Is it necessary to know who will pay? – the individual; a company, or will it be a complimentary room?

Will a blacklist be available? a local hotel association, police, credit card company?

Is a guest history index required to ascertain if a guest has previously stayed and been able to pay?

Filing

How will reservation data be filed? – alphabetically under the date of arrival?

Confirmation and deposits

Is written confirmation of the reservation transaction required? – if so, by whom (hotel in the case of a telephone request; the customer in other cases), and how is it to be given – by standard letter/card; computer print-out; individually typed letter; carbon copy of the

Figure 5.3 *The advantages and disadvantages of the various*

Communication means	Advantages	Disadvantag
Telephone	Allows guest to find out very quickly if accommodation is available	Difficult to sell accommodatic the telephone remember tha enquiry is a p sale
Telex	Combines speed with permanence of a letter. Written message is received through the teleprinter. Instant reply can be sent. Communicate easily with international companies – overcoming expense and time difference. Message can be received even if no one on duty	Expensive to in Space required
Correspondence	Often contains special requests More enforceable as a contract particularly with reference to 'no-shows'.	If not answered may lose the s
Telegram	PROVIDES A WRITTEN MESSAGE	Expensive
Fax	Speed Photocopy of message received Speedy reply possible	Cost and siting Message scraml May have to rej times

mmunication used by the potential guest when making an enquiry

irements of system	Usage
llow check on room availability at a ce ardised pre-printed enquiry card or hone call sheet to record all information. must confirm in writing (Credit Card ber may be accepted by some hotels on a antee of accommodation). se carefully the hours of manning the rvation office e 'hot-line' telephone number for regular omers	Most common – particularly where there is a short lead time
se need carefully – especially if fair ortion of business from industry and merce and international business. and space for teleprinter. tape for international communication. v-up 'leads', ie names and addresses given lex in an endeavour to increase sales	Most large hotels particularly catering for businessmen and conferences
to be stamped and initialled on opening by or secretary. hrough internal mail to Advance rvations for processing. re: details and code main requirements in eviated form at top of letter with native or negative instructions for typist. wer within 24 hours. er alternative means of replying, eg vidually typed letter, standard pro-forma, on copy of reservation form. 'leads' from letter head etc to gain further ness.	Where the lead time is much longer, eg resort hotels
ternational Hotel Telegraph Code	Declined greatly
se need and space	Increasing As for Telex (see above)

Continued . . .

...*Continued*

Personal or chance	Unique opportunity to sell the hotel and the facilities	Inherently suspec short lead time Little information the potential gue Unable to check customer's credi worthiness (unle credit card numl registration).
Computer terminal	Speedy service Often gives alternative room, types or room numbers within price range	

reservation form? How expensive will the confirmation process be?
Is a deposit required? – if so, how much? What accounting record has to be completed?
Is the room availability system and the reservation record to be up-dated on receipt of confirmation or deposit?
How is a cancellation to be dealt with?
When is the reservation to be retrieved? – a month in advance; a week in advance; a day in advance or all three?
Is an arrival and departure list required? – if so, in what format, by whom, and are confirmed and unconfirmed reservations to be segregated?
Will an occupancy forecast be required? – if so, by whom, what period in advance?

The advance reservations system devised must incorporate the following features. It must provide:
— Flexibility to cope with the various means of communication
— The facility to check room availability
— The facility to check customer credit worthiness
— The facility to make an offer and form a contract
— The facility to confirm the reservation request.

5.3.2 Reception, registration and check-in

Arrival

When will the guest generally arrive? – will there be a peak period?
By what mode of transport will the guest arrive? – car; plane/train and/or taxi
If the guest arrives by car, where will it be parked?

fer accommodation under The Innkeepers
ty Act.
one of the following in advance to ensure
t of payment; a deposit; full payment of
st night's accommodation in advance; an
at of the credit card.
e guest the room types during a quiet

colour coded identity card to ensure cash
nly.
'credit limit'

ions on computerisation

Commercial, motor hotels

Computerised links with
other hotels in the
chain, centralised
Reservations Office,
Referral systems

— in the hotel car park? or the local authority park?
— how will the guest know where to park?
— will parking be free or is a charge to be made?
— is the car park well signposted?
— how many cars can be parked?
— will a discount arrangement be negotiated with the local authority?
— will a temporary parking area be allocated for registration and
   unloading?
— will a section be allocated for disabled guests?
Is the guest likely to arrive by train or plane? If so,
— is a courtesy car/minibus service required?
— will it be a free service?
— how will the guest know about this service?
Is a Commissionaire (Linkman) required to receive, meet, greet
   guests, hail taxis, etc?
Is a baggage handling system required? – if so
— which personnel are required and how many?
— will a separate luggage entrance and storage area be required –
   where, how large?
Will the courtesy car driver and the Linkman require training in social
   skills?

Reception
Is the reception easy to find, well signposted and welcoming?
How many guests will arrive at the reception desk in the same time
   period?
Is a traditional reception desk/area required? (some new hotels expect
   the front office personnel to sit down with the arriving guests in the

Figure 5.4 *Comparative details of the alternative systems, whi*

System	Advantages
The hotel diary	Entries in date order
Room rack and Whitney system	Flexible system according to requi Colour coding introduced to denot or room status or room type Remove slip for cancellation
Traditional reservation chart	Separate chart for each month Suitable if great variation in room Allocate specific room no. on reser
Density chart and density/reservation chart	Speedy Suitable for short lead time, short
Computerised system	Alternative formats, eg by date, by type, room price, room number Visual display or print-out if requi

NB None of these systems will work effectively if not kept up to date

front hall and complete the registration process)

Who will be the first person the guest has contact with? – courtesy car driver. Linkman or receptionist?

How much emphasis is to be placed on the importance of the reception/registration process and the establishment of a relationship between front office personnel and the guest?

Registration

What registration details are to be recorded and in what format – card; book, computer print-out? How much data is to be completed by the guest and how much by personnel?

Is any marketing/administrative data to be ascertained and recorded *used for checking and recording room availability*

isadvantages	Possible usage
ntries per page not in alphabetical or room order ay need to physically rule each page 'oss out cancellations if entered in ink	Small establishments
kes up space especially if used for advance reservations ifficult to insert rack slips if too many racks	Medium to large establishments
arge sheet or several sheets per month if large hotel essy if have to rub out, eg cancellations mited room for information ay be difficult to trace one room across whole month quickly ifficult to trace availability of one room across two months ace required	Medium to large establishments – especially those with great variations in room types and tariffs
ust include an overbooking facility into system ight difficulty remembering to record and cancel over several days o guest information included ust file density charts in date order peg board used, pegs may be knocked out	Medium hotels with few room types where one room is much like another
ay be difficult to read on VDU ay be difficult to trace one room over several days ay not have an effective over-booking check	Medium to large hotels

at this time?

How long has the data to be retained after the guest has left, where and in what format?

Room allocation

When will room allocation take place? – on reservation, the day before arrival, the day of arrival, at arrival?

How will rooms be allocated?

— will a priority order of rooms be required eg rooms with views, larger or upgrade rooms before smaller or older rooms, rooms with disadvantages allocated last.

— will a priority order of guests be required, eg confirmed before unconfirmed; long stay before short stay; VIPs and regulars before others; guaranteed reservations before others; company accounts and sources of potential future business before individuals.

Will guests with special needs eg the disabled, single women/business women require special specific rooms?

How will room allocation be recorded? when, what data, in what format? – room letting sheet/bed sheet; whitney system; traditional reservation chart; computerised system?

Who will require this data? – housekeeping, telephonist, reception personnel?

Room status

How will room status be monitored to ensure that the state of every room, whether let (and by whom), vacant and ready for reletting; vacant and dirty; out of order, is known at any one time, eg whitney system, electronic system or computerised system.

Key allocation

Who will issue room keys? – where will they be stored (out of guests sight for security); how will they be stored? – pigeon holes, key board.

Will a key card for identity purposes be required? – if so will it be colour-coded to denote guest status eg conference delegate, VIP, chance customers (chance sales only)

How will mail and messages awaiting guest arrival be stored and distributed?

Room direction

How will the guest be directed to the allocated room?

Will the guest be directed? – if so,

— how will the receptionist know where every room is situated?

— will the room numbers be well sign-posted?

— are the signs legible?

— are the room numbers logically allocated?

Will the guest be taken? – if so,

— by whom?

— what procedure will be followed on arrival at the room?

Luggage handling

Will a luggage handling service be offered? – if so who will do it? Will an identity system be required; how will mass luggage be dealt with?

Booking-out

If over booking occurs how will it be dealt with?

— who will be booked-out? Will the same priority list apply as for room allocation

— where will alternative accommodation be reserved – an hotel in the same group, the nearest hotel, a similar class of hotel?

— how will the guest get there? – will a map be provided, a taxi arranged, by courtesy car?

— who will book out? – the duty manager, front of house manager, head receptionist, duty receptionist?

Chance custom

What proportion of chance custom is usual?

How will they be dealt with?

Will they be expected to pay in advance? – the deposit; the first nights accommodation, each nights accommodation in advance or give a credit card imprint.

Tour business

What proportion of tour business is usual?

How will mass arrivals be dealt with?

Will a separate reception area be required?

Will it be necessary to prepare a room list in advance?

Will it be necessary to allocate rooms in advance?

Can registration cards, keys and hotel information be distributed quickly eg in envelopes in a separate reception area, an empty function room or the coach?

5.3.3 Accounting

Opening the account

When will the guests account card be opened? – on receipt of deposit, day of arrival or on arrival?

How and when will the deposit be entered on the account card?

Posting charges

In which sales outlets will residents accumulate credit sales?

What sales data will be recorded at the point of sales? – and how?

How will details of a specific sale be communicated by the point of sales to the point of guest billing (front office) – by person; point of sales terminal; pneumatic tube?

How often will sales information have to be transferred from the point of sales to the front office?

How up-to-date will guest account cards need to be at any given time?

Is a docket/voucher system required? (see section 5.4 for control features)

How will dockets need to be stored at the front office to await posting and for how long.

Will dockets need 'actioning' after posting to prevent reposting and what happens to the actioned dockets?

What sales information will need to be transferred to a guests account card? – identified sales outlet; date; amount.

When will accommodation charges be posted? – for new arrivals and stay-overs? Who will undertake this and who will monitor?

When will front office accounts be balanced? – at the end of a shift or once per day?

What procedure will be required if the front office accounts do not balance?

What management information is required and how often?

Credit control

Will any credit checking of guest account cards be required? – if so
— why, when and by whom?
— will a credit limit have to be imposed on the guest at any time? How
  much, by whom?

Accounting system

Which accounting system will be the most appropriate? – manual
  tabular ledger; electro mechanical or electronic accounting machine
  or a computerised system.

Check-out

How will front office accounting personnel know which guests are to
  depart.
When will guest account cards be finalised – prior to departure or at
  check-out?
How will guest account cards be checked to ensure all last minute
  credit sales are included?
Will VAT and service charge have to be entered as separate charges?
How will a guest query be dealt with?
By what alternative means may the guest pay their account? – by
  cash; credit card; cheque; direct debit; euro-cheque; travellers
  cheque; foreign currency; travellers agents vouchers or transfer to
  company accounts (transfer to the ledger) See figure 5.5.
Who will require a copy of the finalised account card? – the guest, the
  accounts department, the guests company?
Will a proportion of guests wish to depart in the same time period? –
  thus creating a peak period?
Is a referral system for booking future accommodation a necessary
  service to be provided?
Can guests paying by credit card, with a guaranteed reservation,
  check themselves out at a convenient computer terminal, to relieve
  pressure on the front desk?

Whichever accounting system is selected it must incorporate the
following features:
— Keep the guest's account card up-to-date
— Identify all sales from all sales outlets
— Allow cash sales (eg chance meals, drinks, function payments) as
  opposed to credit sales to be recorded separately
— Balance as required
— Provide the following data for analytical and management purposes:
  — a sales summary from each sales outlet, incorporating a break-
    down of all individual guest transactions
  — a summary of all sales (identified) attributable to one room (guest)
  — a total figure of business done (ie the total revenue from the shift
    or days transactions) by each sales outlet
  — a total of each guest's expenditure (ie normally by room)

Figure 5.5 *Control measures to adopt for each possible method of payment*

Method of payment	Control measures
Cash	Record amount received in payment of account in Cash Received Book
	Total cash received book daily to tally with amount in till
	Record payment on tab ledger/against cash key on electro-mechanical machine/against cash code on computer
	Receipt guests account to denote payment
	Allocate an individual till to all cashiers on duty at one time
	Sign cash floats in and out
Cheques	Check cheque completed properly – date; company name; amount; signature
	Cheque must be signed in presence of cashier
	Check cheque card as means of identification
	Cheque card guarantees payment of a cheque to a certain amount, currently £50
	Only one cheque should be used for one transaction
	If more than £50, cashier must write cheque card number on back – this means transaction is charged as a cash transaction and guest cannot stop it later
Travellers cheques (sterling)	Often proof of identity, eg passport is required before travellers cheques are accepted – to be retained whilst guest signs travellers cheques
	Travellers cheque must have been signed on issue from bank
	Cashier must watch guest make second signature – if not guest must sign on back
	Check two signatures, check with passport signature, check date
Foreign currency	If going to accept foreign currency, have a well organised system
	Know which currencies will and will not be accepted
	Foreign currency legally may only be accepted in payment of account – a foreign exchange should not be set up
	Check exchange rates daily if not more often
	Charge a realistic commission to cover administrative charges and unexpected fluctuations in exchange rate
	Monitor carefully as easier to defraud establishment than with other methods of payment

Credit cards
(a) Visa/Access
	Check individual credit limit if account is over £100
	   – either by phone or computerised terminal
	Complete a sales voucher and credit card imprint
	Guest must sign
	Check validity of credit card – date of expiry,
	   signature against signature on sales voucher
	Give copy to guest and retain copies – one to go to
	   Credit Card Company for payment

(b) Travel/
   Entertainment
   Credit Cards, eg
   American
   Express
	As above
	Establishment must pay a commission to company
	   for franchise

Travel agents vouchers	Check details – company, amount, signature, etc Guest must sign – check signature Retain copy for submission to Travel Agents with commission

Transfer to Outstanding
  Accounts Ledger
	Ensure guest checks and signs account
	Send copy to control/accounts office
	Record form of payment appropriately in
	   accounting system – must be segregated from
	   other forms of payment
	Only credit worthy customers with satisfactory
	   references will be offered this facility
	Require authorised users and credit limits if allow
	   companies/business houses this facility

NB   Some hotel chains offer their own Credit Card Scheme

— a grand total of all business done from all sales outlets – identifying the amount already paid for and the amount still outstanding.

— a grand total of guest expenditure, highlighting the total of the accounts paid and the total of those still outstanding.

— other information as required such as a segregation of VAT, disbursements (VPOs), allowances made, credit card transactions.

— Incorporate control features, including a procedure for rectifying mistakes and making allowances.

5.3.4 Communications

Incoming

How will incoming mail, messages and telephone calls for guests have to be dealt with?

How will the telephonist know who is in which room?

How will guests who are in-house but not in-room be contacted? – what type of paging system will be required?

How will incoming mail be sorted, stored and distributed? and by whom?

Is a pre-printed message sheet required to ensure all relevant data is recorded? How will the guest know that a message is waiting?

Outgoing

How will guests' outgoing mail, messages and telephone calls be dealt with?

What telephone switchboard system is the most appropriate?

Is an efficient, speedy and not too expensive telephone service required?

What attempts will be needed to prevent the telephone service from being a loss maker?

How will telephone charges be transferred to guests account cards, how frequently and how will 'too lates' charges be prevented?

Will a wake-up call or line-barring facility be necessary?

Will stationery, stamps and a post box for outgoing mail be required?

5.3.5 Information services

What type of information will guests require? – about the hotel; about the locality?

What importance is to be placed on this service?

What reference books/materials must be kept at front office?

Will it be more effective to present some of this information in a written format, eg hotel directory of services or 'What's on in town?'

Who will be responsible for the dissemination of this information? – reception personnel; an enquiry clerk; the hall porter.

Will theatre tickets, car hire and tourist agencies be required?

5.3.6 Security

What key controls are required?

How will the safe custody of guests valuables be dealt with?

What is the hotel proprietors liability for loss of guests property within the Hotel Proprietors Act 1956.

Will the entry and exit of all building users be monitored? – if so, how and by whom? – constant portering; security guards; closed circuit television.

5.4 FRONT OFFICE CONTROL

This section is dealt with in two parts. Firstly, the control of the front office activities already discussed including the procedures used, the physical resources and the personnel required to undertake these activities. Secondly, the control of accommodation occupancy to maximise revenue received from accommodation sales, which, it must be remembered, may well affect the revenue received by other sales outlets.

The front office control function cannot be undertaken in isolation. The accounts office is responsible for the overall control process in a hotel operation and for auditing accounting procedures. Marketing and/or conference departments – where they exist and if they operate effectively – will contribute to occupancy and accommodation revenue. The management and the company will impose policies which will affect occupancy and revenue and will require performance data of a financial and non-financial nature, which in turn will affect future decisions and policies imposed.

5.4.1 Controlling the front office activities
Designing appropriate procedures or processes to meet both the requirements of the guest and the establishment is crucial to the effective operation of the front office. With forethought, control features can be incorporated when designing the system in which they then become an integral part. See figure 5.6.

5.4.1.1 Personnel control
The size, type, grading and scope of the operation will greatly affect the organisational structure of the front office, the number of personnel employed and the variety of grades of personnel to be employed.

In a small, privately owned resort hotel, a multi-purpose receptionist may be employed who covers the whole range of activities. In a large city centre, four or five star hotel, different grades of personnel may well be responsible for the different front office functions – with a number of each grade employed, such as advance reservation clerk, receptionist, book-keeper (bill clerk), cashier, information clerk, telephonist. By using simple recording techniques and analysing the guests' behaviour pattern it is possible to determine the mean number of transactions carried out over a period, their nature, and the time periods where peaks and troughs occur daily, weekly and possibly seasonally. This type of information, together with policies on equipment and computers, should influence not only numbers and grades of personnel but also hours of work and scheduling arrangements. Occupancy forecasts will also contribute to the staffing arrangements made. Shift hours will be influenced by the type of operation and pattern of business which in turn will influence the hours of cover to be provided by the front office. A busy metropolitan or an airport hotel will require a 24 hour, three shift coverage, whereas a small resort hotel, where guests stay for one or two weeks at a time may only require a minimal coverage midweek, but a 9 am to 9 pm coverage at the weekends.

In most commercial hotels a two shift system operates, eg 7 am to 3.30 pm, 3 pm to 11.30 pm (an overlap occurring for communication at change-over time). For security, safety and emergency reasons, it may be necessary to employ a night porter and some hotels still employ night auditors to post accommodation charges, carry out a business analysis and produce the required management information (although audits are now easier with the aid of computers). In large front office organisations, a head of section may be required to supervise and control each function, head receptionist, head book-keeper, head cashier, head hall porter. It is essential in any front office to have a designated shift leader on duty, particularly when Heads of Sections are off duty or where the size of operation does not warrant such grades.

Figure 5.6 *Front Office control features. Some front office control features which can be incorporated as an integral part of a system*

Feature	Relevance
ADVANCE RESERVATIONS	
Visual, up-to-date Room Availability chart	Speedy offer
Standard system of recording using pre-printed reservation card	All information recorded. Personnel aide-memoire
Realistic overbooking policy – based on past statistics with a contingency plan for 'booking out'	To maximise revenue but prevent major crises – but have a plan in case
Check customer credit worthiness/ability to pay	Prevent bad debts or fraud
Confirmation and deposit procedure	Increase possibility of guests showing-up Written evidence of offer and acceptance
Time release	Maximise revenue
RECEPTION AND CHECK IN	
Training in social skills and guest care	Welcome, first impressions
Registration	Legal
Standard procedure for chance guests	Prevent bad debts
Well designed, up-to-date room status system	Ensure state of every room known at any time
Priority rating of customers for room allocation	Foster goodwill Prevent booking out certain categories of guests
Identity cards	Security Guest status Control of credit sales
Siting of keys to prevent guest access or viewing	Security

Machine accounting controls

Audit roll	The machine will not operate without it
	Only access with a special key to change it
	Provides a clear audit trail of each transaction
	Consecutive numbering of all transactions
Voucher control	Overprints voucher in 'proving' slot to indicate actioned
Register counter	Show number of postings during a shift to each of the major debit keys
Z Key trip counter	Increases every time the machine is cleared

Cash control

Signing in and out of floats	Security
	Inaccuracies traced to an individual
Limiting number of floats allocated	Security
	Cash flow
Individual cashier code and separate till	Security
	Individual control and monitoring
Recording of all cash received	To check actual cash received
	Security
	Aid cash flow
Efficient processing of foreign currency and administrative charge	Prevent losing out financially

Other controls

Credit check	Highlight peculiar spending patterns or possible bad debts
Impose credit limit	Ensure pay bill in regular amounts
Computer controls	For access and security

ACCOUNTING

Docket/Voucher control	Security
— issue to specified personnel	Prevent fraud
— account for each consecutive docket	Accurate accounting
— speed of transfer from sales outlet to front office	
— store effectively prior to posting	
— action after posting	
— file in case of customer queries	
— forward to Control Office	

Posting of charges	Security
— ensure all charges correctly posted	Prevent fraud
— ensure accommodation charges posted	Accurate accounting
— regular and frequent posting	
— post systematically	
— identify sales outlet	
— speed and method of transfer	
— action docket after posting	
— account posted at a specific time	
— adjustment feature for errors	
Regular balancing	To ensure accurate accounting
	Find inaccuracies
	All totals agree
Sales summary	Analyse sales revenue, guest expenditure, outstanding business

CHECK OUT

Follow a standard procedure	Ensures all aspects covered
Agree the bill with customer	Overcome complaints
	Avoid future problems
Check breakfasts and telephone charges have been posted	Prevent loss of revenue
Set a procedure for dealing with each type of payment method	Aid staff
	Prevent fraud
	Prevent loss

COMMUNICATIONS

Ensure messages are relayed accurately and quickly	Avoid guest frustration and complaints
	Part of image
Ensure speedy system of posting telephone charges	Prevent loss of revenue
Provide information service	Part of image possibly sales producing

SECURITY

Safe custody of guests valuables, with standard procedure	Guest comfort
	Prevent frustration
	Reduce liability
Staff aware to report suspicious events	Safety
Constant staffing in front hall	Safety
Security of main doors at night	Safety

5.4.1.2 Control of physical resources

In this context the physical resources are defined as the front office equipment and accommodation

(1) *Front Office equipment* The range of equipment required, its design and suitability for purpose in relation to the systems to be used, is just as important to the front office as it is to the other departments. The selection and purchasing procedures discussed in chapter 4 are equally pertinent here. The following equipment may be required:

— Telephone network
— Telex; Facsimile
— Filing cabinets, trays, index
— Accounting machine, bill trays, tills
— Computer, printers, VDUs
— Credit card terminal and credit and direct debit card machines
— Photocopier
— Racking and charting systems
— Safe, safe deposit boxes
— Stamps – hotel, date and time
— Staplers and punches
— Calculators
— Key depository
— Mail/key racks
— Typewriter/word processor.

Maintenance arrangements will have to be made for mechanical, electronic and computerised equipment. With rapid advancements in technology, the useful life-span of the complex computerised equipment may be limited, with obsolescence becoming an in-built feature, thus creating the need for an effective replacement cycle to operate, and flexibility in design and layout of the front office. Careful selection and siting of all the equipment is necessary to aid efficiency of workflow, movement and motion economy.

Front office stationery will also be required, which is appropriately designed to satisfy functional and visual requirements. 'Customised' or standard items of stationery may be purchased. In a large concern where corporate image is considered important, design decisions may be imposed from head office.

(2) *The design and layout of the front office* The design elements discussed in chapter 1, section 3.3, are obviously applicable to the design of the front office area. Although the psychological aspects of design, such as the ambience created and the initial impact of the total design scheme of this area on the arriving guest are very important design issues, the practicalities of designing for functional efficiency are also important and will be discussed in this section. Some design features relating to siting and security control have been highlighted already in this chapter. The size and layout of the front office will be influenced by the number of guests and their activities; the front office activities which must occur; the systems devised, the flow of data, the number of transactions to be carried out, the amount of tour and conference business, the required equipment and the number and grades of personnel required to work at a particular time. Conversely, the space available is a constraint when re-designing the layout, an opportunity often created by the decision to install a computer.

5.4.2 Controlling occupancy and revenue

Where accommodation is revenue-producing, the aim must be to achieve capacity occupancy with maximum revenue. Capacity occupancy can only be achieved if someone is sleeping in every bed, with two people in every double, queen-size and king-size bed. Thus, true 100% occupancy is not purely letting every room. Maximum revenue can only be achieved with all customers paying the full room rate. Even if true 100% occupancy can be achieved on occasions, it is very difficult to achieve also maximum revenue as room-rates are subject to discounting for several reasons which are discussed later.

Occupancy and revenue are discussed separately, but their inter-relationship must be established at the outset. If maximum occupancy and revenue are to be achieved, it is essential to:
— determine what the potential maximum occupancy and maximum revenue of the enterprise are
— calculate existing levels of occupancy and revenue being achieved
— monitor achievements and compare with previous periods.

In reality, the emphasis is on ever-improving and increasing occupancy and revenue. The means by which improvements can be made, particularly by increasing the sales effort, must be considered. Occupancy and revenue levels achieved thus become a measurement of performance of the unit or department and often of the manager. Greater pressure to achieve ever greater targets is then placed on personnel, who must be equipped with the knowledge and skills to make improvements, be kept informed of aggregate and individual achievements at regular intervals, and perhaps offered incentives.

Occupancy
Certain essential basic data must be available to ensure occupancy levels can be calculated and monitored such as:
— The total number of rooms available.
— The breakdown of room types and the number of each type.
— The configuration of each room, ie number and types of bed, design and décor.
— The number of Z beds (ie spare, collapsible beds) that can be accommodated if necessary.

From this information the maximum capacity (with and without Z beds) can be calculated. The data required to calculate occupancy levels being achieved at present, is generated, daily, through the normal front office reception and accounting activities. Occupancy statistics of various kinds can be calculated, often by the night auditor which are all useful in their own way, but in isolation do not necessarily reflect an accurate picture. See figure 5.7.

The statistics produced can be summarised weekly, monthly, quarterly or annually as a continuing basis for monitoring achievements and comparing with past performance. They also enable the pattern of occupancy to be analysed, for instance which room types are most popular; are double rooms being let to single occupants; are a high proportion of rooms always out of order? The reasons for these occurences can then be investigated. Over a period of time, fluctuations in occupancy levels can be plotted reflecting peaks and troughs in business, and recurring trends can be identified, such as high occupancy mid-week, low occupancy at the weekend in a commercial hotel.

Break-even analysis can be used to determine the occupancy percentage required to cover fixed and variable costs (assuming that these can be calculated) and to start contributing to profits. This further emphasises the relationship between occupancy and revenue.

Expected future occupancy levels can be forecast from reservation records to highlight anticipated peaks and troughs in business.

It is useful to monitor why reservation requests are turned down as another aid to improving occupancy levels. Is it rate resistance or is it a period of heavy demand and rooms are not available? The former may indicate that prices are too high or the wrong market is being aimed at. The latter may indicate that group or tour business is blocking out more lucrative business which is definitely available at that particular time.

From the data produced it is possible to anticipate periods of high demand and low occupancy and hence consider ways in which occupancy levels can be increased. An increase in occupancy levels should also increase sales in the other sales outlets, if they are effectively promoted. Thus a relationship between accommodation sales and other sales outlets exists.

Suggested ways of increasing occupancy levels are discussed under *Revenue* on page 211, as revenue usually increases when occupancy increases.

5.4.2.2 The characteristics of the clients

Whilst discussing occupancy, it is convenient to consider the occupants and their characteristics. Management can never know enough about their customers. The following questions will give some insight into the characteristics of the occupant, which may be useful when considering ways of increasing occupancy, revenue and sales:

What type of occupants are attracted to the enterprise? (socio-economic group, sex, occupation, income level)

From where do they originate? (Country, county, area of origin or company/organisation and its location)

From what source is business generated? (Travel agents, tour

Type	Calculation	Uses	Limitations
Room occupancy	$\dfrac{\text{Number of rooms sold}}{\text{Total number of rooms}} \times \dfrac{100}{1}$	Indicates % of rooms sold	Does not reflect number of occupants Does not reflect rooms unavailable, for whatever reason
Available room occupancy	$\dfrac{\text{Number of rooms sold}}{\text{Number of total rooms} - \text{Number of rooms not available for letting}} \times \dfrac{100}{1}$	Reflects number of rooms not available for letting, out of order, refurbishing, etc	Still does not reflect number of occupants
Bed occupancy	$\dfrac{\text{Number of beds sold}}{\text{Total possible beds}} \times \dfrac{100}{1}$	Indicates number of beds occupied rather than rooms	Does not reflect number of occupants if double beds are available Does not reflect rooms unavailable
Sleeper occupancy	$\dfrac{\text{Number of sleepers}}{\text{Total possible sleepers}} \times \dfrac{100}{1}$	Indicates number of occupants Can compare room v sleeper occupancy	Does not reflect rooms unavailable
Double occupancy	$\dfrac{\text{Number of doubles let as doubles}}{\text{Total number of doubles}} \times \dfrac{100}{1}$	Includes also number of twins let as twins Reflects number of doubles sold as singles Reflects skill of reservation clerk to 'fill' doubles or twins	
Income occupancy	$\dfrac{\text{Actual accommodation income}}{\text{Number of rooms sold}} \times \dfrac{100}{1}$	Reflects discounts, complimentarys Reflects strategy of doubles sold to single occupants Indicates the percentage of potential income lost on a particular night	

operators, central reservation or agency, business house and companies, organisations, individuals).

How long in advance do they reserve? (what is the lead time?)

What proportion of potential occupants cancel or do not show?

How long do occupants stay? (What is the mean average length of stay per month or how many guests stay 1, 2, 3, 4 or 5 nights, etc in a month)

How much do occupants spend on average? (Generally or per type of guest, eg tours versus individuals, or per nationalities – Japanese versus Americans)

What method of payment do occupants use? (Foreign currency, travellers cheques, cheques or euro-cheques, credit card, direct debit card, cash, transfer to ledger)

How many bed debts are incurred? (This is usually expressed as a percentage of turnover)

Are the occupants satisfied? – what do they like, dislike, complain about?

Much of this information can be extracted from existing records, if they are so designed, and if often summarised on a quarterly, six monthly or annual basis; more frequent summaries are less meaningful. Graphic compilation, such as histograms or pie charts may well aid interpretation of this type of data.

5.4.2.3 Revenue

It is not sufficient to aim purely for capacity occupancy but attempts must be made to maximise revenue. This means, again, that it is essential to know what the maximum potential revenue could be, ie capacity occupancy at full rack rate. Even then extra revenue can be attained from Z beds and a room being sold twice in one day (as a dressing room for instance). This information will help management to realise how much revenue could be achieved, and how much revenue is being lost to the business. It is also useful to know other facts and figures such as:

— The potential revenue at full rack rate with only single room occupancy

— The occupancy percentage required to break even, ie cover variable and fixed costs

Some idea of the number of complimentary rooms allocated and the amount of discounted business, in terms of what type of business, how much discount, how much revenue is lost by discounting and when it tends to occur, may help to decide on the measures to be taken to maximise revenue. Once again it is relatively easy to ascertain each day, from the front office daily trading accounts, how much revenue is being earned. This figure will reflect price variations: discounts, special terms and complimentary accommodation. It can be correlated with occupancy levels and used to monitor performance in financial terms and highlight variances when compared with previous figures.

This can then be analysed to discover the reasons for fluctuation, bearing in mind any price increases which have occurred.

Another statistic, useful when measuring financial performance, is the average room rate being achieved, ie

$$\text{Average room rate} = \frac{\text{accommodation income}}{\text{number of rooms sold}} = £.$$

Alternatively, the average sleeper rate can also be calculated. This statistic provides a useful measure of the quality of room sales, ie an increase in the average room rate achieved reflects maximisation of occupancy, whereas a decrease reflects selling rooms at less than rack rate or lower occupancy. It is possible in most operations to increase the average room rate.

To achieve full potential is an aim rather than an ultimate reality but the following courses of action may be considered:

— Avoid, if possible, letting twins and doubles to single occupants at a single rate. It may be possible to attract a different market

— Is it possible to sell a double or twin at full rack rate even if to a single occupant?

— Offer a special deal for businessmen to bring their wives to fill twin or double rooms

— Is it necessary to sell rooms at discounted or special rates? Would the market pay the full rate?

— Change the bed configuration if necessary. For instance, if twins have to be sold to single occupants, substitute the twin beds for a double. Flexibility remains, the room can still be sold to two people but could be sold as a 'luxury' single at a slightly higher room rate, than an ordinary single

— Charge a higher room rate for rooms with a view, better facilities, better furnishings or more space

— Review the market mix. Are any types of business blocking accommodation which could be sold to a potentially more lucrative type of business. For instance, control the amount or even stop altogether discounted tour business in heavy demand periods when individual business will pay full rack rate

— Consider promoting minimum stay packages. For instance over Bank Holidays it may be possible to sell three nights instead of two if offering a minimum stay package

— Provide a few extras at negligible cost and sell at a higher rate as a speciality package or to a particular market. For instance, provide bathrobe, perfumes and toiletries, hair dryer, curling tongs, iron and ironing board, sewing kit, fruit and cheese basket, floral arrangement to the woman business executive – could even include a portering service and an in-room evening meal service

— Rigidly control 'complimentary' accommodation, only consider for potentially very lucrative future business, eg for a conference executive

— Negotiate a credit card guarantee service with the Credit Card companies to encourage customers actually to arrive and the company to honour payment regardless of arrival

— Scrutinize correspondence or telex messages where information such as job title or professional qualifications of the signatory, the company's letter head or indeed the content of the letter, may give 'leads' for potential sources of future business

— Consider setting up a referral system, particularly in a group or syndicate operation, to pass reservations on to other establishments. The system is reciprocal, reservations will also be passed on to your business. This may be computerised and is more effective if dealt with when the guest checks in rather than at check-out

— Offer future accommodation when turning down reservation requests due to lack of room availability. Presumably the potential guest was interested in staying at your establishment

— Is it possible to find out how much business is lost through personnel ineptitude: at answering the phone; making a favourable impression with the potential client; making it easy for the potential client to talk to or meet the right people quickly; realising the enormity of the potential future business? Carry out 'guest tests' or surveys either personally or by 'employing' a friend, colleague or even a regular well known guest, to evaluate the system. Try 'phoning for accommodation, or to arrange a conference meeting or asking a specific question about facilities and services and see what answers and impressions you are given

— Consider a concerted sales effort (see section 5.5) to attract new business, eg advertising locally; mailing shots or telephone calls to local businesses and organisations; sales brochures – a businessman might just be looking for a venue for a company or professional organisations function or conference

— Organise special promotions, events and activities aimed at very specialised markets and often one-off events. The following list includes actual events offered by a number of hotels:

    Nationality functions

    Space invaders weekend

    Photography, cookery, interior design schools – using key personnel or local experts

    Sporting packages and competitions

    Keep-fit and leisure clubs

— Organise special deals or packages relating to local events and activities, eg races, cricket, shows and fairs, nature spots

— Mini-breaks and weekends

— Employ a selection of front office personnel who speak a range of languages to correlate with the range of nationalities who visit. Arrange speciality 'English' or 'Olde Englishe' events for their benefit.

This list is by no means comprehensive and some of these

suggestions may be of no use in particular enterprises, thus emphasising that extensive knowledge of the business, the product and the market, is essential. As revenue from accommodation tends to make the largest contribution to the profitability of the enterprise, it is usual to determine the extent of this contribution in percentage terms compared to the percentage contribution made by all the other sales outlets in the establishment.

5.4.2.4 Pricing

As the price level will affect the volume of sales, revenue, and consequently profitability, it is essential that the price level is correct. The price level must not be so high as to dissuade custom or so low that it fails to cover variable and marginal costs. At the same time it must be competitive. Pricing policy is so critical and complex that it is rarely up to the unit manager, let alone the accommodation or front office manager, to decide on room rates (unless it is a privately owned enterprise). However, it is useful to understand the nature of a room charge.

The room price charged has to cover the cost of items used by the guest, such as stationery, room and water heating, soap, laundering of bed linen. This is the *marginal cost* (defined as the cost of producing another unit), which is negligible and does not include those costs involved in providing accommodation whether or not it is sold, such as labour, rent and rates, cleaning and heating of public areas, telephone and television rental, most of which are fixed but may incorporate semi-variable elements. The gap between the marginal cost and the selling price, which is often referred to as the *price discretion*, gives rise to the possibility of varying the price between covering marginal costs and the stated selling price, hence the practice of discounting room rates to attract more business.

The room rate is usually subject to more variations and fluctuations in price than any other sales item. The price charged may vary for the following reasons:

— The room type, whether single, twin, etc. The greater the number of room types, the greater the number of different room rates
— The convenience of the room, ie its size, décor, facilities and services
— The number of occupants in a room. A twin room sold to a single occupant will be sold at less than normal rack rate, whereas, if a Z bed is put up, a higher room rate will be charged
— The market segment or type of customer
  — a businessman not paying his own account is not as sensitive to the price charged
  — high prices attract a certain segment of the population who prefer to use the most expensive hotel
  — a business executive may be willing to pay more for a little extra service
  — regular customers may receive discounts

— celebrities may be offered complimentary accommodation for
the publicity
— The guest attending a function, wedding, dinner dance may be
offered a discounted room rate
— Discounts for bulk reservations, conferences and tours
— Complimentary accommodation for promotional reasons, as prizes,
for visiting personnel, etc

Fluctuations in price may occur for instance:
— at certain times of the year. This usually relates to supply and
demand, lower rates being charged in the low season
— at certain times of the week. Midweek may be very busy and
businessmen will pay rack rate, but a lower price may be charged at
the weekend 'o encourage occupancy
— special events and promotion, eg Christmas or New Year events
— to undercut competition
— after a certain time in the evening, prices of vacant rooms may be
lowered in an attempt to encourage extra sales.

The nature of the room price also means that an extra room sale
contributes more to profits than an extra sale from any other sales
outlet, where the marginal cost tends to be a much larger percentage
of the selling price, eg a meal. Prices tend to fluctuate according to
occupancy trends. For instance, prices may be lowered at periods of
low occupancy in an attempt to attract more business and the
established rack rate charged at periods of higher demand. A lowering
of room rates does not automatically lead to an increase in room sales,
owing to a phenomenon known as *elasticity of demand*.

Where price changes do not necessarily affect changes in the
quantity of rooms demanded there is an inelastic demand which tends
to be the case in the hotel industry. According to M L KASAVANA[2]
'research (*viz à viz* the hotel industry) has illustrated that there is only
an indirect relationship between price and demand, and that within
certain percent changes in price, demand may be totally unaffected'.

The optimal room price, according to KASAVANA must reflect all the
internal and external factors listed below.

Internal considerations

A reasonable rate of return, over and above the standard rate of
interest, for taking the risks of going into business

The proportion of services which incur costs but do not receive direct
revenue to be covered in part by room revenue

Overheads (cost centres) which are apportioned to the rooms department

Fluctuations and variations in room rates according to the market
segment, eg commercial rates, complimentary rates, family rates,
weekend rates, etc.

External considerations

Competitive factors – the intensity of competition; the type of competition; the market share (of rooms sold); and whether a price leader exists

Elasticity of demand (defined as the change in room price as related to changes in the number of rooms sold).

Other factors

Location within the market area. The geographical location will influence the demand for rooms and, therefore, the price that can be charged.

Location and convenience (ie size, décor what it contains) of a room within the hotel in terms of views and proximity to other facilities, will influence the specific price to be charged for that room.

Belief that pricing must be dynamic and responsive to market forces (a belief shared by M L KASAVANA[2] and HCITB[4] – now HCTC) has led to the development of pricing philosophies rather than a strict adherence to mathematical models.

These mathematical models, all of which are explained in hotel accounting text books (see end of chapter for references) include the following:

— Cost – plus pricing
— Rate of return/HUBBART room formula
— Marginal or contribution pricing
— Break-even analysis
— Rule of thumb (1:1000)

One of the problems associated with using mathematical models is that the price calculated is an average one which has to be charged over a period of time rather than an actual price to be quoted.

Market forces pricing basically involves reconciling the following three factors:

1 *Cost*
   — what is the customer prepared to pay?
   — what is the customer expecting to pay?
   — what can the customer afford to pay?
   — what has happened to the customers spending power, ie what economic factors have affected the customer?
   — what must the business charge in order to make a profit or at least survive.
2 *Competition*
   — how many competitors are there?
   — do they cater for the same potential customer?
   — are they offering the same standard, services, facilities?
   — how do they price their product?
   — is there a price leader?
3 *Governmental influences*
   — what effect does VAT have on prices?

— what percentage VAT has to be charged?
— is there any legislation affecting pricing policy
— what is the governments attitude to tourism?
— what grants and subsidies are available?

Consideration must also be given to whether the room rate is inclusive of certain services or facilities, such as early morning tea, breakfasts or other meals, or whether the guest is expected to pay for every single extra, such as iron and ironing board. In reality so many different prices may result if the hotel has a great variation of room types; a variety of tariffs; special rates or discounts for different types of business; and high and low season rates, that it becomes extremely confusing for front office personnel. Clients too may be upset if they realise another client has the same room type at a lower price.

5.5 SELLING

Endeavouring continually to increase occupancy and revenue levels means that personnel must always be attempting to increase sales, ie attract new business and increase in-house sales.

The attitude towards the selling function and increasing sales has had to change in the last few years. Hotels (and other types of operations) can no longer afford to sit back and wait for business to come to them or for guests to ask for things.

A positive sales policy may well have to be adopted. This will involve other departments, such as conference and banqueting, Sales and Marketing, which are possibly more concerned with generating new business, while the Front Office is more concerned with increasing in-house sales. JAMES LAVENSON[3] suggests that all personnel, from the Manager to the Doorman, are sales people as they are responsible for caring for the guests and satisfying their needs. He suggests that personnel 'sell' to guests in everything they say and do, and that the relationship created between personnel and guest creates also a unique opportunity for increasing sales. Of course, the attitude and approach of personnel could, likewise, have a negative effect on sales.

COLIN DIX[1] suggests that 'selling by reception employees involves finding the needs of the customers, converting them into wants and providing the facilities to fulfill them'.

If a positive sales policy is to be introduced, certain characteristics associated with selling accommodation must be understood, particularly those which impose constraints.
— Accommodation provides a greater contribution to fixed costs and subsequently to profits than any other sales outlet.
— As a saleable commodity, accommodation is constrained by two characteristics:

1 *Time*. Accommodation and its associated facilities and services can be perceived as a perishable product which if not sold tonight the

revenue is lost forever, unlike food and beverages, where items can be stored for a while and sold on another occasion.

2 *Quantity*, the quantity of rooms is static and cannot fluctuate to meet demands (apart from changing bed configurations and using Z beds).

— The selling price is subject to fluctuations and variations over a period of time according to supply and demand and other influences.
— Accommodation is an intangible product which is difficult to describe.
— Unlike many products on sale, accommodation cannot be sampled or tried out before purchase. Although if guests have stayed before they will have previously sampled and will have a particular impression in mind when re-purchasing. On some occasions it may be possible to view the accommodation before purchase, but even then the guest will not really know what it is like until it is too late and it has to be paid for anyway.

5.5.1 Sales opportunities
If effective selling is to take place, all sales opportunities within the guest cycle must be identified.

Advance reservations A great opportunity may occur to convert an enquiry into a sale if the potential guest is undecided. The selling of accommodation over the telephone is extremely difficult, and training in telephone and selling techniques is recommended to allow personnel to capitalise on this opportunity. The voice can be regarded as a sales tool and the way in which the telephone is answered and the telephone manner can make or break a sale. Personnel must be able to visualise accurately the room they are selling and use the right descriptive words to convey a mental picture to the potential guest.

Check-in
After the guest has registered, the facilities and services which the hotel has to offer, which may otherwise go unused, can be promoted. The receptionist has to use some discretion. If the guest arrives late, he may wish room service or a snack in the coffee shop. Even simple questions such as 'May I book dinner in the restaurant for you, Mr Jones?', may result in increased dinner sales.

En route to the bedroom
There are a number of opportunities which can be exploited en route to the room:
— Details of sales outlets, facilities and services can be advertised in the lift, especially special promotions and activities.
— The porter can mention particular items which maybe of interest, like saunas, hairdressing, entertainment, while conducting the guest to their room.

In-room

Directories of services may be placed in rooms and the in-room video may be used to publicise facilities, services and events.

Check-out

Even opportunities occur at check-out to encourage the guest to return in the future or promote other hotels in the group. Reply-paid reservation postcards or the reservations 'hotline' telephone number may be issued to aid future bookings. Some hotels offer incentives, such as discounts or the use of services free of charge, to encourage return or usage of other hotels in the group. Even asking the guest if he has enjoyed his stay, and if he has any complaints or comments, may help to re-establish goodwill before departure and encourage the guest to consider future patronage.

To make the most of these opportunities, personnel must have time to give undivided attention to guests, so making correct staffing levels essential.

5.5.2 Product knowledge

Accommodation can be perceived as a product, comprising a complex package of tangible and intangible benefits and services, such as physical accommodation, facilities and services and intangible or psychological experiences, such as hospitality, ambience, décor, image, personal service, status and security.

The accommodation package may well be only a part of the total product which the guest experiences. Food and beverage services, entertainment and other leisure activities may also be experienced. These other services, facilities and benefits may well only be purchased because the guest's initial need was for accommodation, and they may go unused if not drawn to the guest's attention, which is part of the sales effort as previously intimated.

If personnel are to sell the accommodation package effectively they must possess a precise knowledge of the product, as the guest requires other services and facilities, beyond the scope of the accommodation package, eg food.

There are many reasons why full product knowledge is required, including the following:

— to be able to describe the product effectively to the potential guest, particularly over the telephone, personnel must be able to visualise rooms and use the right descriptive words to convey an accurate mental picture to the client in an attempt to equate expectations with reality.
— To produce the brochure and written sales and marketing literature required.
— To evaluate the product on offer, comparing it with competitors' products and determine strengths and weaknesses. The strengths can then be emphasised when selling to a potential guest.

In order to know the product intimately, a combination of t
procedures can be used:

1 conducting a product analysis
2 sampling the product.

Product analysis
When analysing the product, all factors which make up the product or
package have to be considered. A systematic approach to the analysis
is always useful and the product analysis checklist, outlined in figure
5.8, may be of value.

When conducting a product analysis it is usual to compare the
product with that of the competition. This checklist can subsequently
be developed by management for use when evaluating the quality
standards and efficiency of the product.

Sampling
To know the product it is beneficial to sample it. Stay overnight in a
bedroom, see the in-room video, experience room service and so on.
This creates a unique experience to perceive the product objectively
from the guests' viewpoint. Although it is easier for Supervisory and
Management personnel to sample for themselves, it may be beneficial
to other grades of personnel, such as a new maid or receptionist to stay
overnight, or at least to have a comprehensive tour of the whole
establishment. Costs may be incurred with this exercise, but the
benefits may outweigh the expense involved.

5.5.3 Training
If personnel are expected to promote this sales policy, it is only fair
that they understand the reasons for the enforcement, know the
product, know where the sales opportunities occur in the guest cycle
and have undertaken appropriate training in salesmanship.

5.5.4 Control
Monitoring performance, and analysing increases and decreases in
sales, whether in occupancy or revenue terms, have already been
discussed. However, if personnel are to maintain motivation, they
require some feedback on performance to show how effective their
efforts are collectively and individually. An incentive scheme may be
necessary to encourage and maintain motivation.

5.5.6 Market research
Market research is invaluable when considering increasing sales. All
the data collected about the clients and their characteristics, in
conjunction with an evaluation of the product on offer, will enable
management to decide if the most suitable market segments are being
attracted; the optimum market mix is being achieved; where improvements can be made; and what strengths are possessed which can be
highlighted and featured in the sales campaigns.

Figure 5.8 *Product analysis checklist*

---

1 *Name of establishment*

2 *Location*
Where is it?
What is the address?
What is the telephone number?
What is the telex number?
What is the postal code?
How do you approach it? — by car
                          — by air
                          — by rail

3 *Site*
Where is it (city centre/suburbs)?
What type (garden/concrete)?
How much land (acreage)?
Is there a car park?
What is the capacity of the car park?
If no car park – what arrangements?

4 *Premises –*
How old is the building?
Was it purpose build?
In what style was it constructed? (Victorian/Chalet)
What is its image?
How many floors/storeys?
What size is it? (number of rooms/beds/customers)

5 *Accommodation*

Bedroom/Sleeping Facilities
— How many?
— Range of types?
— Location of rooms?
— Room numbering system?
— Décor/theme/colour schemes?
— Size and convenience? (ie facilities and benefits)
— Price range?

Non-residential
Public areas — Lounge
             — Bars
             — Restaurants

How many?
What type?
Location?
Decor/theme/colour schemes?
Opening times?
Price range?

Conference areas — Conference rooms
                 — Meeting rooms
                 — Function/Banqueting rooms
                 — Exhibition halls

How many?
Location?
Capacities with alternative seating arrangements?
Décor/theme/colour schemes?
Services and facilities?
Prices?

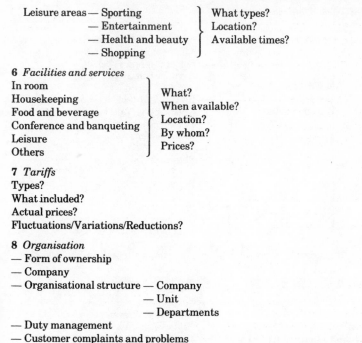

Leisure areas — Sporting ⎫ What types?
            — Entertainment ⎬ Location?
            — Health and beauty ⎭ Available times?
            — Shopping

6 *Facilities and services*
In room ⎫
Housekeeping ⎪ What?
Food and beverage ⎪ When available?
Conference and banqueting ⎬ Location?
Leisure ⎪ By whom?
Others ⎭ Prices?

7 *Tariffs*
Types?
What included?
Actual prices?
Fluctuations/Variations/Reductions?

8 *Organisation*
— Form of ownership
— Company
— Organisational structure — Company
                               — Unit
                               — Departments
— Duty management
— Customer complaints and problems

Questionnaires are also useful to evaluate customer satisfaction, if guests can be persuaded to complete them, again highlight strengths and weaknesses and determine what facilities and services could be provided which are not at present.

5.6 CONFERENCE ORGANISATION

There is no doubt that conference business is very lucrative, and attracting a conference market, if facilities permit, may be one way of increasing sales. Universities and colleges with residential accommodation which is only occupied for about two-thirds of the year, cannot afford to sit back and lose a considerable amount of potential revenue which could be used to improve standards and the facilities available to students. Sometimes this revenue is used to supplement the local authority educational budget.

This section is more concerned with planning and organising a conference, than developing the market and increasing conference sales.

Organising a conference involves identifying in great detail the clients' requirements to ensure ultimate satisfaction, planning, preparing and actually directing the conference activities at the particular time, besides dealing with the accounting and follow-up procedures. See figure 5.9 for conference cycle of activities.

Figure 5.9 *Conference cycle*

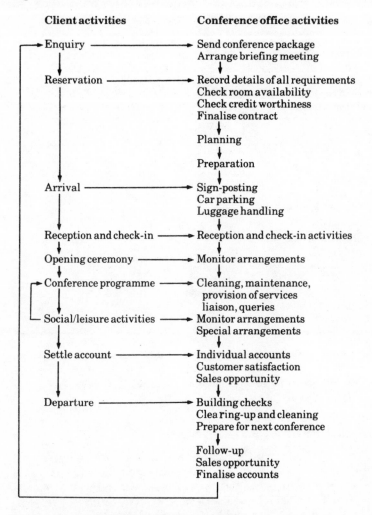

Client activities	Conference office activities
Enquiry	Send conference package Arrange briefing meeting
Reservation	Record details of all requirements Check room availability Check credit worthiness Finalise contract
	Planning
	Preparation
Arrival	Sign-posting Car parking Luggage handling
Reception and check-in	Reception and check-in activities
Opening ceremony	Monitor arrangements
Conference programme	Cleaning, maintenance, provision of services liaison, queries
Social/leisure activities	Monitor arrangements Special arrangements
Settle account	Individual accounts Customer satisfaction Sales opportunity
Departure	Building checks Clea ring-up and cleaning Prepare for next conference
	Follow-up Sales opportunity Finalise accounts

5.6.1 Enquiries and reservations

Enquiry and reservation procedures must be designed for dealing with conference clients separately from normal day to day business, mainly as more time is required to sort out all arrangements as larger numbers of guests are involved.

Links must be maintained with the normal front office activities, particularly in the case of room availability. It is imperative that a good impression is created from the moment a potential client contacts the organisation.

Correspondence must be dealt with quickly and the telephonist or reservations clerk geared up to realise the potential importance of the call and direct it speedily to someone who can help. The potential guest is not impressed when told 'the conference officer is out or off-duty ring back tomorrow'. The initial enquiry and reservation stages should be made as easy as possible for the potential client. Unfortunately, this is not always the case.

A total package, incorporating liaison between all departments concerned, must be promoted to the potential guest, otherwise business may be lost. Often the potential guest experiences difficulties in arranging to see all the key personnel at one time.

5.6.2 Briefing meeting

By far the best way of finding out what the potential client requires and explaining the product is a face to face meeting incorporating a tour of the premises and facilities. Many potential clients may never have organised a conference or function before and many others may wish to devote their energies to organising the programme, the reception and involvement of delegates and the needs of their guest speakers and not to the practicalities of the arrangements.

It is the client representative who will be criticized in the first place by delegates if the physical details are not satisfactory. It is beneficial to both parties if the manager uses his expertise to ask the right questions and make suggestions. As with normal reservations, a standard checklist may be used to record all the relevant details, but it will be a more complex document. See figure 5.10.

Generally speaking, the arrangements discussed will fall under the following headings:
General details
Sleeping accommodation
Food and beverage arrangements
Conference programme
Social programme and leisure facilities
Reception and registration arrangements.

Room availability will be checked and standard and negotiable prices will be discussed. The potential client may have to go back to his committee for confirmation and the manager may well wish to research the credit worthiness of the potential client organisation where potentially large accounts are concerned. A formal contract may be signed by both parties, incorporating the important details and the procedure for cancellation, deadline for numbers, damage to property and payment arrangements.

5.6.3 Planning and preparation

The comprehensiveness of the briefing details and the efficiency of the communication system set up will affect the planning and preparation stages and the actual outcome, ie how satisfactory the conference is. From the data collected at the briefing stage, supplemented through liaison with the client, it is possible to plot the time scale (the lead time

Figure 5.10 *Conference organisers checklist*

Client organisation details	Client's name
	Address
	Telephone number
	Telex number
General conference details	Dates
	Function type
	Length of stay
	Arrival and departure times
	Conference programme — number of sessions
	session titles
	starting and
	finishing times
	break times
	Non-delegates programme
	Childrens programme
Delegate details	Minimum and maximum number
	Number of residents/non-residents
	Age range
	Sex
	Marital status
	Number of non-delegates, eg spouse and children
	Any handicapped/disabled
	Any special diets
Guest speakers	How many?
	Who?
	Any special arrangements, eg security
	Number of nights staying
	Arrival and departure times
	Room type
	Any extra facilities/services
Accommodation	
Conference	Number and types of conference rooms
	Size of rooms
	Layout style
	Demonstration/exhibition areas
	Storage of equipment and audio-visual aids
	Specialised equipment requiring special installation – by whom, when will it arrive?
	Conference equipment – flip charts, lectern, OHP, microphone, simultaneous translation, audio-visual equipment
Residential	Room types/price range
	Number of rooms
	Number per room/room sharing
	Provision of any extras

Reception	Client organisation reception area — where? — how much space?
Administrative	Client organisation office area Secretarial/duplicating service
Social/Leisure/ Entertainment activities	What? When? Numbers

Catering arrangements	Meals on arrival/departure days
	Break times
	Meal times
	Menu types/price range
	Service style
	Special diets
	Childrens meals
	Bar facilities – when
	Official functions — sherry reception
	                — menu/price
	                — service style
	                — seating plan
	                — menu/place name printing
	                — flowers
	                — microphones
	                — guest speaker
	                — toast master
	                — dance band/disco

Miscellaneous	Flowers Newspapers Laundry services Baby-minding Transport

tends to be long – one hotel is known to reserve conference space 10 years in advance) and decide at what point in time various activities must occur and which departments are involved.

Network analysis and a checklist system are useful aids to planning and control. Figure 5.11 shows the decisions and activities to be considered at the planning and preparation stages. Attention to detail during these stages can make a great deal of difference to the final standards of the conference. Liaison must be maintained with the client and it is beneficial if a specific member of the conference office is designated as liaison officer between the client and the operation throughout the entire planning, preparation and execution of the conference.

The client must know whom to contact, and always deal with the same person who has the interests of that specific conference at heart. Frequent liaison between the conference office and all relevant departmental heads is also essential.

Figure 5.11 *Planning and preparation checklist*

	Planning	Preparation
Conference	Decide which facilities/room to use Plan room layouts Decide what audio/visual equipment is required Planning staffing arrangements	Order audio/visual aids Check all equipment Install any equipment necessary Assemble displays Prepare layout Set up with requirements – water, chalk, felt-tip pens, etc Arrange technicians Arrange secretarial and duplicating services Clean all areas Provide sufficient ashtrays or 'no smoking' signs
Residential accommodation	Decide which rooms are to be allocated Decide what facilities/provisions have to be provided Decide how much linen is required Plan staffing arrangements	Allocate specific rooms to delegates Check linen, allocate, make up rooms Allocate provisions Check fire notices Prepare sanitary areas, provide cleaning agents Prepare pantries, provide utensils and beverages Conduct maintenance inspection Clean all rooms
Reception area	Decide where it will be	Set up area

The Client and the Front Office 227

...rooms and leisure areas	Decide which areas will be used	Clean areas
	Plan times of usage	Prepare and layout area
	Plan layouts	Order and arrange flowers
Catering	Plan meal and break-times	Order food and liquor stocks
	Decide which restaurants/dining rooms required	Print menus, name cards, table plans
	Plan menus and types of service	Check cutlery, glassware, crockery, linen stocks
	Plan room layouts	Procure licences
	Plan bar times and location	Clean rooms
	Plan formal conference function	Prepare layouts, set up
	Estimate cutlery, glassware, crockery, linen requirements	
	Plan staffing arrangements	
	Book band/disco	
Staffing	Estimate all staffing requirements	Brief staff
	Plan staff schedules and rotas	Train staff if necessary
Miscellaneous	Decide on portering arrangements	
	Plan sign-posting	

The activities involved in the preparation stage particularly will differ from a hotel to an educational establishment.

In a university student accommodation will obviously be used, and provisions, such as soap and towels, coat hangers, beverages, which are not allocated to students, will have to be provided for conference delegates.

Students will have to be notified to clear their rooms, so provision for storing student belongings may be required. Delegates name cards may be stuck on doors, and room lists put up in prominent places. Unlicensed premises will have to obtain licences; decide where the bar facilities will be sited; and what security arrangements are required. Many educational premises do not have a physical reception desk, so one may have to be organised.

Some educational establishments actually possess special conference stocks of those items either which they do not generally provide for students or of a higher quality than those they do provide. These stocks may include bed linen, towels, soaps, cutlery, crockery, glassware and table linen for example.

5.6.4 The conference

Once everything is prepared, a final inspection should be made to ensure that the standards are being achieved, nothing has been overlooked, and the existing condition of the premises noted in case of accidents and vandalism occurring during the conference.

Figure 5.12 shows the activities which occur during the conference.

Liaison with the client representative must be maintained throughout the duration of the conference and an effective monitoring system established to ensure all arrangements proceed smoothly and according to plan.

At the end of the conference, customer satisfaction may be investigated to ascertain the delegates views, preferences and perceived strengths and weaknesses of the conference package.

5.6.5 Follow-up

At the end of the conference a physical check of the premises used may take place to estimate any damage or misplaced items for which a charge may be made, depending on the extent of the damage and the agreed contractual arrangements. Missing keys may be chased up and lost property sent to the client organisation, depending on company policy.

Outstanding accounts will have to be finalised and submitted for payment. A sales opportunity occurs to encourage not only the re-booking of this particular conference but all delegates are a potential source of future business and conference or other marketing campaigns may be conducted.

Finally, a de-briefing session with Departmental Heads may highlight strengths and weaknesses in the conference organisation.

Figure 5.12 *Flow chart to show delegate and conference activities throughout duration of conference*

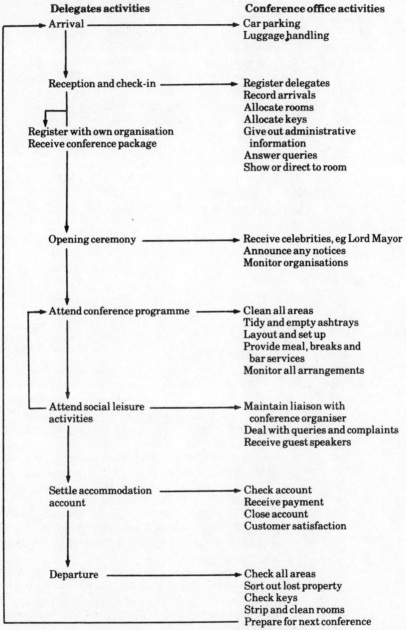

Delegates activities	Conference office activities
Arrival	Car parking Luggage handling
Reception and check-in	Register delegates Record arrivals Allocate rooms Allocate keys Give out administrative information Answer queries Show or direct to room
Register with own organisation Receive conference package	
Opening ceremony	Receive celebrities, eg Lord Mayor Announce any notices Monitor organisations
Attend conference programme	Clean all areas Tidy and empty ashtrays Layout and set up Provide meal, breaks and bar services Monitor all arrangements
Attend social leisure activities	Maintain liaison with conference organiser Deal with queries and complaints Receive guest speakers
Settle accommodation account	Check account Receive payment Close account Customer satisfaction
Departure	Check all areas Sort out lost property Check keys Strip and clean rooms Prepare for next conference

The accounting arrangements will vary – sometimes delegates will pay individually for accommodation prior to arrival or on departure, sometimes delegates pay for accommodation with their conference fee and their Conference Organiser then pays all accommodation costs.

5.7 Computerising Front Office Activities

Technological development has certainly made a great impact on front office activities. The decision to computerise the front office was often forced by the breakdown of the electro-mechanical accounting machine, and many operations have commenced by computerising the accounting activities and then extending the system to encompass other front office activities. Software packages are available covering virtually every front office function from reservations, registration, room allocation, guest history, billing and accounting, to producing management information. Room management systems, such as room status, message waiting, early morning calls, baby listening, fire detection, security systems and electronic keys, drinks dispensers, in-room video, teletext, telephone logging, and energy control systems, can all be inter-linked with a networked computer system. Some operations have computerised central reservations and referral systems and have terminal links with transport such as airlines and car hire companies.

To be of value, the computerised system must be a cost effective and viable proposition. Although the cost of computer systems is decreasing, they are still expensive to purchase, and selection of both hardware and software, installation, staff introduction and training, are not easy problems with which to deal. Initially, a feasibility study involving the consideration of anticipated functions, siting, installation, staffing and customer implications, breakdown, security and control, should be undertaken to decide whether or not a system would be advantageous, to whom and in what ways.

If the costs outweigh the advantages, as may well be the case in a small operation, it is unwise to proceed. If the outcome is to purchase, then great care must be taken to define requirements (ie specify what the computer is required to do and the data required) and purchase the most suitable system. Even though prices are decreasing, it is unwise to purchase rashly and end up with a system that does not really carry out the required function or produce the data in the formats required.

When identifying the software package required, it is necessary to consider the type of business, market segments, existing systems and general occupancy trends, and use the guest cycle as a guide to estimate the number of transactions over a period and the specific inputs, outputs, storage capacity and number of calculations required. It is possible to estimate how many advance reservations are taken over a period of time, and specify the mean length of 'lead' time between reservation and arrival as a means of estimating the disc storage capacity for the advanced reservation function. The following aspects may be specified for the advanced reservations programme:

(1) Allow room availability check
— by date of arrival
— for period of intended stay
— by room type within date of arrival

— by price range within date of arrival
(2) Input potential guests reservation details (specify data)
— Store until date of arrival
— File trace by date of arrival
— File trace by surname
— File trace by 1st initial of surname
— Then store as registration card
— Printout registration card (store for 12 months)
— Update room availability
(3) Allow overbooking facility
— Manager to be able to change percentage daily or as required
(4) Input confirmation received
— Update guest file
— Update room availability file
— Update arrival and departure list
(5) Input deposit received (specify data)
— Update guest file
— Update room availability file
— Update arrival and departure list
(6) Output arrival and departure list
— Confirmed and unconfirmed
— By date of arrival for day
    for next week
    for next month
(7) Output occupancy forecasts (state specific data)
(8) Output marketing data (state specific data)

If a system is to be purchased then installation and staff training become reality.

5.7.1 Installation

It is useful for the system to be available somewhere in the building for a period of time before installation in the front office to allow for training and familiarisation. It is sensible actually to install the computer in the front office (having already decided where it will be sited and made any physical alterations) at the quietest time of the week to minimise inconvenience to personnel and customers. In a commercial hotel with a high occupancy during the week, the most convenient time for installation is at the weekend. If physical installation in this example took place during Friday night, relevant data could be fed into the system during the weekend and the system could probably be operational after balancing at the end of the first shift on Monday morning, a procedure adopted by at least one large hotel chain.

5.7.2 Staff training

Training is essential to ensure a smooth changeover from the previous system to the computerised system. Training must commence well in advance of installation so that staff have time to overcome their feelings of insecurity and doubt in their own ability to cope, which are very frequent problems of which management must be aware.

Once the initial barrier is overcome staff must not only be taught how to operate the system but also be given time to build up confidence, so that when the system is physically sited in the front office and 'goes live', operation is second nature.

It is useful to identify which groups of personnel require training, what knowledge and skills they require, and the duration of their training. One known example is where a hotel chain identified the following groups of personnel and placed them in the priority order indicated for training purposes:

Group 1   Front office manager, head receptionist and cashier
Group 2   General Manager, Assistant and Duty Manager
Group 3   Controller, night auditor, control/accounts clerk
Group 4   Front office personnel
Group 5   Housekeeping personnel
Group 6   Other sales outlet personnel
Group 7   Porter

Staff training should also involve discussing any changes in grading, scheduling arrangements and daily routine.

The installation of a computer may require personnel to cover a whole range of front office activities, so becoming multi-skilled as opposed to retaining traditional grades with specified responsibilities. Their daily routine will certainly change and personnel may have much more 'spare' time due to speedier processing of data and management information and statistics being produced by the system. This available time may be used for greater customer contact and increased sales effort but personnel must be aware that this is so and be trained to cope with changing responsibilities, otherwise frustration might result.

5.7.3

Control measures must be implemented to ensure efficiency, security and operation is continually maintained.

The following control measures may be considered:

— Training, supervision and frequent monitoring
— No personnel allowed to eat or drink in the area whilst using the system.
— Storage of discs to be organised in encased filing tray
— Care to be taken with floppy discs
  — not put on window sills or radiators to be affected by heat
  — coffee cups, etc, not to be stood on them
  — to be treated with respect
— Duplicate copies – on file – of vital information
— Regular data validation checks in programmes to ensure right data

is fed in and rubbish is rejected
— Prevent static occurring in the area

Security
— All personnel to be issued with a password control code for access into the system
— Personnel only to have access to that part of the programme to which they need access to carry out their duties
— All confidential information and vital financial data on disc to be stored securely
— Duplicate copies of vital information kept off site in case of fire or other emergencies
— Vital discs may need to be kept in fire proof storage cabinets (which will prevent discs melting in the case of fire)
— No personnel to have access to the operating system
— Management audit trail for checking purposes.

Maintaining operation
— Planned maintenance of system
— Effective 24 hour call-out in case of breakdown
— Duplicate VDUs or printers in case of failure (may consider 'Duplex' system, ie two processing units)
— Regular print-outs, at least at the end of each shift, so that in case of a break-down it is only necessary to back-track to the last print-out to commence a manual system.

References
[1] DIX, C, *Accommodation Operations*, MacDonald and Evans 1982
[2] KASAVANA, M L, *Hotel Information Systems*, CBI Publishing Co 1978
[3] LAVENSON, J, *Think Strawberries*, Paper delivered to American Medical Association, New York, 7 February 1974
[4] HCITB, Small Business Aid 'What Price Should I Charge?' 1979

Further reading
HARRIS, P and HAZZARD, P, *Accounting and Financial Management in the Hotel and Catering Industry*, Northwood 1977
KOTAS, R, *Management Accounting for Hotels and Restaurants*, Surrey University Press 1977
PAIGE, G and J, *The Hotel Receptionist*, Holt, Rinehart and Winston 1984

6

Unified Themes

In the system of Accommodation Management, an analysis of the sub-systems has been made and the response of each sub-system to environmental constraints and influences (which dictate the specific form and characteristic of any system of Accommodation Management) have been considered. A specific environmental influence may affect just one specific sub-system, or several, but there are four particular influences which deserve special attention, since they have far reaching effects in each sub-system in any specific system of accommodation management (be it in the XYZ hotel, in the EFG military base or any other enterprise). These influences are:

1 Finance   3 Health and safety
2 Energy   4 Security

Finance is, more often than not, a limiting factor in any enterprise and the preparation and control of a budget by the Accommodation Manager will determine the pattern of development of his or her department. Energy usage can, in general terms, be considered as a financial constraint, but due to the technical implications of the resource it will be looked at separately. Health, safety and security will be considered together. Influencing the sub-systems here, are legal, moral and practical constraints.

6.1 FINANCE

Any good manager must ensure that all the resources available to him are used to their maximum effect to achieve both the specific objectives of the department and the overall aims of the enterprise. The resources available to the Accommodation Manager are:

Personnel   The Building
Equipment   Energy
Materials   Own experience.

If maximum efficiency is to be achieved this may not mean that resources must be used to their maximum capacity, rather that they should operate at an optimum level.

Optimum staffing types, levels and deployment must be determined and controlled; the most appropriate materials and equipment selected, stored and utilised; the building must be maintained to facilitate optimum occupancy levels, and power usage must be identified, monitored and controlled. Probably the most important document which the manager produces will be the annual budget, whereby detailed plans are developed for the department in the coming year and expressed in financial terms. In this way he or she aims to influence the allocation of monies – a resource of the overall enterprise. (In some enterprises, a budget may be imposed on the Accommodation Manager. This automatically reduces his or her authority and ability to determine the best course of action for the department to assist most effectively in the achievement of the over-all goals of the enterprise. Nevertheless, the manager is bound to endeavour to use the financial resource to its best effect.

6.1.1 Budgetary control

The terms *budget* and *estimates* are often used as if synonymous, but here *estimates* are defined as 'plans developed within broad financial targets' whereas 'budgets' will relate to a financial expression of an intention to take a specific course of action. Budgetary control begins with scrutiny of this planned expenditure and, essentially, is a control over the resources devoted to the actions, not just an exercise in the overall control of money.

The Accommodation Manager will need to prepare annual budgets, along with other departmental managers, probably three to six months in advance. When approved and amalgamated these will then constitute the master budget. The cost centres will vary from one establishment to another and from one accounting system to another. They will also vary with the size, scope and organisation of the operation. The Accommodation Department's cost centres will include some of the following:

1 *Labour* These will include total costs for each grade of staff employed, also any enhanced rate costs or bonus figures and train-ing, uniform costs, etc. These can be calculated from the whole-time-equivalent figures, deployment schedules and duty rotas.

2 *Supplies* These may include costs for cleaning agents, cleaning equipment (stock and capital items) depreciation of capital equip-ment or equipment replacement, guest supplies, stationery, crock-ery, uniforms. These figures may be assessed by considering past budget figures and any changes in supplies systems. Work pro-cedures and task frequency figures will also give an indication of costs.

3 *Linen and laundry* This may include all types of soft furnishings repairs, cleaning and replacement. It may also include laundry equipment (and maintenance) and product costs where there is an on-premises laundry. Again, to assess these costs, historic data will be valuable.

4 *Maintenance* These may include external maintenance, eg grounds, gardens and external fabric and internal costs, eg surfaces, structures, plant and equipment.

5 *Contract service*, eg window cleaning, floral arrangements, redecorating.

6 *Furniture and furnishings* This may include all types of furniture, some fittings, carpets, etc.

No item should be included on the budget which is outside the scope of the manager's authority. Where unit costings are to be calculated, the total figure, from the calculations above, can be divided by the number of units (a 'unit' could be a patient's bed or, say, 100 sq m in a hospital, a room or a student in a hall of residence, a bed or bedroom in an hotel).

In addition to operational costs, other costs which must be calculated and apportioned for unit costs to be complete are the 'service costs'.

With the standard system of hotel accounts the 'service costs' tend to be classified as 'Service Department Costs' (including administration; sales, advertising and promotion; heat light and power) and General Expenditure (including any item which cannot be allocated to another heading). In this standard system of hotel accounts, repairs and maintenance, plant and machinery and property cost centres are not included in the figures used to calculate the hotel operating profit. This is so that a common classification, up to and including general expenditure, can produce information on income, expenditure and profit which is reasonably uniform and comparable throughout the industry.

Within the Health Service there tends to be two classes of expenditure:

Patient care services
General services (amongst others, administration, domestic and cleaning, portering, linen and laundry services and 'estate' management which includes energy costs).

A budget is produced for each department within each unit (a unit being, in this case, a hospital).

6.1.2 Budget preparation
In order to prepare a realistic budget, the following comparisons can be made with the budget for the current financial year:

Total costs
Costs per cost centre
Actual expenditure to date.

To facilitate budget preparation and also to enable the ongoing process of budgetary control to operate, *cost statements* or *operating statements* produced at certain fixed intervals, eg weekly or monthly can be produced. These reports compare the actual expenditure with the budgetary figure and any unsatisfactory variances can be investigated and, hopefully, controlled. In such a way, problems might be identified and rectified at an early stage.

The style of presentation of budget varies with the operation and its accounting system, but there does need to be a standard format within an organisation. One style of layout is shown in figure 6.1.

Figure 6.1 *XYZ hospital: domestic departmental budget*

Code No.	Staffing	Percentage of budget
01	Domestic services manager	3
	Assistant domestic services manager	2
02	Domestic supervisors	5
03	Domestic assistants	35
04	Ward orderlies	–
05	Housekeepers and teams	–
06	Window cleaners	–
07	Temporary staff	–
08	Domestic supervisors bonus	–
09	Domestic floor team bonus	–
10	Domestic assistant bonus	–
11	Ancillaries domestic	–
		45
	Non-staffing	
29	Hardware and crockery	0.01
30	General equipment cleaning materials	0.01
31	General equipment general items	0.60
32	General equipment repairs and maintenance	0.03
33	Cleaning materials catering	0.50
34	Cleaning materials domestic	1.50
35	Cleaning materials other	1.50
36	Replacement cleaning equipment	0.50
37	Contract services window cleaning	1
38	Contract services general cleaning	49
39	Contract services housekeeping	–
40	Contract services other	0.30
41	Travel and subsistance	0.02
42	Miscellaneous	0.03
43	Staff uniforms	–
44	Services received from other units	–
45	Services provided to other units	–
46	General equipment special items	–
		55
		100

To operate maximum control over the budget, the Accommodation Manager should be responsible for its preparation, within policies set by higher management. Whilst the manager's budget proposals may not be accepted in their entirety, he or she must be involved in any decision made involving its amendment and given the opportunity to justify his or her financial plans. Ultimately the manager may have to operate the department under different (probably tighter) financial constraints and must be aware of all expenses incurred. A regular operating statement will facilitate this, as will any other information appertaining to costs, eg copy invoices of supplies received, information of changing wage rates, bonus payments. Much routine information associated with budgetary control, can be compiled systematically and readily processed by computer for the assistance of the budget holder.

6.2 ENERGY CONSERVATION

The standard system of hotel accounting does not provide for the reallocation or recharging of the costs of 'service departments' (including heat, light and power) to operated departments, eg rooms department. In the Health Service, each unit, eg a hospital, has an energy budget but separate departments within that hospital generally do not. Thus, in the past, probably the only information available on energy consumption in buildings was in the annual accounts. Even then, annual variations in building energy costs were generally apportioned to changes in energy prices and analyses of energy utilisation were rarely pursued. Gradually, the realisation of a predicted 'world energy crisis' is dawning in this country. In recent years, sharp increases in energy prices have developed public awareness, at least in the consequence of the problem, and green policies are being developed.

At present some 30% of the total UK prime energy consumption is used in buildings (more than that used by industry for production purposes). In order to stop this predicted world energy crisis, many would argue that a corporate responsibility must be fostered, mainly through a massive educational programme. Reduction in the use of heat, light and power can be encouraged by reduced fuel bills, but the savings must go further. Economic use of all things (from the use of disposables to the use of wall coverings) must be strived for and energy reclamation must be developed, eg recycling waste, if significant world energy conservation is to be achieved.

Tackling the problem on a much smaller scale, that is within a single building, the Accommodation Manager must be aware of the energy consumption of his or her department and probably the process towards conservation should follow a similar pattern. Reducing fuel bills in public buildings is, however, inevitably more difficult than cutting fuel bills in a private residence. The commitment and the direct financial incentives of most building users is lacking. Educating users in energy awareness must be the key. Setting up training sessions for staff is relatively easy. The success of this training is another matter, as is the education of customers.

One way of ensuring more economic use of energy is to create an environment where excessive uses are neither desired by users nor, in any case, easily achieved and such an environment is best developed in the design and planning stages of a new building. The Department of Health and Social Security commissioned the design and construction of a low energy hospital and the project received sponsorship from the EEC. Much was learned from the project and some features incorporated would not be recommended for future buildings, however, a 50% reduction of energy usage over comparable establishments was achieved – a significant financial reward over the life of a hospital.

A list of some design and construction features is given below, together with their implications:

1 *Siting of the building*

Exposed sites with high windspeeds give reduced U values and increased ventilation rates. Elevated sites are cooler. Polluted sites, eg noise or air require mechanical ventilation.

2 *Volume, shape and layout of the building envelope*

Smaller volumes give better energy economy. Smaller surface areas reduce heat loss. Open planned buildings require additional heating. Orientation of windows affects solar gain.

3 *Construction*

Structural insulation (wall and roof), double glazing and reduced window sizes minimise heat loss

4 *Heating systems*

Heat sources should be centrally located for insulation. Zoned heating, thermostatically controlled is recommended. Fuel selection is vital, boilers easily converted to all alternative fuels may be cost effective. Exhaust heat may be reclaimed. Heat pumps are advocated. Waste incineration might be one heat source.

5 *Fittings*

Internal surfaces should reduce heat losses. Lighting systems should be cost effective, eg high efficiency lighting. Humidifiers may be needed where windows are reduced.

Monitoring usage in certain areas may be an incentive. Tight environmental monitoring and control can be achieved through computerisation.

Providing a low energy building is by no means the total solution. Such a building encourages economic use of energy and probably focuses attention of users on energy conservation but control must be on-going. The employment of energy managers has been seen by some establishments as a means of ensuring a constant awareness of energy usage. One of the first tasks of an energy manager may well be to establish regular energy audits, whereby usage of power in different sections is monitored and analysed. Downward trends can be encouraged and upward trends quickly identified and any faults hopefully rectified.

Training staff in awareness of energy use may be a significant means of encouraging the development of processes which require less energy. Equipment and materials may then be selected with energy conservation in mind and suitable maintenance programmes developed to ensure that all items work at their optimum efficiency. To encourage the best use of energy, emphasis must be placed on the control of usage rather than on the monitoring of wastage.

6.3 HEALTH AND SAFETY

Under the Health and Safety at Work Act (1974) the manager has legal responsibilities both as an employer and as an employee. As an employer he is required:

1 To provide and maintain safe plant and systems
2 To ensure, so far as reasonably practicable, safety and absence of risks to health in connection with the use, handling, storage and transport of articles and substances.
3 To provide such information, training, instruction and supervision as is necessary to maintain health and safety standards.
4 To maintain safe places of work, including entrances and exits.
5 To provide a working environment which is, so far as is reasonably practicable, safe and without risks to health and adequate regarding facilities and arrangements for welfare.

To comply with these responsibilities, it is useful to refer to the resources available to the Accommodation Manager and assess his responsibility for each. The first resource is staff and here the manager must ensure that their working environment is safe, the materials and equipment they use are safe and that they are trained for their job and appropriately supervised. The next two resources are equipment and materials and here, to ensure that they are safe in use, they must be selected with due care, stored and maintained as appropriate and staff must be trained and supervised in their use.

Power and plant (the Building) are the final resources of the Accommodation Manager and to ensure that these are safe for all building users their components must be selected and maintained, hazard notices displayed, where there are unavoidable defects these should receive attention and again staff must be trained and supervised in their safe use. Further provisions will often be appropriate for the security of the building and its users.

From this brief analysis, major responsibilities under the heading of Health and Safety can be identified, but the Accommodation Manager will need to delve deeper than this and prepare a policy document:

1 To identify health and safety hazards with respect to his or her specific department
2 Explain how these risks will be minimised.

Such a Health and Safety policy would vary from one establishment to another but some of the broader issues are identified in the sample Health and Safety Policy. Two further sample policies are also included, namely a Fire Policy and a Security Policy. To some extent fire and security threats are covered in the general health and safety policy but these are two topics demanding considerable attention of the practising Accommodation Manager and worthy of further comment here.

Sample: *Accommodation Department Health and Safety Policy*

The promotion of Health and Safety measures is to be regarded as a joint management and employee objective. The manager places great importance on the safety and well being of employees together with other building users. Employees together with management will assist in deciding the necessary precautions to be taken. To ensure co-operate effort, management and employee representatives, together with safety officers will inspect all working areas and equipment every few months and recommendations to improve standards of health and safety will be progressed.

The general identified potential hazards and the proposals to minimise risks are given below:

1 Equipment is seen as a potential hazard where it is used incorrectly, inappropriately or in a badly maintained condition.
   Proposed controls of these risks are:

(a) Equipment will be selected with due care to be used for identified tasks in specific situations.
(b) Provision will be made for appropriate accessories including attachments or warning notices to indicate work in progress.
(c) Equipment users will be given training and retraining where necessary in the safe use and care of equipment. Employees will not use equipment for which they have not received training.
(d) Adequate supervision will be provided for equipment usage.
(e) Scheduling of work will make adequate allowance for tasks to be completed safely.
(f) Regular preventative maintenance will be practised and procedures developed for dealing with defective equipment.
(g) Suitable storage conditions will be provided for all equipment.

2 Surfaces could represent slip, trip, fire, noise, infection or other hazards where they are defective, inappropriate or otherwise unsafe.
   Proposed controls of these risks are:

(a) Selection of surfaces including floors, walls, furniture and sanitary fittings will be performed with due care.
(b) Appropriate planned preventative cleaning and maintenance routines will be applied.
(c) Adequate systems of inspection, hazard spotting and reporting will be devised.
(d) Design and layout of the interior will, wherever possible, make for safe conditions. Where hazards are unavoidable, suitable warnings will be used.

3 Chemicals represent a potential hazard, possibly causing adverse effects on users, on the building users and on surfaces through

chemical reactions, odours and other means. Some may represent a fire risk or be a poison risk.

Proposed control of these risks are by the following:

(a) Careful selection of the chemicals which will be appropriate to specific surfaces in specific situations.

(b) Provision of appropriate protective clothing, eg rubber gloves and overalls.

(c) Provision of adequate training in the use and storage of chemicals.

(d) Provision of adequate supervision of use.

(e) Provision of warning notices or instruction information on usage, dilutions, etc, will be made.

(f) Appropriate equipment will be provided for use with chemicals.

(g) Provision will be made for appropriate storage facilities and stores control systems to monitor and control usage and availability of chemicals.

(h) Chemicals will be issued to authorised users only.

4 The general physical and psychological environment may represent health and safety risks through various ergonomic defects, eg temperature levels, privacy requirements, security needs and job satisfaction.

Proposed controls of these potential threats are:

(a) The monitoring and control of the environment to ensure healthy and comfortable conditions.

(b) The development of an efficient and sensitive personnel function which will provide staff welfare.

(c) The use of a well staffed occupational health department.

(d) The efficient operation of safety representatives.

Sample: *Fire Policy*

Probably the greatest risk threatening any property owner is that of fire. Fire safety is regarded with great importance as it can threaten lives and livelihoods of all building users. Maximum co-operation of staff is sought to minimise the risks of fire by ensuring safe working practices are followed and any hazards reported with urgency.

The potential hazards and proposals made to minimise the risks are as follows:

1 The building itself is identified as the first risk. This includes the main structure, internal design and layout and all furniture, fittings and furnishings. Many of these components may be flammable, some may hamper fire detection, safety of escape or effectiveness of fire fighting.

Controls of these risks are:

(a) The building, its components and uses are scrutinised by the Fire Authority before the issue of the Fire Certificate. Any faults found by the Fire Authority are dealt with urgently to comply with requirements and recommendations.

(b) Selection procedures for any new items incorporate consideration of fire hazards.

(c) Smoke and fire detectors, smoke doors, alarms, alternative escape routes, exit signs, emergency lighting and extinguishers are fitted and maintained in line with recommendations.

2 Absence of appropriate procedures to deal with fire prevention, detection, alarm and escape would constitute fire hazards.

Procedures devised include the following:

(a) Daily inspection checks are implemented to identify any fire hazards and problems so identified are dealt with urgently.

(b) Stores areas are included in the regular inspection and items in storage are stored in line with requirements and recommendations.

(c) Procedures to follow, on the detection of fire and on hearing the alarm raised, are included in all staff's training and communicated to other building users on the approved fire notices.

(d) When normal procedures become temporarily inappropriate due to building work or other reasons, alternative procedures are devised and communicated to those concerned.

(e) Security procedures will be maintained to reduce the risk of arsonists, terrorists or the like gaining access to the building and a Bomb Threat procedure will be devised and implemented.

3 All building users represent a fire risk when unsafe practices occur. To minimise this risk:

(a) Regular staff training and retraining incorporates procedures to be followed to: promote fire prevention; deal with the detection of a fire hazard; deal with the detection of a fire; effect the safest means of escape for themselves and other building users in the case of fire; operate fire extinguishers where appropriate.

(b) Procedures to follow when a fire is detected or the alarm raised are communicated to other building users on approved notices posted as is required and recommended.

4 Items in short or longer term storage represent a fire risk, particularly during the periods where personnel are not in their immediate vicinity to identify hazards.

To minimise this risk:

(a) Highly flammable items will not be stored in the long term and when short term storage is necessitated, such items will be stored in separate fire proof confines as recommended by the Fire Authority.

(b) Flammable items will receive strict stock control, minimum quantities will be kept and recommendations of the Fire Authority will be sought and followed.

(c) No smoking will occur in any stores areas.

(d) All items of stock and the physical stores areas themselves will be monitored and controlled with fire risks in mind.

6.4 SECURITY

Sample: *Security Policy for XYZ Hotel*

The promotion of security within this establishment is to be regarded as a joint management and employee objective. The safety and security of employees, guests, personal belongings, plant, equipment and furnishings will be best achieved through a co-operative effort.

Potential security risks are outlined below, together with current policies on minimising these:

1 *Staff, guests and other bona-fide users*
The possible risks here, are from personal attack, bomb threats or terrorist attack, unauthorised disclosure of personal information and theft or damage to personal belongings. To minimise these risks the following procedures are operative:

(a) Access to and use of the building is restricted through means of identifying bona-fide users. Guests are issued with identifying 'key cards' and their luggage with similar luggage tags.

(b) References are taken up on all staff on employment to ensure honesty and trustworthiness.

(c) Personal records and confidential information appertaining to staff or guests are held by authorised staff and access to these is restricted to authorised users only. Such records, when disposed of are shredded or otherwise defaced and destroyed to prevent unauthorised use.

(d) Access to such records on computer is again restricted to authorised users of the records. Disposal is absolute when implemented.

(e) Lockers are provided for all staff and locker rooms are open to inspection by management.

(f) Hand luggage may not be carried by staff further than the locker room.

(g) Facilities are provided, on a short term basis, for the safe keeping of valuables for staff and guests.

(h) A bomb threat procedure has been devised and is included in staff induction programmes.

2 *Building, fabric, fittings and furnishings*
Vandalism and theft (apart from bomb threats and terrorist attack mentioned above) are the major problems foreseen in this area and precautions are as follows:

(a) Entry to the building is restricted to identified bona-fide users ; authorisation of all building users is checked.

(b) Anti-intrusion devices including alarms and barred windows are installed where considered appropriate.

(c) Doors are fitted with locks as appropriate and strict key-control is exercised.

(d) A security patrol is employed for surveillance of hotel grounds.

(e) Part of all staff's training includes security training and the importance of reporting suspicious persons or situations.

(f) Staff are also trained in a bomb scare procedure devised for our hotel.

3 Cash and keys

Theft of wages, from tills, metered telephones and hotel takings are seen to be a potential risk. Theft or dishonest use of keys are also risks to be minimised. Procedures adopted are as follows:

(a) Security guards are employed for the handling of large quantities of money.

(b) Personnel are identified by a supervisor at wage payouts.

(c) Cash points and tills are frequently emptied.

(d) Regular balancing and auditing of accounts is ensured.

(e) References of all recruits are taken up prior to employment.

(f) Identification/Key cards must be produced by guests before occupied room keys are handed to them.

(g) Sub-master, master and grand master keys are used and access to each restricted to authorised users.

(h) Keys are only issued to authorised users on signature. Returned keys are similarly received and signed for.

4 Stores

Theft of goods delivered in stores areas or issued and 'in use' is controlled by the following means:

(a) Strict stores control operates and usage is monitored. Issues and receipts are checked.

(b) Access to stores keys is restricted to authorised persons.

(c) Appropriate record systems of stores are kept and access, including access to computerised records, is restricted.

(d) Supervision of staff and spot checking of staff leaving the premises is undertaken.

Glossary

A.D.M. Association of Domestic Management.

Air count A term related to the number of microbes present in the air. Measured using an agar plate.

Antiseptic A product intended for use on or in human tissues, capable of killing or preventing growth of micro-organisms.

Asepsis The exclusion of putrefying bacteria from the field of operation.

Audit trace A check through the audit roll of an electro-mechanical or electric front office accounting machine or through a computer trace through the accounting transactions to verify transactions.

Autoclave Apparatus for sterilisation by steam at high pressure.

Bacterial counts – see *Swab tests* and *Air counts*

Biodegradable Detergents and other surface active agents are decomposed by normal sewage treatments or are broken down and absorbed by bacteriological cycles, leaving no toxic matter.

Booking out Arranging accommodation in another hotel for guests with a reservation at one's own hotel when over booking has occurred and there are more guests than rooms available.

Break even analysis An examination of how much profit or loss will be made by a business at different levels of turn-over.

Break even point The point at which all costs are covered and there is neither a profit nor a loss.

Buffing A process to harden the polish film applied to the floor surface and create a gloss finish.

Cationic detergent A detergent in which the active part of the molecule carries a positive charge.

Chemical disinfectant A product capable of destroying micro-organisms, but not usually spores, not necessarily killing all micro-organisms but reducing numbers to a level not normally harmful to health.

Compression Where mechanical load forces atoms closer together.

Contract furniture/contract use Designed for other than domestic use.

Contribution costing An approach to pricing seeking to achieve a target contribution towards fixed costs and profits. The general philosophy is that although individual sales may not achieve a net profit, the sum total of contributions from all sales will be sufficient to cover fixed costs and provide an adequate net profit.

Cost plus costing A pre-determined amount or percentage ('mark-up') is added to an estimated cost to arrive at the selling price.

Credit limit   A limit to the amount of credit allowed to a guest before account is paid.

Deadleg   A pipe serviced by hot water which does not form part of the circulation system.

Density chart   A reservation system used in modern hotel types with few room types. It involves reserving a room-type rather than a room by number.

Density reservation chart   A density chart representing a week rather than a day.

Deposits ledger   A composite account in which advance deposits are credited to the guest.

Disbursement   A payment made by the hotel on behalf of the guest which is then charged to the guest.

Disinfection   Removal or destruction of sufficient numbers of micro-organisms to avoid danger to health. Achieved by dry or moist heat or chemicals.

Dye spinning   A fibre forming chemical is dissolved in a volatile solvent which evaporates in warm air after filaments leave the spinneret.

Emulsification   Creating a colloidal suspension of one liquid in another.

Fixed costs   Costs which remain constant irrespective of changes in volume of business.

Guest history index   Specified details relating to guests who have stayed in the past, usually including legally required registration details.

Hard water   Hardness is caused mainly by calcium and magnesium salts and is measured in parts per million, eg soft, 0–50 parts per million.

Heat pump   Works on the principal of latent heat of vapouristation. A liquid refrigerant is used in combination with a low temperature source to generate heat energy.

High efficiency boiler   Designed to heat water as necessary rather than to provide stored hot water.

HCIMA   Hotel Catering and Institutional Management Association.

HCITB   Hotel and Catering Industrial Training Board. Now HCTC.

Hotel diary   A reservation system using a diary for entering details.

Hubbart room formula   A method of pricing based on the rate of return method of pricing yielding a minimum average room rate sufficient to earn a stated rate of return on capital.

Hydrolysis   The formulation of an acid and a base from a salt by interaction with water; it is caused by the ionic dissociation of water.

Lead time   The length of time between the reservation and the guest's arrival.

Life cycle   The length of time of an item before replacement is necessary.

Link man   An hotel commissionaire.

Marginal cost   The cost of producing the next unit.

Marginal costing See contribution pricing.

Melt spinning Hard polyester is melted, extruded through a spinneret and cooled in air to solidify filaments.

No show Guests with prior reservations who do not arrive.

Open tender All organisations are invited to submit tenders.

Outstanding accounts ledger May be referred to as *Bad Debts Ledger*, a guest bill being paid by a company or an individual on account is debited here after the guest's account is finalised by the front office. It remains a debt until payment is received and credited.

Overbooking Accepting more reservations than there is accommodation available.

Paramedical Hospital functions, other than medical associated with patient care.

pH Potential of hydrogen; a means of quantifying the acidity or alkalinity of a solution.

Pool system Where a central pool of linen exists to be shared by all users and a pre-determined quantity is issued on a regular basis in exchange for dirty items.

P45 Personal taxation summary.

Quantity surveyor Advises on all cost matters, rendering procedures and contractual arrangements and acts as accountant.

Rate of return pricing Designed to ensure the correct relationship between capital invested and the resultant net profit.

Referral system Referring reservations to other hotels in the group or syndicate.

Replacement cycle Analysing when an item needs replacing or renewing, based on knowledge of rates of deterioration.

Reservation chart A traditional charting system for reserving a specific room.

Rooms list A list of which guests are staying in which rooms.

Room rack An old-fashioned wooden rack used for filing advanced and current reservations, largely replaced by the Whitney System.

Room status The state of every room at a given time, ie occupied, vacant, ready for re-letting, out of order.

Rule of thumb pricing Used to give an instant estimate of room rate based on construction costs. This suggests that £1 charge is made for every £1000 of the total construction cost.

Secondary infection When a patient contracts another illness, usually as a result of cross infection.

Selective tendering Organisations are picked out and only these invited to submit a tender.

Semi variable costs These move in sympathy with, but not in proportion to, the volume of sales.

Sepsis The invasion of bodily tissues by non-specific pathogenic organisms.

Slit sampler A suction machine capable of taking timed quantities of air from the atmosphere and measuring bacterial loading in the air.

Soap A product formulated by the saponification or neutralisation of fats, oils, resins, waxes or their acids with organic or inorganic bases. Usually natural components are used.

Solvent The component of a solution which is present in excess, or whose physical state is the same as that of the solution.

Spray burnishing/buffing A method of floor maintenance whereby a fine mist of cleaning solution or floor polish is applied and buffed whilst still damp, until the surface drys and hardens and dirt is removed.

Static Change in charge caused by the transfer of electrons from one surface to another as a result of abrasion. Unless there is some means by which the charge can leak to earth it will accumulate.

Sterilisation The destruction or removal of all microbial life.

Stop list A list of stolen and invalid credit cards issued by the card company.

Stop–Go chart A summary of room availability prominently displayed so that time is not spent checking room availability system. High demand periods will be indicated with overbooking instructions.

Surface tension A property of liquid surfaces whereby they appear to be covered by a thin elastic membrane in a state of tension.

Surfactant Capable of breaking down the surface tension.

Swab test A method of analysing the microbes present.

Synthetic detergent/syndet Products manufactured from processed organic chemicals usually derived from petroleum.

Synthetic time values Time standards built up from element times previously obtained from direct time study.

Tariffs The pricing structure quoted to the consumer which may be bed only, bed and breakfast, half board, full board, inclusive terms, special package.

Tension Where mechanical loads force atoms further apart.

Toilet cleanser An acidic cleaning agent comprising sodium bisulphate and chlorine compounds of hydrochloric acid or phosphoric acid specially formulated for cleaning inside toilet bowls.

Traditional reservation chart See *Reservation chart*

Valance A textile frill or trim around the bed base.

Variable cost Costs which move in proportion to the volume of sales.

VPO Visitors Paid Out. See *Disbursement*

Wet spinning Filaments from the spinneret emerge directly into chemical baths which cause the viscous liquid to solidify.

Whitley Council An organisation associated with the NHS, comprising Management and Staff (including Trade Unions and NHS professional bodies) representatives whose functions are to determine conditions of service and rates of pay. There is a General Council and nine functional councils.

Whitney system A system of metal room racks patented by a USA company used for advanced and current reservations.

Appendix 1

Legislation affecting the work of the Accommodation Manager

Some of the legislation has been classified below into laws affecting:

(a) Employment
(b) Operations
(c) Licensing laws
(d) Building Standards.

These may overlap in many areas.

(a) Laws dealing with employment

Employment of Women, Young Person's and Children's Act 1920
Young Persons (Employment) Acts 1938 and 1964
The Disabled Persons (Employment) Acts 1944 and 1958
Payment of Wages Act 1960
Factories Act 1961
Employers Liability (Defective Equipment) Act 1961
Offices, Shops and Railway Premises Act 1969
Redundancy Payments Act 1965 and 1969
Race Relations Act 1976
Employers Liability (Compulsary Insurance) Act 1969
Equal Pay Act 1970
Attachment of Earnings Act 1971
Contract of Employment Act 1972
Trade Union and Labour Relations Act 1974
Health and Safety at Work Act 1974 (including COSHH Regulations 1988)
Rehabilitation of Offenders Act 1974
Sex Discrimination Act 1974
Employment Protection Act 1975
Wages Council Act 1979

(b) Laws dealing with operations

Sale of Goods Act 1893
Hotel Proprietors Act 1956
Shops, Offices and Railway Premises Act 1963
Health and Safety at Work Act 1974
Equal Pay Act 1970
Sex Discrimination Act 1975
Race Relations Act 1976
Trades Descriptions Act 1968
Contracts of Employment Act 1972
Fire Precautions Act 1971

Misrepresentation Act 1967
Part III of the Development of Tourism Act 1969
Consumer Protection Act 1973
Licensing Laws
Laws of Contract
Gaming Act 1968
The Immigration (Hotel Records) Order 1972
The Innkeepers' Right of Lien and The Innkeepers Act 1878

(c) Licensing laws
Laws and regulations are very complex. Full details may be found in Paterson's Licensing Laws, which is published annually. The ABC of Licensing Laws published by the Licensed Victuallers Central Protection Society of London is also a useful book.

(d) Laws relating to the building
Health and Safety at Work Act 1974
Town and Country Planning Act 1971
Public Health Act 1936 and 1961
Building Regulations 1976
Housing Act (Section 4) 1957
Factories Act 1961
Offices, Shops and Railway Premises Act 1963
Fire Precaution Act 1971
Control of Pollution Act 1974.

Appendix 2

Training Package

The development of a training package involves initially identifying a large scale training need which will warrant the time and effort of formulation and the expense of production, and provision to the end user. The formulation usually undertaken by a small group will involve defining the aims and objectives, writing the content and suggesting suitable training techniques and aids to use. Suggestions for organising and running the training package may also be included.

The benefits of such a concept are that the costs of formulation and production are shared by a number of users over a period of time, thus resulting in more economic training. Standardisation of training and content material, and a systematic approach to training will also result. The training package must be piloted initially in order to eliminate teething problems and be evaluated and updated on a regular basis. It must be flexible to amend to meet local training needs and allow for learners with different learning rates.

The Domestic Supervisors Training Kit

This kit has recently been upgraded and is the first of a comprehensive series of training packages in NHS hotel services. The kit comprises a Manager's Pack and a Supervisor's Pack. It is designed to help Domestic Services Managers train their supervisors, so that they in turn can 'cascade' that training on to their staff.

The packs comprise 11 modules containing technical notes and learning material on the core skill areas.

Module   1 – Introduction
         2 – General Principles of Cleaning
         3 – Cleaning Agents
         4 – Equipment
         5 – Furniture, fixtures and fittings
         6 – Sanitary areas
         7 – Walls, windows and ceilings
         8 – Hard floors
         9 – Textile floor coverings
        10 – Isolation and special risk areas
        11 – Hotel services

The Laundry Supervisor's Manual
This series of handbooks includes:

1 Classification and marking   7 Welfare
2 Washhouse plant   8 Mechanical handling
3 Washing materials   9 Services and safety
4 Washing processes   10 Process and quality control
5 Planning, communications   11 Supervisory skills
6 Drying and finishing

This manual will shortly be upgraded.

Appendix 3

Work Study

The basic work study procedure involves eight basic steps:
1 The task, procedure, job, process, operation is SELECTED and defined.
2 Everything which happens must be directly observed and RECORDED, using the most appropriate techniques (see the Method Study section below).
3 Each step of the whole process, must be critically EXAMINED to identify:
— the purpose
— where it takes place
— in what sequence it occurs
— who is involved
— what means/methods are used.

Where appropriate, the task under review should be considered in the context of the whole operation. It may be beneficial to break-down the task and study the man-process and the work activities and their inter-relationship.

At this stage in the work study procedure the following types of problems may have been highlighted:
— inefficiencies
— clumsy procedures
— double-handling or delays
— productive or non-productive areas
— facilitation or restriction by other activities or the physical environment
— waste in terms of time or energy.

4 The most economic method can be DEVELOPED by using method study techniques.
5 By using work measurement techniques, the quantity of work can be MEASURED and a standard time calculated for the performance.
6 The new method and the related time must be DEFINED for ease of identification.
7 The new method can then be INSTALLED as a standard practice with a defined time allowance.
8 The new standard must be MAINTAINED by using proper control measures.

BASIC WORK STUDY STEPS
Identifying those relevant to method study and work measurement

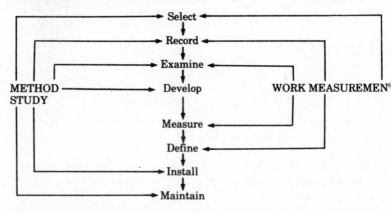

Method study

The British Standards definition of Method Study is: 'the systematic recording and critical examination of existing and proposed ways of doing work, as a means of developing and applying easier and more effective methods and reducing costs.'

Method Study includes six of the eight work study steps:

Select	Develop
Record	Install
Examine	Maintain

1 Select

When selecting the problem(s) to be examined, it is highly likely that the urgent problem(s) will be considered first. However, three issues must be borne in mind.

(a) *Economics*
— is it feasible financially to commence this method study?
— will it be feasible financially to continue to the next stage of this method study?

(b) *Technical knowledge and expertise*
— the appropriate technical knowledge and expertise must be available in order to conduct this method study.

(c) *Human considerations and reactions*
— these are very difficult to assess but mental and emotional reactions to investigations must be anticipated. It may be necessary to offer some form of training in Work Study Appreciation to Trade Union Officials and personnel to ensure they are conversant with basic principles and objectives.

Method study will be more readily accepted by workers if unpopular tasks (which are dirty, heavy, often complained about) are selected in the first place. Personnel are more likely to accept present and future studies if they can see unpopular features removed and effort and fatigue reduced.

2 Record
The success of the whole procedure depends on the accuracy with which facts are recorded. The data recorded will provide the basis for critical examination and the development of the improved method.

The following methods of recording and charting may be used although process and flow-process charts are possibly the widest used methods.

Charts
Process charts – manufacturing or product handling
Flow-process charts – activities of personnel, materials or equipment
Two-handed process charts – activities of a worker's two hands
Multiple activity charts – activities of personnel or machines on a common time scale
Simultaneous Motion Charts (SIMO charts) – activities of a workers' hands, legs and other body movements on a common time scale.

Diagrams and models
Flow and string diagrams – paths of movement of personnel, materials and equipment
Two and three dimensional models – layout of work place or plants
Cyclegraphs or Chronocycle graphs – films of high speed, short cycle operations.

See references at end of section.

3 Examine
This stage involves the use of a series of 'questioning sequences' in an impartial and objective manner and normally follows a well established pattern, with a view to:
— identifying productive and non-productive stages
— eliminating, combining, rearranging or simplifying activities.

Initially, the aspects already listed under Work Study are challenged, namely:
— the purpose for which ⎱
— the place at which ⎪
— the sequence in which ⎬ the activities are undertaken.
— the person by whom ⎪
— the means by which ⎰

These aspects are then developed further by asking another series of questions: what, why, when, who, how in relation to each of the above (see figure A). The non-productive stages such as delays and storages are particularly challenged.

Figure A

Questioning sequences

PURPOSE — What is done?
Why is it done?
What *else* might be done?
What should be done?

PLACE — Where is it done?
Why is it done there?
Where *else* might it be done?
Where should it be done?

SEQUENCE — When is it done?
Why is it done then?
When might it be done?
When should it be done?

PERSON — Who does it?
Why does that person do it?
Who else might do it?
Who should do it?

MEANS — How is it done?
Why is it done that way?
How else might it be done?
How should it be done?

---

4 Develop
The responses to the series of questions will be analysed to see if a new method can justifiably be developed. If so, the proposed new method must be constructed and recorded using the same recording techniques as previously used. Again the flow process chart is particularly relevant. The present and proposed methods will be compared to ensure that nothing has been overlooked and improvements have been made. The new proposals must define clearly how the new method will achieve its aims and objectives; affect other departments; comply with health and safety and other regulations and result in being cost saving.

5 Install
The improved method can then be installed as long as it is a practical proposition and and is acceptable to all groups of personnel involved. If personnel have been consulted at earlier stages for their advice and opinions and regularly briefed throughout the whole process, there is likely to be less resistance and installation may proceed smoothly. Training or re-training of personnel is essential, so the new method must be standardised and specified (for instance, in a job breakdown format).

6 Maintain

Once the method has been installed, it should be maintained in its specified form and personnel not allowed to revert to the old method or introduce elements not allowed for unless there is some good reason. Obviously the new method must be clearly defined and specified beyond risk of misinterpretation. The onus is firmly on supervisory staff to ensure the new method and its standards are maintained and monitored as far as is possible.

Method Study may also be used to:
— improve layout of the work environment
— improve design of plant and equipment
— reduce unnecessary fatigue and economise on human effort
— improve the allocation and use of resources
— develop a better physical environment.

Work measurement

Work Measurement as defined by British Standards is 'the application of techniques designed to establish the time for a qualified worker to carry out a specified job at a defined level of performance'.

There are also British Standards definitions for 'an average worker' and 'normal performance' which are relevant. 'A *representative* (or average) worker in relation to any given class of work is one with the intelligence and physique necessary to undertake that work, adequately trained and with sufficient experience to perform it to satisfactory standards of quality, whose skill and performance are average to the group under consideration.

'*Normal performance* (or pace) is the working rate of the average worker working under capable supervision but without the stimulus of an incentive wage-payment plan. This pace can easily be maintained day after day without undue physical or mental fatigue and is characterised by the fairly steady exertion of reasonable effort.'

Work measurement techniques provide a means of measuring time taken in an individual or series of operations to identify ineffective time and/or set a standard time for performing the operation(s).

Work Measurement may be used to:
— compare the efficiency of alternative methods in terms of continuous working and cost savings
— balance the work of team members
— determine the number of machines an operative can control
— provide the basis for estimating optimum personnel and equipment requirements for carrying out a programme of work
— provide the basis for estimating tender prices and selling prices
— set standards of equipment utilisation and personnel performance which are particularly applicable as the basis for Incentive Bonus Schemes
— Provide data for analysing and controlling labour costs

Appendix 4

A comparison of linen systems

	Capital outlay OP Laundry	Capital outlay Comm. Laundry	Linen hire Comm. Laundry
Linen	Bought to the personal specification in line with OP laundry capabilities	Bought to personal specification	May be from standard pool stock or purchased by the hire company to meet customer's specification
Equipment	Capital costs involved. Running costs include management and supervision of the laundry and sewing room	May need repair facilities in addition to hire charges. Staff costs involved in checking, sorting, dispatching and receiving linen	As capital outlay for commercial laundry, with exception of no repair facilities
Standards	Set and controlled by staff	Some direct control by linen purchase. Control of standards of laundered items is indirect	Indirect control of standards

Spatial requirements	Maximum space required, ie for laundry, sewing room, central linen store, peripheral stores	Reduced space required for central and peripheral linen stores. Also, possibly repair room	Only store area required
Flexibility of service	Flexibility within constraints of laundry capacity, and number of pieces owned	Constraints are the number of pieces owned (though the laundry may hire out extras). Contracted items not sent to laundry may still be chargeable	Excessive peaks in demand may easily be covered by short term additional hire. Contracted items not sent to laundry may still be chargeable

Index